The Common Core in Action

**Recent Titles in the Libraries Unlimited
SLM Hot Topics Series**

Protecting Intellectual Freedom and Privacy in Your School Library
Helen R. Adams

The Common Core in Action

Ready-to-Use Lesson Plans
for K–6 Librarians

Deborah J. Jesseman

SLM Hot Topics

LIBRARIES
UNLIMITED™

An Imprint of ABC-CLIO, LLC
Santa Barbara, California • Denver, Colorado

Library of Congress Cataloging-in-Publication Data

Jesseman, Deborah J.
    The common core in action : ready-to-use lesson plans for K-6 librarians / Deborah J. Jesseman.
        pages cm. — (SLM hot topics)
    Includes bibliographical references and index.
    ISBN 978-1-61069-717-0 (pbk : alk. paper) — ISBN 978-1-61069-718-7 (ebook)   1. Elementary school libraries—Activity programs—United States.   2. School librarian participation in curriculum planning.   3. Education—Standards—United States.   4. Education, Elementary—Curricula–United States.   5. Elementary school libraries—Collection development.   I. Title.
    Z675.S3.J47   2015
    027.8'222—dc23   2015002528

ISBN: 978-1-61069-717-0
EISBN: 978-1-61069-718-7

19 18 17 16 15   1 2 3 4 5

This book is also available on the World Wide Web as an eBook.
Visit www.abc-clio.com for details.

Libraries Unlimited
An Imprint of ABC-CLIO, LLC

ABC-CLIO, LLC
130 Cremona Drive, P.O. Box 1911
Santa Barbara, California 93116-1911

This book is printed on acid-free paper ∞
Manufactured in the United States of America

AASL's *Standards for the 21st-Century Learner* used in lesson plans are excerpted from *Standards for the 21st-Century Learner* by the American Association of School Librarians, a division of the American Library Association, copyright © 2007 American Library Association. Available for download at www.ala.org/aasl/standards. Used with permission.

Contents

Introduction

OVERVIEW OF THE COMMON CORE STATE STANDARDS

What are they?

The Common Core State Standards were developed under the guidance of the National Governors Association Center for Best Practices and the Council of Chief State School Officers. The process began in 2007 and the final Common Core State Standards were nationally released in 2010. A separate validation committee, consisting of 28 individuals noted in the educational standards community, concluded that the standards were appropriate in terms of their level of clarity and specificity, informed by available research or evidence, and the result of processes that reflect best practices for standards development. The National Governors Association Center for Best Practices and the Council of Chief State School Officers are in the process of developing a long-term governance structure to monitor the quality of the Common Core State Standards.

The Common Core State Standards are not part of the No Child Left Behind legislation, were not developed with federal funds, and are not a federal program. State adoption is voluntary. The standards have currently been adopted in 43 states, the Department of Defense Education Activity, Washington, D.C., Guam, the Northern Mariana Islands, and the U.S. Virgin Islands.

How are they different from the content standards?

The Common Core State Standards were developed to be reflective of the core knowledge and skills that students need to be ready for college and career. They currently focus on English Language Arts and Mathematics, with a minimal content requirement for each set of standards. The English Language Arts minimal content includes classic myths and stories from around the world, America's founding documents, foundational American literature, and Shakespeare. The Mathematics minimal content includes elementary concepts of whole numbers, addition, subtraction, multiplication, division, fractions, and decimals while the upper levels focus on problem-solving skills. The focus was to avoid the inconsistency of having different states cover different topics at different grade levels and to promote a solid starting point for adoption of cross-state Common Core standards.

What are the implications for schools using Common Core State Standards?

The Common Core State Standards are not a curriculum but a set of goals and expectations for English Language Arts and Mathematics instruction. The decisions on implementation of the standards are the responsibility of the individual states and their local school districts. The standards outline what students should know at different levels but allow for teacher-led instruction and curriculum tailored to the needs of the student demographic at the classroom level.

OPPORTUNITIES THE COMMON CORE STATE STANDARDS PROVIDE FOR THE SCHOOL LIBRARIAN

Collaborating with teachers and providing instructional resources

The school librarian can become a key participant in facilitation of instructional resources by becoming familiar with the Common Core State Standards and the grade-specific curriculum. This knowledge allows the school librarian to suggest and provide additional curriculum resources to the classroom teacher and encourages collaboration through the development of co-teaching opportunities. The more involved school librarians are with the classroom curriculum and co-teaching opportunities, the more efficient they will be in developing a supportive school library collection of resources.

Co-teaching

The lessons included in this book are co-teaching opportunities that encourage the school librarian to collaborate with classroom teachers in providing resources and instructional support. Each lesson includes Common Core State Standards aligned with the subject content. It is important that the school librarian become familiar with the Common Core State Standards attached to each co-teaching lesson in order to work successfully with classroom teachers.

Collection development planning to reflect the instructional needs of the Common Core State Standards curriculum

Successful collaboration and co-teaching between the school librarian and the classroom teacher allows for greater understanding of the content to be addressed at each grade level through collaborative goals and objectives in each lesson. Further understanding of the content in the classroom provides the school librarian with the knowledge to seek resources that will complement the content lessons, meet the needs of the teachers, and support the curriculum.

If a classroom teacher assigns a Social Studies unit about famous people and the school librarian has collaborated in planning the unit, this will not only promote collection development of biographies and autobiographies but will encourage an expanded lesson on primary and secondary sources. An English lesson on poetry will prompt collection development resources beyond a few anthologies and look to a vast array of possible resources that will be used each year. The Common Core State Standards focus on inquiry is a boon for increasing the library collection of nonfiction materials, but familiarity with the level-specific curriculum will ensure that purchases will be utilized effectively.

Active participation by the school librarian on a school or district curriculum committee that addresses the Common Core State Standards is a proactive way to understand the needs of the curriculum and develop the library collection to support the curriculum needs.

Collection development adjustments and additions since adoption of the Common Core State Standards curriculum

From North Carolina:

I think that Common Core has changed what I have purchased, and what I am planning to purchase. I have placed more importance on acquiring information books with some meat in them. I have de-emphasized picture books and popular fiction mainly because information books are expensive. So I have had to reallocate funds to expand the media center's nonfiction collection. There is an increased emphasis on classroom collections and the procurement of book sets by the administration. The main criticism I have for this is that the teachers have little or no training.

From Georgia:

I concentrated on updating my 1979 and older fiction collection to get the kids back in the library for my first five years at this school. The past couple of years I have emphasized nonfiction and try to pair it with fiction. It is still a hard sell to get the teachers to buy in—current non-fiction books are shorter than older books, and teachers generally don't think they are long enough, regardless of Lexile level.

I also heavily weeded nonfiction, bought as many short story collections as I could find as well as all of the *No Fear Shakespeare* titles, and had my shop classes cut down my 7-foot shelves to 5 feet for increased light and visibility. Also purchased some add-on displays to put some nonfiction face out. Traffic and circulation have picked up.

From New Jersey:
Simply, we are focusing more on nonfiction texts and when I do read aloud, my questioning/discussion is somewhat modified. But to be honest, a lot of Common Core is just good teaching and people do it anyway. There is more interest in text evidence and less on personal connections.

From Iowa:
We have looked more at books that are "Common Core Aligned" when purchasing items. It has helped us in the nonfiction with teachers needing books for units. I also try to find some fiction that is aligned with the Core or goes along with similar topics I know teachers talk about with students.

From Iowa:
It hasn't affected my collection development at all to this point. Our district has found that the curriculum we have in place is meeting the Common Core standards and I haven't had to look for materials to specifically fit with the Common Core. My administrators haven't talked with me at this point about planning for adding materials that specifically address CCSS either.

From Maryland:
I spend more of my resources on nonfiction than before. The needs of the curriculum were limited in the nonfiction areas, and the new standards promoted a need for additions in this area.

From New York system office:
I provide support to school librarians throughout New York City, and through my office we have offered grants to the field for collection development focusing on building up the nonfiction acquisitions in schools. We also offer professional development on nonfiction book groups and collection development.

SUMMARY

Most school library staff have the primary responsibility for selecting library materials in accordance with the school's curriculum and instructional program. The selection process is one that may include consultation with school administrators, teachers, and parents, and the library materials should support, enrich, and extend the curriculum. This aligns with the basis of the Common Core State Standards, which are learning goals that outline what a student should know and be able to do at the end of each grade. The standards were created to ensure that all students graduate from high school with the skills and knowledge necessary to succeed in college, career, and life, regardless of where they live. School librarian familiarity with the school curriculum and standards will support and encourage student success.

HOW TO USE THIS BOOK

Many of the lessons in this book were adapted from "Into the Curriculum" lessons from *School Library Monthly* and have been attributed to the original author. The remaining lessons were created specifically for this book by the author.

Each lesson includes:

- A lesson summary
- Specific AASL and CCSS standards that align with the lesson
- Roles of the teacher and the school librarian
- Step-by-step instructions to complete the lesson
- Handouts are included in the Student Resource site found at http://www.abc-clio.com/Libraries Unlimited/product.aspx?pc=A4367P
- Assessment rubrics
- Boxed area that includes additional ideas for the school librarian
- Bibliography of additional books or online resources to use for the lesson or to expand the lesson.

Each lesson has been aligned to both the AASL and CCSS standards. When utilizing these standards it is suggested that the school librarian become familiar with the requirements of the standards to tailor questions or discussions that will incorporate the expected student learning.

Chapter 1

English

ENGLISH   Grade Levels: K–1

Fiction/Nonfiction

Lesson Summary: The lesson introduces the idea of fiction and nonfiction books and materials to young students by looking at real and not real items and materials. They will listen to fiction and nonfiction stories about pumpkins, discuss the real and not real aspects of the stories, and sort books into fiction and nonfiction piles.

Standards Addressed:

AASL *Standards for the 21st Century Learner*

- Inquire, think critically, and gain knowledge (1.1.1; 1.1.2; 1.1.9; 1.2.2; 1.4.2)
- Draw conclusions, make informed decisions, apply knowledge to new situations, and create new knowledge (2.1.1; 2.1.3; 2.1.5; 2.3.1)
- Share knowledge and participate ethically and productively as members of our democratic society (3.1.2; 3.1.3; 3.2.2; 3.2.3; 3.3.1)
- Pursue personal and aesthetic growth (4.1.1)

Common Core State Standards

- CCSS.ELA-Literacy.RL.K.1; RL.K.3; RL.K.4; RL.K.5; RL.K.10
- CCSS.ELA-Literacy.RI.K.1; RI.K.2; RI.K.4; RI.K.5; RI.K.6; RI.K.9; RI.K.10
- CCSS.ELA-Literacy.SL.K.1; SL.K.2; SL.K.3; SL.K.4; SL.K.6
- CCSS.ELA-Literacy.RL.1.1; RL.1.3; RL.1.5; RL.1.6; RL.1.9
- CCSS.ELA-Literacy.RI.1.1; RI.1.2; RI.1.3; RI.1.4; RI.1.5; RI.1.6; RI.1.7; RI.1.8; RI.1.9; RI.1.10
- CCSS.ELA-Literacy.SL.1.1; SL.1.2; SL.1.3; SL.1.4; SL.1.6

Instructional Resources:

- *Required*
  - o Nonfiction book about pumpkins
  - o Fiction book about pumpkins
  - o Fiction and nonfiction book covers or books
  - o Diagram handout
  - o Crayons, markers
  - o Exit Tickets handout

Adapted from an SLM learning plan by Jennifer Evans. Reading/Language Arts: It's the Great Pumpkin Fiction, Non-fiction Lesson. *School Library Media Activities Monthly*, Volume XXIV, Number 2, October 2007, pp. 17–18.

All handouts are included in the Student Resource site found at http://www.abc-clio.com/Libraries Unlimited/product.aspx?pc=A4367P

- *Recommended*
  - Real pumpkins
  - Fake pumpkins

Instructional Roles:

This lesson may be co-taught by the classroom teacher and the school librarian. The school librarian will lead the instruction on fiction and nonfiction books and where they are located in the library. Both instructors may read books aloud and assist the students while they are working on the assignment.

Procedure for Completion:

Step One: The school librarian reads a nonfiction book about pumpkins and then a fiction book about pumpkins to the students. The students are given the Diagram handout to complete while discussing what makes a pumpkin real and what makes a pumpkin not real. It would add to the lesson to have real pumpkins and fake pumpkins available if possible.

Step Two: The school librarian explains that students are going to look at real (nonfiction) and not real/made-up (fiction) books. Real books present facts and true things and not real books present made-up stories. In the large group the co-teachers will hold up several examples and ask the students where the book belongs: next to the real pumpkin or next to the fake pumpkin.

Step Three: The students are divided into table groups and are given an assortment of book covers (or books) they will sort according to fiction or nonfiction. The co-teachers will circulate to discuss with students why they are sorting them into particular piles.

Completion: Students will be provided with an Exit Ticket where they will circle the fiction book covers.

Completion of Project:

The final product will be the completed Exit Tickets.

Student Assessment/Reflection:

The Exit Ticket and group work will be the object of the main student assessment and are based on the rubric for the project. Conversations with the teacher and school librarian throughout the process are important in the assessment process.

Professional Reflection—Librarian Notes:

The subject of this lesson does not need to be pumpkins but can be any topic that can be included in a "real" and "not real" discussion, such as apples or animals.

Fiction/Nonfiction Rubric

	Excellent	Satisfactory	Unsatisfactory
Step One: Contribution to Discussion	Student contributed to the discussion.	Student needed encouragement to contribute to the discussion.	Student did not contribute to the discussion.
Step Two: Table Group	Student worked well in the group and contributed to the assignment.	Student needed encouragement to work well in the group and contribute to the assignment.	Student did not work well in the group.
Step Three: Exit Ticket	Work completed on time and correct.	Work completed but with assistance.	Work not completed or incorrect.
Staying on Task	Student working as assigned and not disengaged or causing a disruption.	Student working well on assignment most of the time.	Student not on task or was a disciplinary problem.

Student Name:
Fiction/Nonfiction Grade:

	Excellent	Satisfactory	Unsatisfactory
Step One: Contribution to Discussion			
Step Two: Table Group			
Step Three: Exit Ticket			
Staying on Task Daily			

SUGGESTED BIBLIOGRAPHY

Bunting, E. (1988). *Scary, Scary Halloween.* New York, NY: HMH Books for Young Readers.

Esbaum, J. (2009). *Seed, Sprout, Pumpkin, Pie.* Washington, DC: National Geographic Children's Books.

Ffeffer, W. (2004). *From Seed to Pumpkin.* New York, NY: HarperCollins.

Fridell, R., & Walsh, P. (2010). *Life Cycle of a Pumpkin.* Mankato, MN: Capstone Classroom.

Hubbell, W. (2000). *Pumpkin Jack.* Park Ridge, IL: Albert Whitman.

Jackson, A. (2002). *I Know an Old Lady Who Swallowed a Pie.* New York, NY: Puffin.

Kroll, S. (1993). *The Biggest Pumpkin Ever.* New York, NY: Cartwheel Books.

Levenson, G. (2002). *Pumpkin Circle.* Berkeley, CA: Tricycle Press.

Lewis, K. (2008). *The Runaway Pumpkin.* New York, NY: Orchard Books.

McNamara, M. (2007). *How Many Seeds in a Pumpkin?* New York, NY: Schwartz & Wade.

Saunders-Smith, G. (1998). *Fall Harvest.* Mankato, MN: Capstone Classroom.

Schulz, C. M. (2008). *It's the Great Pumpkin, Charlie Brown.* Philadelphia, PA: Running Press Kids.

Silverman, E. (1995). *Big Pumpkin.* New York, NY: Aladdin.

Titherington, J. (1990). *Pumpkin Pumpkin.* New York, NY: Greenwillow Books.

White, L. (1997). *Too Many Pumpkins.* New York, NY: Holiday House.

Williams, L. (1986). *The Little Old Lady Who Wasn't Afraid of Anything.* New York, NY: HarperCollins.

Wing, N. (1999). *The Night Before Halloween.* New York, NY: Grosset & Dunlap.

ENGLISH

Grade Levels: K–1

"Advice for Anansi"

Lesson Summary: This unit is a series of lessons that introduce young students to the concept of the literary character and gives them the opportunity to discover for themselves the traits that define the character of Anansi the Spider.

Standards Addressed:

AASL *Standards for the 21st Century Learner*

- Inquire, think critically, and gain knowledge (1.1.1–1.1.3; 1.4.2)
- Draw conclusions, make informed decisions, apply knowledge to new situations, and create new knowledge (2.1.1; 2.1.2; 2.1.3; 2.1.5; 2.2.4; 2.3.1)
- Share knowledge and participate ethically and productively as members of our democratic society (3.1.1–3.1.5; 3.2.2; 3.2.3; 3.3.2; 3.3.4)
- Pursue personal and aesthetic growth (4.1.1; 4.1.2; 4.1.3; 4.1.6; 4.1.8)

Common Core State Standards

- CCSS.ELA-Literacy.RL.K.1; RL.K.3; RL.K.4; RL.K.6; RL.K.7; RL.K.9; RL.K.10
- CCSS.ELA-Literacy.L.K.1; L.K.2; L.K.4; L.K.5; L.K.6
- CCSS.ELA-Literacy.SL.K.1; SL.K.2; SL.K.3; SL.K.4; SL.K.5; SL.K.6
- CCSS.ELA-Literacy.W.K.2; W.K.5; W.K.6; W.K.7; W.K.8
- CCSS.ELA-Literacy.RL.1.1; RL.1.3; RL.1.5; RL.1.6; RL.1.7; RL.1.9; RL.1.10
- CCSS.ELA-Literacy.L.1.1; L.1.2; L.1.4; L.1.5; L.1.6
- CCSS.ELA-Literacy.SL.1.1; SL.1.2; SL.1.3; SL.1.4; SL.1.5; SL.1.6
- CCSS.ELA-Literacy.W.1.1; W.1.5; W.1.6; W.1.7; W.1.8

Instructional Resources:

- *Required*
  - Stories about *Anansi the Spider* by Eric A. Kimmel
  - Chart paper
  - Advice Planning handouts
  - Large drawing paper and markers, crayons, or paint

All handouts are included in the Student Resource site found at http://www.abc-clio.com/Libraries Unlimited/product.aspx?pc=A4367P.

Instructional Roles:

This lesson may be co-taught by the classroom teacher and the school librarian as a series of lessons to complement the classroom English Language Arts instruction.

Procedure for Completion:

Step One—Building a Foundation: The school librarian reads *Anansi and the Moss-Covered Rock* aloud to introduce the character of Anansi to the students. In subsequent classes other Anansi books are read

Adapted from an SLM learning plan by Elizabeth Griffin. English/Language Arts: Advice for Anansi. *School Library Monthly*, Volume XXVII, Number 5, February 2011, pp. 12–14.

to build students' background knowledge about the character. To help students begin thinking about Anansi's character traits, the teacher makes comments such as: "There goes Anansi, stealing food again, just like he took the animals' fruit in our last book!" or "I wonder if this trick will work out better for Anansi than the moss-covered rock did."

Step Two—Constructing a Character: The co-teachers introduce students to the concept of a character, explaining that a character is someone in a story that we can recognize because he or she looks and acts a certain way. The same character can appear in many different stories, such as Anansi, Curious George, Clifford the Big Red Dog, or the Berenstain Bears. The students are asked to reflect on what they have learned so far about the character of Anansi. If they were going to tell a friend who had never read an Anansi book what Anansi is like, what would they say? The student responses are recorded on chart paper with like ideas grouped together.

The school librarian reads *Anansi and the Talking Melon* and asks the students to look for examples of the character traits they listed on the chart and to seek new ones they find in the current book.

Step Three—Applying New Knowledge: The co-teachers begin the third stage of the unit referencing the list of character traits the students developed in the prior lesson and announce that they will be using what they know about Anansi to create a book of their own. They are to imagine that Anansi is coming to visit their school and, based on what they know about his character traits, they will give him some advice on how to behave.

Students are assigned to groups of two to four, given an Advice Planning handout to complete, and work together to develop a plan to address one of Anansi's character flaws. Each group will form a plan and illustrate their advice to Anansi to be included as a page in the class book.

Completion: Publishing the Book

The school librarian compiles each group's page into a class book, typing the accompanying text from the Advice Planning handout or allowing time for students to type their own text.

Completion of Project:

The final product is the class book.

Student Assessment/Reflection:

The Advice Planning handout, the completed advice book, and group work will be the object of the main student assessment and are based on the rubric for the project. Conversations with and observations by the teacher and school librarian throughout the process are important in the assessment process.

Professional Reflection—Librarian Notes:

The class book can be compiled in a variety of ways. The book can be spiral-bound and included in the classroom or library collection. It can be uploaded as an online slide show or as a digital book using a site such as PhotoSnack or TeacherTube, making it available for students and parents to read online.

Advice for Anansi Rubric

	Excellent	Satisfactory	Unsatisfactory
Advice Planning Handout	Student completed the handout as assigned.	Student needed assistance or did not complete the handout on time.	Student did not complete the handout.
Group Work	Student worked well in the group and contributed to the assignment.	Student needed encouragement to work well in the group and contribute to the assignment.	Student did not work well in the group.
Completed Book Page	Work completed on time, neat and creative.	Work not completed on time or messy.	Work not completed.
Staying on Task	Student working as assigned and not disengaged or causing a disruption.	Student working well on assignment most of the time.	Student not on task or was a disciplinary problem.

Student Name:

Advice for Anansi Grade:

	Excellent	Satisfactory	Unsatisfactory
Advice Planning Handout			
Group Work			
Completed Book Page			
Staying on Task Daily			

From *The Common Core in Action: Ready-to-Use Lesson Plans for K–6 Librarians* by Deborah J. Jesseman. Santa Barbara, CA: Libraries Unlimited. Copyright © 2015.

SUGGESTED BIBLIOGRAPHY

Kimmel, E. A., & Stevens, J. (1992). *Anansi Goes Fishing.* New York, NY: Holiday House.

Kimmel, E. A., & Stevens, J. (2002). *Anansi and the Magic Stick.* New York, NY: Holiday House.

Kimmel, E. A., & Stevens, J. (1990). *Anansi and the Moss-Covered Rock.* New York, NY: Holiday House.

Kimmel, E. A., & Stevens, J. (2008). *Anansi's Party Time.* New York, NY: Holiday House.

Kimmel, E. A., & Stevens, J. (1995). *Anansi and the Talking Melon.* New York, NY: Holiday House.

Online Resources:

Eric Kimmel: http://ericakimmel.com/

TeacherTube: www.teachertube.com

PhotoSnack: http://www.photosnack.com/

ENGLISH   **Grade Levels:** 2–3

Writing and Storytelling

Lesson Summary: In this lesson students will write and illustrate a story about their journey to and from school.

Standards Addressed:

AASL *Standards for the 21st Century Learner*

- Inquire, think critically, and gain knowledge (1.1.1–1.1.6; 1.2.1–1.2.7; 1.3.1–1.3.5; 1.4.1–1.4.4)
- Draw conclusions, make informed decisions, apply knowledge to new situations, and create new knowledge (2.1.1–2.1.6; 2.2.4; 2.3.1; 2.4.1–2.4.4)
- Share knowledge and participate ethically and productively as members of our democratic society (3.3.1–3.3.6; 3.3.1–3.3.7; 3.4.1–3.4.2)
- Pursue personal and aesthetic growth (4.1.1; 4.1.4; 4.1.6–4.1.8; 4.2.1–4.2.3; 4.4.1–4.4.6)

Common Core State Standards

- CCSS.ELA-Literacy.RL.2.1; RL.2.2; RL.2.3; RL.2.4; RL.2.5; RL.2.6; RL.2.7; RL.2.10
- CCSS.ELA-Literacy.RF.2.3; RF.2.4
- CCSS.ELA-Literacy.L.2.1; L.2.2; L.2.3; L.2.4; L.2.5; L.2.6
- CCSS.ELA-Literacy.W.2.3; W.2.5; W.2.6; W.2.8
- CCSS.ELA-Literacy.RL.3.1; RL.3.2; RL.3.3; RL.3.4; RL.3.5; RL.3.6; RL.3.7; RL.3.10
- CCSS.ELA-Literacy.RF.3.3; RF.3.4
- CCSS.ELA-Literacy.L.3.1; L.3.2; L.3.3; L.3.4; L.3.5; L.3.6
- CCSS.ELA-Literacy.W.3.3; W.3.4; W.3.5; W.3.6; W.3.8; W.3.10

Instructional Resources:

- *Required*
  - Pens, pencils, paper, crayons, markers
- *Recommended*
  - Computer access for word processing

Instructional Roles:

This lesson may be co-taught by the classroom teacher and the librarian. Both may assist the students in developing their stories by asking questions and making suggestions while the students describe their journeys to and from school.

Procedure for Completion:

Day One: The school librarian will read the Dr. Seuss book *And to Think That I Saw It on Mulberry Street*. Students will be led in a discussion of what Marco really saw and how he exaggerated the simple things to make his journey appear more exciting. For the first part of the assignment each student will write down their path to school, whether it is walking, a bus ride, or part of a car pool. Everyone may have a unique perspective. The homework assignment will be to observe and write down what they see on each part of the journey.

Day Two: Students will complete writing the details of their journey to or from school and submit the first draft for review by the co-teachers.

Day Three—Completion: The first draft will be returned and students will use this as a basis for making up or exaggerating aspects of their journey. They will write and illustrate this story.

Completion of Project:

The final project is an illustrated story, which the teachers may have bound or digitally scanned.

Student Assessment/Reflection:

The final project is the object of the main student assessment and is based on the rubric for the project. Questions asked during the writing process as well as conversations with the teacher and school librarian throughout the project will be included in the assessment process.

Professional Reflection—Librarian Notes:

The school librarian may want to suggest that this be an assignment during a Dr. Seuss Day or week. Resources on observing and noticing things would be an added bonus to student learning.

Story Rubric

	Excellent	Satisfactory	Unsatisfactory
Step One: Basic Outline	Work completed as assigned and on time.	Work completed but not on time or extensive corrections needed before moving to next step.	Work not completed or having several revisions before moving to next step.
Step Two: Basic Story	Work completed on time and well written.	Work completed but not on time or extensive corrections needed before completing the final product.	Work not completed or having several revisions before moving to next step.
Step Three: Story with Illustrations	Work completed on time, all requirements are included, and the final product is neat and appealing.	Work not completed on time; some elements may be missing; the final product is messy, incomplete, or not accurate.	Work not completed or missing major elements.
Staying on Task Daily	Student working as assigned and not disengaged or causing a disruption.	Student working well on assignment most days.	Student not on task daily or was a disciplinary problem.

Student Name:

Story Grade:

	Excellent	Satisfactory	Unsatisfactory
Step One: Basic Outline			
Step Two: Basic Story			
Step Three: Story with Illustrations			
Staying on Task Daily			

From *The Common Core in Action: Ready-to-Use Lesson Plans for K–6 Librarians* by Deborah J. Jesseman. Santa Barbara, CA: Libraries Unlimited. Copyright © 2015.

SUGGESTED BIBLIOGRAPHY

Benke, K. (2010). *Rip the Page!: Adventures in Creative Writing.* Boston, MA: Roost Books.

Dr. Seuss (1989 Reprint). *And to Think That I Saw It on Mulberry Street.* New York, NY: Random House Books for Young Readers.

Fletcher, R., & Portalupi, J. (2001). *Writing Workshop: The Essential Guide.* Portsmouth, NH: Heinemann.

Holub, J., & Sweet, M. (2013). *Little Red Writing.* San Francisco, CA: Chronicle Books.

Hurni-Dove, K. (2006). *Teaching the Craft of Writing: Leads & Endings.* New York, NY: Scholastic Teaching Resources

Leograndis, D. (2008). *Launching the Writing Workshop: A Step-by-Step Guide in Photographs.* New York, NY: Scholastic Teaching Resources.

Levine, G. C. (2006). *Writing Magic: Creating Stories That Fly.* New York, NY: HarperCollins.

Scholastic (2010). *Scholastic Success with Writing, Grade 3.* New York, NY: Scholastic Teaching Resources.

Spectrum (2002). *Writing, Grade 2.* Victoria, Australia: Spectrum Publications.

Spectrum (2006). *Writing, Grade 3.* Victoria, Australia: Spectrum Publications.

Tunks, K. W., & Giles, R. (2007). *Write Now!: Publishing with Young Authors, PreK–Grade 2.* Portsmouth, NH: Heinemann.

ENGLISH   Grade Levels: 2–3

Fiction/Nonfiction

Lesson Summary: This lesson introduces the idea of fiction and nonfiction books and materials to students by comparing prior knowledge of Abraham Lincoln with new information presented to them.

Standards Addressed:

AASL *Standards for the 21st Century Learner*

- Inquire, think critically, and gain knowledge (1.1.1–1.1.6; 1.1.9; 1.2.4; 1.4.2; 1.4.4)
- Draw conclusions, make informed decisions, apply knowledge to new situations, and create new knowledge (2.1.1–2.1.3; 2.1.5; 2.1.6; 2.2.4)
- Share knowledge and participate ethically and productively as members of our democratic society (3.1.1; 3.3.4; 3.4.1)
- Pursue personal and aesthetic growth (4.1.1; 4.1.4; 4.1.6; 4.3.1; 4.3.2)

Common Core State Standards

- CCSS.ELA-Literacy.RI.2.1; RI.2.2; RI.2.3; RI.2.4; RI.2.5; RI.2.6; RI.2.9; RI.2.10
- CCSS.ELA-Literacy.SL.2.1; SL.2.2; SL.2.3; SL.2.4; SL.2.6
- CCSS.ELA-Literacy.L.2.1; L.2.2; L.2.3; L.2.6
- CCSS.ELA-Literacy.RI.3.1; RI.3.2; RI.3.3; RI.3.4; RI.3.5; RI.3.6; RI.3.7; RI.3.8; RI.3.9; RI.3.10
- CCSS.ELA-Literacy.SL.3.1; SL.3.2; SL.3.3; SL.3.6
- CCSS.ELA-Literacy.L.3.1; L.3.2; L.3.3; L.3.6

Instructional Resources:

- *Required*
  o KLW handout
  o Character Cluster handout
  o Timeline handout
  o Pencils, crayons, scissors, glue, construction paper
  o Easel chart or whiteboard

All handouts are included in the Student Resource site found at http://www.abc-clio.com/Libraries Unlimited/product.aspx?pc=A4367P.

Instructional Roles:

This lesson will be co-taught by the classroom teacher and the school librarian. Together they will determine the pre- and post-assessments and determine how to transfer the learning through other curriculum subject areas.

Procedure for Completion:

Day One: The students will be shown the cover of the fiction book *A. Lincoln and Me* and asked to predict what the story may be about. They will then discuss what they already know about Abraham Lincoln, utilizing the KLW handout, and the teachers will chart the information on the board. The teachers will lead

Adapted from an SLM learning plan by Leila Reigelsperger. Social Studies/Language Arts: Learning about Abraham Lincoln Using Fiction and Nonfiction Materials. *School Library Monthly,* Volume XXVII, Number 1, September–October 2010, pp. 16–17.

a discussion of what the students want to learn about Abraham Lincoln and tell them that the story may not answer all the things they want to know, but they will use additional resources to gain that information.

The school librarian will point out the call number of the book and tell the students that this is a fictional story about a boy who shares the same birthday as Abraham Lincoln. Students will be reminded of the differences between fiction and nonfiction books. The school librarian will read the story to the students, pausing to point out anything on the chart that is covered in the story.

Day Two: The school librarian will define the word *biography* and point out the call number for books that are biographical and where they are located in the library. The teachers will review the information from the KWL chart and show the students the cover of the book *Honest Abe*. The school librarian will read the story aloud and encourage discussion. Any new information gained in the discussion will be added to the chart.

Students are introduced to the Character Cluster handout and are to complete the chart listing adjectives that describe Lincoln and provide an example to support their adjective. Example: Abe Lincoln was a *hardworking* person because he helped his father build a log cabin for his family to live in.

Day Three—Completion: The school librarian will review biography information, read *A Picture Book of Abraham Lincoln,* and ask the students to think about what information they have learned about Abraham Lincoln. The last page of the story includes "Important Dates." The teachers will demonstrate how these dates can be placed in a chart to create a timeline of Lincoln's life.

Discuss how students can create a timeline of their own lives. For example: What did they do as a 1-year-old? As a 2-year-old? Students will begin their own Timelines and may include real photos or draw pictures of themselves at various ages in their lives.

Completion of Project:

The final product will be the completed KWL handout, Character Cluster handout, and Personal Timeline handout.

Student Assessment/Reflection:

The students' handouts will be graded on the lesson rubric, but contributions to the group discussion and conversations with the teacher and school librarian throughout the process are included in the assessment process.

Professional Reflection—Librarian Notes:

This general lesson may be extended to other units that may include: Math—Lincoln is on the five-dollar bill and the penny; Social Studies—the Lincoln Memorial, comparison between Martin Luther King, Jr. and Lincoln; English Language Arts—read *Abe Lincoln Remembers* and have students write interview questions they might ask Lincoln.

Fiction/Nonfiction Rubric

	Excellent	Satisfactory	Unsatisfactory
KLW Worksheet	Work completed on time, accurate, and well written.	Work not completed on time or missing elements.	Work not completed or not handed in.
Character Cluster Worksheet	Work completed on time, accurate, and creative.	Work not completed on time or may have inaccurate statements.	Work not completed.
Personal Timeline	Work completed on time, creative, and neat.	Work completed but elements missing; work was late or messy.	Work not completed.
Staying on Task	Student working as assigned and not disengaged or causing a disruption.	Student working well on assignment most of the time.	Student not on task or was a disciplinary problem.

Student Name:

Fiction/Nonfiction Grade:

	Excellent	Satisfactory	Unsatisfactory
KLW Worksheet			
Character Cluster Worksheet			
Personal Timeline			
Staying on Task Daily			

SUGGESTED BIBLIOGRAPHY

Adler, D. A. (1989). *A Picture Book of Abraham Lincoln.* New York, NY: Holiday House.
Borden, L. (2009). *A. Lincoln and Me.* New York, NY: Scholastic.
Kunhardt, E. (1993). *Honest Abe.* New York, NY: Greenwillow.
Turner, A. (2001). *Abe Lincoln Remembers.* New York, NY: Harper-Collins.

Video Resources:

A. Lincoln and Me. Nutmeg Media, 2005. 14 min.
Abraham Lincoln. Great Americans for Children series. Schlessinger Media, 2003. 23 min.

Online Resources:

America's Story: http://www.americaslibrary.gov/aa/index.php
Lincoln Bicentennial: http://www.lincolnbicentennial.org/
Lincoln Home: http://www.nps.gov/liho/index.htm

ENGLISH

Adjectives Wordle

Grade Levels: 3–4

Lesson Summary: This lesson reinforces grammar skills, applies thesaurus skills, and explores adjectives while students create a personal Wordle.

Standards Addressed:

AASL *Standards for the 21st Century Learner*

- Inquire, think critically, and gain knowledge (1.1.1–1.1.3; 1.3.5; 1.4.4)
- Draw conclusions, make informed decisions, apply knowledge to new situations, and create new knowledge (2.1.1; 2.1.2; 2.1.4; 2.1.5; 2.1.6; 2.2.4)
- Share knowledge and participate ethically and productively as members of our democratic society (3.1.4; 3.1.6; 3.4.1; 3.4.2)
- Pursue personal and aesthetic growth (4.1.6; 4.1.8; 4.4.2)

Common Core State Standards

- CCSS.ELA-Literacy.L.3.1; L.3.2; L.3.3; L.3.4; L.3.5; L.3.6
- CCSS.ELA-Literacy.RF.3.3
- CCSS.ELA-Literacy.L.4.1; L.4.2; L.4.3; L.4.4; L.4.5; L.4.6
- CCSS.ELA-Literacy.RF.4.3

Instructional Resources:

- *Required*
  - *Sloppy Joe* by Dave Keane
  - Adjective Collection handout
  - Creating a Wordle handout
  - Dictionaries, thesaurus
  - Projector
  - Computers with Internet access
  - Printer
  - Enlarged sample of a thesaurus entry
  - Enlarged Wordle projects describing the Cat in the Hat, the Grinch, Junie B. Jones, and Harry Potter

All handouts are included in the Student Resource site found at http://www.abc-clio.com/Libraries Unlimited/product.aspx?pc=A4367P.

- *Recommended*
  - Printer with color printing capability
  - Wordle displays

Instructional Roles:

The classroom teacher and school librarian collaborate in the teaching of three sequential lessons. The classroom teacher is responsible for preteaching the concept of adjectives as part of the English

Adapted from an SLM learning plan by Diane Fawcett. English Language Arts: Adjectives about Us! *School Library Monthly*, Volume 28, Number 4, January 2012, pp. 52–53.

Language Arts curriculum and leads the students as they brainstorm their personal adjective lists. The school librarian introduces the story and the procedure for using a thesaurus, either print or online, and leads the students through the process of creating a personal Wordle.

Procedure for Completion:

Step One: The school librarian reads aloud *Sloppy Joe* by Dave Keane, drawing students' attention to the adjective "sloppy" as a descriptor for the main character.

After students hear the book, the classroom teacher reviews the concept that adjectives can describe how we look (tall, blonde), the ways we act toward others (friendly, kind), how we feel (cheerful, shy), and what we are able to do with our special talents (athletic, artistic, intelligent). Both teachers review selected pictures from *Sloppy Joe* to elicit other adjectives from the students that describe Joe and record the adjectives on easel paper.

The school librarian informs students that they will be making special computer projects describing themselves using adjectives and will share premade, enlarged Wordle projects describing familiar characters from literature: the Cat in the Hat, the Grinch, Junie B. Jones, and Harry Potter.

Step Two: Students view the list made to describe Sloppy Joe and complete the Adjective Collection handout to record a minimum of 10 adjectives to describe themselves. The school librarian introduces students to the thesaurus as a solution for overused words. An enlarged sample of a thesaurus entry may be on display. Students look up their overused adjectives in the thesaurus and upgrade their lists.

Step Three—Completion: The school librarian uses an Internet-connected computer and projector to demonstrate the process of making a Wordle word cloud. The set of adjectives describing Sloppy Joe is used to demonstrate the steps from the Creating a Wordle handout.

The students will create a personal word cloud using their Adjective Collection handout and the Creating a Wordle handout.

Completion of Project:

The final project is a printed, personalized student Wordle.

Student Assessment/Reflection:

Student assessment is based on the rubric for the Wordle project, the Adjectives Collection handout, and conversations with the teacher and school librarian throughout the process.

Professional Reflection—Librarian Notes:

This is a good differentiation lesson for English Language Arts, English as a Second Language students, and language-disabled students. It can also be adapted to a variety of contents to include a bit of fun technology in any lesson.

Adjectives Wordle Rubric

	Excellent	Satisfactory	Unsatisfactory
Adjective Collection	The Adjective Collection was completed on time, accurately, and creatively.	The Adjective Collection was not completed on time or missing some required elements.	The Adjective Collection was not completed or not handed in at all.
Wordle	Wordle was completed as assigned.	Wordle was completed but not on time.	Wordle was not completed or not handed in at all.
Staying on Task Daily	Student working as assigned and not disengaged or causing a disruption.	Student working well on assignment most days.	Student not on task daily or was a disciplinary problem.

Student Name:
Adjectives Wordle Grade:

	Excellent	Satisfactory	Unsatisfactory
Adjective Collection			
Wordle			
Staying on Task Daily			

From *The Common Core in Action: Ready-to-Use Lesson Plans for K–6 Librarians* by Deborah J. Jesseman. Santa Barbara, CA: Libraries Unlimited. Copyright © 2015.

SUGGESTED BIBLIOGRAPHY

Keane, D. (2009). *Sloppy Joe*. New York, NY: Scholastic.

Online Resource:

Wordle: http://www.wordle.net/create

ENGLISH
Photo Story

Grade Levels: 4–5

Lesson Summary: *The Polar Express* by Chris Van Allsburg is a classic Christmas story that may provide various instructional connections through text and illustrations. This lesson allows students to demonstrate their understanding of fiction while creating their own version of the story.

Standards Addressed:

AASL *Standards for the 21st Century Learner*

- Inquire, think critically, and gain knowledge (1.1.1; 1.1.2; 1.1.9; 1.2.2; 1.2.3; 1.3.1; 1.3.5; 1.4.4)
- Draw conclusions, make informed decisions, apply knowledge to new situations, and create new knowledge (2.1.1; 2.1.2; 2.1.5; 2.1.6; 2.2.2; 2.2.4)
- Share knowledge and participate ethically and productively as members of our democratic society (3.1.1; 3.1.3; 3.1.4; 3.2.1; 3.2.2; 3.3.4)
- Pursue personal and aesthetic growth (4.1.1; 4.1.3; 4.1.5; 4.1.6; 4.1.7; 4.1.8; 4.2.4)

Common Core State Standards

- CCSS.ELA-Literacy.RI.4.1; RI.4.2; RI.4.3; RI.4.4; RI.4.6; RI.4.7
- CCSS.ELA-Literacy.RF.4.3; RF.4.4
- CCSS.ELA-Literacy.L.4.1; L.4.2; L.4.3; L.4.4; L.4.5; L.4.6
- CCSS.ELA-Literacy.W.4.3; W.4.4; W.4.5; W.4.6; W.4.8; W.4.10
- CCSS.ELA-Literacy.RI.5.1; RI.5.2; RI.5.3; RI.5.4; RI.5.5; RI.5.6; RI.5.7
- CCSS.ELA-Literacy.RF.5.3; RF.5.4
- CCSS.ELA-Literacy.L.5.1; L.5.2; L.5.3; L.5.4; L.5.5; L.5.6
- CCSS.ELA-Literacy.W.5.3; W.5.4; W.5.5; W.5.6; W.5.8; W.5.10

Instructional Resources:

- *Required*
  - *The Polar Express* by Chris Van Allsburg
  - Other Chris Van Allsburg books
  - Computer access/laptops
  - Computer paper
  - Blank CD-R CDs
  - Photo Story for Windows
  - Wordle Pathfinder
  - Photo Story Pathfinder
  - 30 preselected photos saved to a shared drive

All handouts are included in the Student Resource site found at http://www.abc-clio.com/Libraries Unlimited/product.aspx?pc=A4367P.

Instructional Roles:

The school librarian and classroom teacher are co-teachers in this lesson. The school librarian will introduce and read the book *The Polar Express* by Chris Van Allsburg to the class. The co-teachers will

Adapted from an SLM learning plan by Mary Tolson. Reading/Language Arts: All Aboard! Your Own Polar Express. *School Library Monthly*, Volume XXVII, Number 3, December 2010, pp. 18–20.

discuss with the students the author's choice of vocabulary, style, and illustrations as well as what makes this book fiction or nonfiction. The school librarian will work with the students to retell *The Polar Express* using Photo Story.

Procedure for Completion:

Day One: The school librarian gathers books by author Chris Van Allsburg and displays them in the library. When the students arrive they are directed to the display and asked if they have ever read or heard of any of the books. The school librarian reads *The Polar Express* to the students, and the co-teachers will discuss the style, vocabulary, and characteristics of the book and lead the students in generating a list of descriptive words relating to the story.

Students use the *Wordle Pathfinder* to open a blank Wordle page. They will type in the blank box all of the words listed that Van Allsburg used in the story to make it more interesting, add their one wish for a holiday gift, then customize and print their Wordle. This Wordle will be shared with the class.

Day Two: Students will create a rough draft of their own version of *The Polar Express* using their Wordle and their own words. They are given the Rough Draft Outline handout, which is based on prior knowledge of the parts of a story, and fill in each block with at least two complete sentences.

Day Three—Completion: The school librarian and the classroom teacher guide the students in using the Photo Story Pathfinder to write their story using the rough draft and inserting preselected images saved on a selected drive. The students will create a Photo Story consisting of at least six slides, music, and pictures.

Completion of Project:

The final project is a Photo Story that the students will share with the rest of the class.

Student Assessment/Reflection:

Student assessment is based on the rubric for the Photo Story project and conversations with the teacher and school librarian throughout the process.

Professional Reflection—Librarian Notes:

This would be a good lesson to use just prior to the winter break and may include showing the students the video of *The Polar Express*. Providing each student with a CD that contains their story to take home and share would add to the activity.

Photo Story Rubric

	Excellent	Satisfactory	Unsatisfactory
Step One: Wordle	Wordle completed as assigned.	Wordle was completed but not on time.	Wordle was not complete or not handed in at all.
Step Two: Rough Draft	The rough draft was organized and completed on time.	The rough draft was not completed on time or missing some required elements.	The rough draft was not completed or not handed in at all.
Step Three: Final Photo Story	Work completed on time, accurate, and creative.	Work not completed on time and may not include all requirements.	Work not completed or is missing major elements.
Staying on Task Daily	Student working as assigned and not disengaged or causing a disruption.	Student working well on assignment most days.	Student not on task daily or is a disciplinary problem.

Student Name:

Photo Story Grade:

	Excellent	Satisfactory	Unsatisfactory
Step One: Wordle			
Step Two: Rough Draft			
Step Three: Final Photo Story			
Staying on Task Daily			

SUGGESTED BIBLIOGRAPHY

Van Allsburg, C. (1979). *The Garden of Abdul Gasazi.* New York, NY: HMH Books for Young Readers.

Van Allsburg, C. (1981). *Jumanji.* New York, NY: Scholastic Book Services.

Van Allsburg, C. (2011). *Just a Dream.* New York, NY: HMH Books for Young Readers.

Van Allsburg, C. (1985). *The Polar Express.* New York, NY: Houghton Mifflin.

Van Allsburg, C. (1988). *Two Bad Ants.* New York, NY: HMH Books for Young Readers.

Van Allsburg, C. (1992). *The Widow's Broom.* New York, NY: HMH Books for Young Readers.

Van Allsburg, C. (1991). *The Wretched Stone.* New York, NY: Houghton Mifflin.

Van Allsburg, C. (1987). *The Z Was Zapped: A Play in Twenty-Six Acts.* New York, NY: HMH Books for Young Readers.

Van Allsburg, C. (2002). *Zathura.* New York, NY: Houghton Mifflin.

Online Resource:

Wordle: http://www.wordle.net

Photo Story Download:

For Windows: http://microsoft-photo-story.en.softonic.com/
For Mac: http://en.softonic.com/s/photo-story-3-mac:mac

ENGLISH   Grade Levels: 5–6

Shakespeare's Midsummer Night's Dream

Lesson Summary: Students will read Susan Cooper's *King of Shadows* independently. They will also utilize a reader's theater script to perform Shakespeare's play *A Midsummer Night's Dream* and conduct research about Shakespeare's time. The guided research topics may include exploring the language and accent of the play, the bubonic plague, sights and smells specific to the time period, and the Globe Theatre.

Standards Addressed:

AASL *Standards for the 21st Century Learner*

- Inquire, think critically, and gain knowledge (1.1.1–1.1.9; 1.2.1–1.2.7; 1.3.1–1.3.5; 1.4.1–1.4.4)
- Draw conclusions, make informed decisions, apply knowledge to new situations, and create new knowledge (2.1.1–2.1.6; 2.2.1–2.2.4; 2.3.1–2.3.3; 2.4.1–2.4.4)
- Share knowledge and participate ethically and productively as members of our democratic society (3.1.2–3.1.6; 3.2.1; 3.3.7; 3.4.1–3.4.2)
- Pursue personal and aesthetic growth (4.1.1; 4.1.3–4.1.8; 4.2.1–4.2.3; 4.3.1–4.3.4; 4.4.1–4.4.6)

Common Core State Standards

- CCSS.ELA-Literacy.RF.5.3; RF.5.4
- CCSS.ELA-Literacy.RI.5.1; RI.5.2; RI.5.3; RI.5.4; RI.5.5; RI.5.6; RI.5.7; RI.5.8; RI.5.9; RI.5.10
- CCSS.ELA-Literacy.RL.5.1; RL.5.2; RL.5.3; RL.5.4; RL.5.5; RL.5.6; RL.5.7; RL.5.9; RL.5.10
- CCSS.ELA-Literacy.SL.5.1; SL.5.2; SL.5.3; SL.5.4; SL.5.6
- CCSS.ELA-Literacy.W.5.2; W.5.4; W.5.5; W.5.7; W.5.9; W.5.10
- CCSS.ELA-Literacy.RI.6.1; RI.6.2; RI.6.3; RI.6.4; RI.6.5; RI.6.6; RI.6.7; RI.6.8; RI.6.9; RI.6.10
- CCSS.ELA-Literacy.RL.6.1; RL.6.2; RL.6.3; RL.6.4; RL.6.5; RL.6.6; RL.6.7; RL.6.9; RL.6.10
- CCSS.ELA-Literacy.RH.6–8.1; RH.6–8.2; RH.6–8.3; RH.6–8.4; RH.6–8.5; RH.6–8.6; RH.6–8.8; RH.6–8.9; RH.6–8.10
- CCSS.ELA-Literacy.SL.6.1; SL.6.2; SL.6.3; SL.6.4; SL.6.6
- CCSS.ELA-Literacy.W.6.2; W.6.4; W.6.5; W.6.7; W.6.9; W.6.10

Instructional Resources:

- *Required*
  - Student access to the book *King of Shadows* by Susan Cooper
  - Reader's theater version of *A Midsummer Night's Dream* by William Shakespeare
  - 10 Facts handout
  - Reference materials that may include print or online sources

All handouts are included in the Student Resource site found at http://www.abc-clio.com/Libraries Unlimited/product.aspx?pc=A4367P .

Instructional Roles:

The classroom teacher and the school librarian are co-teachers in this assignment. The assigned reading will be completed as homework, and the research on Shakespeare's era and reader's theater performance of *A Midsummer Night's Dream* will utilize the library.

Procedure for Completion:

Day One: The students are assigned readings in *King of Shadows* in their classroom. Moving to the school library they will be introduced to Shakespeare's *A Midsummer Night's Dream* and given the 10 Facts about What Life Was Like in Shakespeare's Time handout. Students will choose a topic to research that results in a brief paper.

Day Two—Completion: Each day the students will perform the reader's theater version of *A Midsummer Night's Dream*, discuss the readings from *King of Shadows*, and explore the facts about Shakespeare's era. For example, the book discusses the accents of Shakespeare's England compared to those of current England and the United States. The author comments that the main character has a South Carolina accent, which is closest to Shakespeare's original play, because the English and Scots who settled in the Appalachian Mountains areas of Carolina and Georgia were isolated from the main colonies.

Completion of Project:

Students are assessed on their participation in the *King of Shadows* discussion, participation in the reader's theater performance, and their paper.

Student Assessment/Reflection:

Student assessment is based on the rubric for the project and conversations with the teacher and school librarian throughout the process.

Professional Reflection—Librarian Notes:

Points for further discussion and exploration may include the contrasts and similarities of London within the 400-year time span; the surroundings of the Globe Theatre in the different time periods; personal habits, food, lodging, and bedding; the bubonic plague; and the noise at that time versus the current day.

Shakespeare's *Midsummer Night's Dream* Rubric

	Excellent	Satisfactory	Unsatisfactory
Step One: *King of Shadows* Reading Assignments	Readings completed as assigned.	Readings completed but not always on time as assigned.	Readings were not complete, late, or only partially completed.
Step Two: Reader's Theater Participation	Student volunteered and participated in the reader's theater production.	Student did not volunteer for a reader's theater part but participated when assigned.	Student did not participate in the reader's theater production.
Step Three: Report	Work completed on time, accurate, and well written.	Work not completed on time and may have some inaccuracies, and not well written.	Work not completed or is missing major elements.
Staying on Task Daily	Student working as assigned and not disengaged or causing a disruption.	Student working well on assignment most days.	Student not on task daily or was a disciplinary problem.

Student Name:

Shakespeare's *Midsummer Night's Dream* Grade:

	Excellent	Satisfactory	Unsatisfactory
Step One: *King of Shadows* Reading Assignments			
Step Two: Reader's Theater Participation			
Step Three: Report			
Staying on Task Daily			

SUGGESTED BIBLIOGRAPHY

Blackwood, G. (1999). *Shakespeare Stealer.* New York, NY: Puffin.

Blackwood, G. (2002). *Shakespeare's Scribe.* New York, NY: Puffin.

Blackwood, G. (2005). *Shakespeare's Spy.* New York, NY: Puffin.

Blackwood, G. (2004). *Shakespeare Stealer Series: The Shakespeare Stealer / Shakespeare's Scribe / Shakespeare's Spy.* New York, NY: Dutton Children's Books, NY.

Cooper, S. (2001). *King of Shadows.* New York, NY: Margaret K. McElderry Books.

Poulsen, J. (2013). *Shakespeare for Reader's Theatre: Hamlet, Romeo & Juliet, Midsummer Night's Dream.* Neustadt, ON, Canada: Five Rivers Chapmanry.

Shuter, J. (2014). *Shakespeare and the Theatre.* Mankato, MN: Capstone Classroom.

Reader's Theater Scripts:

http://www.teachingheart.net/readerstheater.htm

http://www.bard.org/education/insights/midsummerinsights.pdf

http://stclareslanguagecenter.wikispaces.com/file/view/Simply+Shakespeare%3B+Readers+Theatre+for+Young+People.pdf

ENGLISH   **Grade Levels:** 5–6
Poetry Book

Lesson Summary: In this lesson students develop a book that includes examples of the different styles of poetry they have studied. These types of poems will include limerick, haiku, free verse, cinquain, lyric, and concrete. For each style they will write a poem and include a professional example.

Standards Addressed:

AASL *Standards for the 21st Century Learner*

- Inquire, think critically, and gain knowledge (1.1.1–1.1.9; 1.2.1–1.2.7; 1.3.1–1.3.5; 1.4.1; 1.4.2; 1.4.4)
- Draw conclusions, make informed decisions, apply knowledge to new situations, and create new knowledge (2.1.6; 2.2.4; 2.4.1)
- Share knowledge and participate ethically and productively as members of our democratic society (3.1.2–3.1.4; 3.1.6; 3.4.2)
- Pursue personal and aesthetic growth (4.1.6; 4.1.8; 4.2.1–4.2.2; 4.3.2; 4.3.4; 4.4.2; 4.4.3)

Common Core State Standards

- CCSS.ELA-Literacy.RF.5.3; RF.5.4
- CCSS.ELA-Literacy.L.5.1; L.5.2; L.5.3; L.5.4; L.5.5; L.5.6
- CCSS.ELA-Literacy.W.5.5; W.5.6
- CCSS.ELA-Literacy.L.6.1; L.6.2; L.6.3; L.6.4; L.6.5; L.6.6
- CCSS.ELA-Literacy.W.6.5; W.6.6

Instructional Resources:

- *Required*
  - Paper, pencils, markers, crayons
  - Computer access for word processing
  - Access to a computer and projector or Smartboard
- *Recommended*
  - Access to a spiral binding machine

Instructional Roles:

The teacher guides the students in the elements of the poetry styles they will include in their projects. The school librarian is the resource for the teacher and the guide for student research. Both instructors will provide support and guidance for students as they research and develop their projects.

Procedure for Completion:

Day One: The teacher introduces the poetry unit and explains the project. Students are read limerick poem examples, shown examples on the Smartboard, and search both online and in poetry books for other examples they would like to use. Assigned homework is to write a limerick poem.

Day Two: Students will type up both the example and their poem and print the pages. They will either decorate the pages by hand or utilize computer graphics.

Day Three—Completion: Each of the above steps is repeated for haiku poems, free verse, cinquain poetry, lyric poems, and concrete poetry. It is anticipated that two days will be allowed for each style and a final two days for completing the books.

Completion of Project:

The students will organize their poetry pages and create a title page and table of contents. The pages can be put together with staples, sewed with yarn or ribbon, or spiral bound.

Student Assessment/Reflection:

The final project is the object of the main student assessment and is based on the rubric for the project. Observations and conversations with the teacher and school librarian throughout the process will also be included in the assessment process.

> **Professional Reflection—Librarian Notes:**
>
> It is encouraging to provide students bound copies of their poetry books if at all possible. A local copy store may provide this service for a minimal fee or the school district may have access to a binding machine.

Poetry Book Rubric

	Excellent	Satisfactory	Unsatisfactory
Step One: Professional Poems	Work completed as assigned on time and the poems reflect the correct style.	Work completed but not on time or extensive corrections needed before moving to next step.	Work not completed or having several revisions before moving to next step.
Step Two: Student-Created Poems	Work completed on time, well-written poems that reflect the correct style.	Work completed but not on time or extensive corrections needed before completing the final product.	Work not completed or having several revisions before moving to next step.
Step Three: Completed Book	Work completed on time, all requirements are included, and the final product is neat and appealing to view.	Work not completed on time, some elements may be missing, and the final product is messy, incomplete, or not accurate.	Work not completed or missing major elements.
Staying on Task Daily	Student working as assigned and not disengaged or causing a disruption.	Student working well on assignment most days.	Student not on task daily or is a disciplinary problem.

Student Name:
Poetry Book Grade:

	Excellent	Satisfactory	Unsatisfactory
Step One: Professional Poems			
Step Two: Student-Created Poems			
Step Three: Completed Book			
Staying on Task Daily			

From *The Common Core in Action: Ready-to-Use Lesson Plans for K–6 Librarians* by Deborah J. Jesseman. Santa Barbara, CA: Libraries Unlimited. Copyright © 2015.

SUGGESTED BIBLIOGRAPHY

Creech, S. (2001). *Love That Dog*. New York, NY: HarperTrophy.

Hirsch, R. (2002). *FEG: Stupid (Ridiculous) Poems for Intelligent Children*. New York, NY: Little Brown.

Janeczko, P. B. (2014). *Firefly July: A Year of Very Short Poems*. Somerville, MA: Candlewick Press.

Levine, G. C., & Cordell, M. (2012). *Forgive Me, I Meant to Do It: False Apology Poems*. New York, NY: Harper.

Lewis, J. (2005). *Please Bury Me in the Library*. Florida: Gulliver Books, Harcourt.

Prelutsky, J. (2005). *Read a Rhyme, Write a Rhyme*. New York, NY: Random House.

Salas, L. (2011). *Bookspeak!: Poems about Books*. New York, NY: Clarion Books.

Salas, L. P. (2012). *Picture Yourself Writing Poetry: Using Photos to Inspire Writing*. Mankato, MN: Capstone Classroom.

Salas, L. P., & Salerno, S. (2009). *Stampede: Poems to Celebrate the Wild Side of School*. New York, NY: Clarion Books.

Shakur, T. (1999). *The Rose That Grew from Concrete*. New York, NY: Pocket Books.

Silverstein, S. (1992). *Don't Bump the Glump! And Other Fantasies*. New York, NY: HarperCollins.

Silverstein, S. (2004). *Where the Sidewalk Ends*. New York, NY: HarperCollins.

Singer, M. (2010). *Mirror Mirror: A Book of Reversible Verse*. New York, NY: Penguin Group.

Stevenson, R. L., Corvino, L., & Schoonmaker, F. (2000). *Poetry for Young People: Robert Louis Stevenson*. New York, NY: Sterling.

Stockland, P. M., & Rojo, S. (2004). *Cobwebs, Chatters, and Chills: A Collection of Scary Poems*. Minneapolis, MN: Compass Point Books.

Online Resources:

http://www.poetry4kids.com/index.php_
http://www.gigglepoetry.com/
http://pbskids.org/arthur/games/poetry/what.html

ENGLISH   **Grade Levels:** 5–6

Book Trailers

Lesson Summary: Students will read a book, then create a short book trailer using Animoto or another video program. Through the process students will illustrate their understanding of the book and communicate it to others.

Standards Addressed:

AASL *Standards for the 21st Century Learner*

- Inquire, think critically, and gain knowledge (1.1.2; 1.1.4; 1.1.8; 1.1.9; 1.1.2; 1.2.3; 1.3.1; 1.3.3; 1.3.5; 1.4.2; 1.4.4)
- Draw conclusions, make informed decisions, apply knowledge to new situations, and create new knowledge (2.1.2; 2.1.4; 2.1.6)
- Share knowledge and participate ethically and productively as members of our democratic society (3.1.4; 3.1.6)
- Pursue personal and aesthetic growth (4.1.1; 4.1.7; 4.1.8; 4.2.4; 4.3.4; 4.4.1)

Common Core State Standards

- CCSS.ELA-Literacy.RI.5.1; RI.5.2; RI.5.4; RI.5.5; RI.5.6; RI.5.10
- CCSS.ELA-Literacy.RF.5.3; RF.5.4
- CCSS.ELA-Literacy.L.5.1; L.5.2; L.5.3; L.5.4; L.5.5; L.5.6
- CCSS.ELA-Literacy.SL.5.2; SL.5.5; SL.5.6
- CCSS.ELA-Literacy.RI.6.1; RI.6.2; RI.6.3; RI.6.4; RI.6.6; RI.6.10
- CCSS.ELA-Literacy.L.6.1; L.6.2; L.6.3; L.6.4; L.6.5; L.6.6
- CCSS.ELA-Literacy.SL.6.2; SL.6.5; SL.6.6

Instructional Resources:

- *Required*
  - Library or classroom book
  - Book Trailer Characteristics handout
  - Storyboard Template handout
  - Storyboard Example handout
  - Computers with Internet access
  - Access to a computer and projector or Smartboard
  - Access to Creative Commons: http://search.creativecommons.org for free images; Animoto: http://animoto.com, a free tool for online video creation

All handouts are included in the Student Resource site found at http://www.abc-clio.com/Libraries Unlimited/product.aspx?pc=A4367P.

- *Optional*
  - Digital camera, video camera, and microphone

Instructional Roles:

The school librarian and the classroom teacher co-teach this lesson, work together to guide the students in developing the book trailers, and oversee the assessment.

Adapted from an SLM learning plan by Melissa Purcell. English Language Arts: Lights, Cameras, Action, and Books!: A Book Trailer. *School Library Monthly*, Volume 29, Number 4, January 2013, pp. 56–58.

Procedure for Completion:

Day One: Prior to the assignment students are to choose a library book to read or use a required classroom reading assignment. The co-teachers will review the elements of a story—characters, plots, setting, and themes—and show several examples of grade-appropriate trailers. The co-teachers will brainstorm with the students to identify the elements of a quality book trailer as they complete the Quality Book Trailer Characteristics handout.

Day Two: Students create a storyboard for a 30-second book trailer by using a blank Storyboard Template handout and a Storyboard Example handout. After the storyboards are completed, the co-teachers will guide students as they search for images and videos utilizing the Creative Commons website or other free sources and provide a lesson on proper use of sources and citations.

Day Three—Completion: Students work on creating their book trailer.

Completion of Project:

The completed project is the storyboard and a 30-second book trailer created in Animoto, or other video software.

Student Assessment/Reflection:

Student assessment is based on the rubric for the project. Conversations and observations with the teacher and school librarian throughout the process will be included in the assessment.

Professional Reflection—Librarian Notes:

It would be most beneficial if the school librarian creates several trailers for this lesson using books from the library. The student-completed book trailers can also be used to promote books to other students by posting on the library website, through morning announcements, or setting up the trailers to run continuously on a station in the library.

Book Trailer Rubric

	Excellent	Satisfactory	Unsatisfactory
Book Summary and Storyboard	Summary is clear and concise with sufficient detail, no spelling or grammatical errors.	Summary is not clearly presented or spoils the story for a reader by giving away too many details. One or two spelling or grammatical errors.	Summary is incomplete, off topic, or presented in a way that gives too many details. Three or four grammatical errors.
Creativity and Pictures	High-quality pictures represent a significant element from the book and originality enhances the viewing experience.	Pictures are not the best quality and do not represent the most significant elements from the book. Shows some creativity but needs improvement to draw the viewer in.	Pictures seem random, making it hard to understand how they represent the book, or are of poor quality. Lacks creativity and originality, which makes it boring or not engaging.
Overall Construction	Book title and author are clearly identified, thoughts are organized and flow smoothly, and citations are properly included.	Book title is clearly identified but author is not, thoughts are organized but does not flow smoothly, and citations have some errors.	Book title and author are not clearly identified, layout is not organized, and no credit slide at the end.
Staying on Task	Student working as assigned and not disengaged or causing a disruption.	Student working well on assignment most of the time.	Student not on task or is a disciplinary problem.

Student Name:

Book Trailer Grade:

	Excellent	Satisfactory	Unsatisfactory
Book Summary and Storyboard			
Creativity and Pictures			
Overall Construction			
Staying on Task Daily			

From *The Common Core in Action: Ready-to-Use Lesson Plans for K–6 Librarians* by Deborah J. Jesseman. Santa Barbara, CA: Libraries Unlimited. Copyright © 2015.

SUGGESTED BIBLIOGRAPHY

Howard, D. A., & Hunter, A. M. (2014). *Teaching the Video Production Class: Beyond the Morning Newscast.* Santa Barbara, CA: ABC-CLIO, Libraries Unlimited.

Lanier, T., & Nichols, C. (2010). *Filmmaking for Teens: Pulling Off Your Shorts.* Studio City, CA: Michael Wiese Productions.

Online Resources:

Animoto: http://animoto.com, a free tool for online video creation

Creative Commons: http://search.creativecommons.org for free images

Book Trailers:

The False Princess by Eilis O'Neal and *Now Is the Time for Running* by Michael Williams can also be shared.

http://tinyurl.com/thefalseprincess

http://tinyurl.com/runningbywilliams

ENGLISH
Persuasive Text

Grade Levels: 5–6

Lesson Summary: In this lesson students will gain skills in identifying, reading, and understanding persuasive text. It is a lesson that can be repeated to encourage growth in this area while providing helpful strategies and connections to real-world issues as students develop skills related to required assessments.

Standards Addressed:

AASL *Standards for the 21st Century Learner*

- Inquire, think critically, and gain knowledge (1.1.1–1.1.3; 1.1.6–1.1.9; 1.2.4; 1.3.4; 1.4.2; 1.4.4)
- Draw conclusions, make informed decisions, apply knowledge to new situations, and create new knowledge (2.1.1–2.1.5; 2.2.3)
- Share knowledge and participate ethically and productively as members of our democratic society (3.1.1; 3.1.2; 3.1.5; 3.2.1; 3.2.2; 3.2.3; 3.3.1; 3.3.4)
- Pursue personal and aesthetic growth (4.1.4; 4.1.6; 4.3.1)

Common Core State Standards

- CCSS.ELA-Literacy.RI.5.1; RI.5.2; RI.5.4; RI.5.8; RI.5.10
- CCSS.ELA-Literacy.SL.5.1; SL.5.3; SL.5.4
- CCSS.ELA-Literacy.RI.6.1; RI.6.2; RI.6.3; RI.6.4; RI.6.5; RI.6.6; RI.6.8; RI.6.10
- CCSS.ELA-Literacy.SL.6.1; SL.6.3; SL.6.4; SL.6.6

Instructional Resources:

- *Required*
  - Persuasive Notes handout
  - Newspaper editorials
  - Persuasive Analysis handout
  - Persuasive Notes Discussion example

All handouts are included in the Student Resource site found at http://www.abc-clio.com/Libraries Unlimited/product.aspx?pc=A4367P.

- *Recommended*
  - Computer connected to projector or Smartboard access

Instructional Roles:

The classroom teacher and the school librarian are co-teachers in this lesson and work together to instruct, guide, and assess student learning.

Procedure for Completion:

Day One: Students are asked what it means to persuade someone and to give examples (persuading a parent to let them stay up late, go somewhere, or buy a video game). The co-teachers explain that persuasion can happen through talking, through written materials, or through media advertising like

Adapted from an SLM learning plan by Amy Brownlee. English Language Arts: Persuasive Reading with Newspaper Editorials. *School Library Monthly*, Volume 28, Number 6, March 2012, pp. 55–57.

television and radio commercials. Learning and utilizing persuasive reading is a lifelong skill that can help in making decisions such as buying a car or voting for the president.

The co-teachers provide the students with the Persuasive Notes handout. They will facilitate discussion about each question utilizing the Persuasive Notes Discussion Sample. "Bias" may be a new word for many students and extra time may be needed to explain the term. Some examples of bias may include advertising during a presidential campaign or believing that their high school football team is better than their closest rival. Students are reminded to take notes on the handout to be used later.

Day Two: The co-teachers will begin with a review of *Day One* and project a copy of a short editorial on the screen while guiding the students through the Persuasive Analysis handout. The class will be divided into small groups and given a new article and a Persuasive Analysis handout to complete. When each group has completed the handout they will present it to the class.

Day Three—Completion: Students will each be given an editorial and a Persuasive Analysis handout to complete individually for the final assessment.

Completion of Project:

The final product of this lesson will be the individual editorial and Persuasive Analysis handout.

Student Assessment/Reflection:

Students are assessed on their participation in the group Persuasive Analysis and presentation, their individual editorial and Persuasive Analysis handout, and conversations with the teacher and school librarian throughout the process.

Professional Reflection—Librarian Notes:

This lesson is one that can easily be differentiated for a variety of learners or grade levels by providing students with simpler or more complex examples of persuasive writing. It may be expanded to an analysis of television commercials or print advertising.

Persuasive Text Rubric

	Excellent	Satisfactory	Unsatisfactory
Persuasive Notes	Student completed the handout as assigned.	Student completed the handout but not handed in on time or needed assistance in completing it.	Student did not hand in the assignment or it was partially complete.
Group Persuasive Analysis	Student actively participated in the group work and presentation.	Student participated minimally in the group work and presentation.	Student did not participate in the group work and presentation.
Individual Persuasive Analysis	Work completed on time, accurate, and well written.	Work not completed on time, incomplete, or not well written.	Work not completed or is missing major elements.
Staying on Task Daily	Student working as assigned and not disengaged or causing a disruption.	Student working well on assignment most days.	Student not on task daily or is a disciplinary problem.

Student Name:
Persuasive Text Grade:

	Excellent	Satisfactory	Unsatisfactory
Persuasive Notes			
Group Persuasive Analysis			
Individual Persuasive Analysis			
Staying on Task Daily			

SUGGESTED BIBLIOGRAPHY

Backman, B. (2010). *Persuasion Points: 82 Strategic Exercises for Writing High-Scoring Persuasive Essays.* Gaines-
     ville, FL: Maupin House.
Clifford, T. (2007). *Crafting Opinion and Persuasive Papers.* Gainesville, FL: Maupin House.
Newspaper editorials.

Chapter 2

Science

SCIENCE/TECHNOLOGY   **Grade Levels:** K–1

Designing a House for the Three Little Pigs

Lesson Summary: This lesson will engage students in problem solving to save the three little pigs from the big bad wolf by examining how best to build a house.

Standards Addressed:

AASL *Standards for the 21st Century Learner*

- Inquire, think critically, and gain knowledge (1.1.1–1.1.2; 1.2.2; 1.4.2)
- Draw conclusions, make informed decisions, apply knowledge to new situations, and create new knowledge (2.1.1–2.1.3; 2.1.5; 2.2.4; 2.3.1)
- Share knowledge and participate ethically and productively as members of our democratic society (3.1.1; 3.1.3; 3.3.4)
- Pursue personal and aesthetic growth (4.1.l; 4.1.8; 4.4.4)

Common Core State Standards

- CCSS.ELA-Literacy.RL.K.1; RL.K.2; RL.K.3; RL.K.4; RL.K.7; RL.K.9
- CCSS.ELA-Literacy.SL.K.1; SL.K.2; SL.K.3; SL.K.4; SL.K.5; SL.K.6
- CCSS.ELA-Literacy.RL.1.1; RL.1.2; RL.1.3; RL.1.6; RL.1.7; RL.1.9
- CCSS.ELA-Literacy.SL.1.1; SL.1.2; SL.1.3; SL.1.4; SL.1.5; SL.1.6

Instructional Resources:

- *Required*
  - Marshall, James. *The Three Little Pigs.* Penguin, 1996
  - Handout: A House for the Three Little Pigs—one per student
  - Large pictures of five types of houses
  - Pencils, markers, crayons

All handouts are included in the Student Resource site found at http://www.abc-clio.com/Libraries Unlimited/product.aspx?pc=A4367P.

- *Recommended*
  - Computer with online access and projector

Adapted from an SLM learning plan by Marisa Congelio. Science/Technology: Problem Solving. *School Library Monthly,* Volume 29, Number 1, September–October 2012, pp. 53–54.

Instructional Roles:

The classroom teacher and school librarian collaborate to facilitate discussion with the students. The librarian reads the story aloud and the teacher models critical thinking skills during the story. At the end of the lesson, both the teacher and the school librarian individually question students to ensure understanding of the material taught.

Procedure for Completion:

Step One: The school librarian explains to the group that they are going to learn about building houses. To activate prior knowledge, the librarian asks the students:

> Have you ever seen a house being built (a house before it was a house)?
> What did it look like?
> What was it made out of?

Step Two: The school library reads the story *The Three Little Pigs* by James Marshall. At the point in the story when each pig is building his house, the teacher models critical thinking skills, saying something like: "This pig is building his house out of _____. I think this is a good idea because _____. I think this is a bad idea because _____. I know this because _____."

Step Three: At the end of the story the school librarian and the classroom teacher prompt a class discussion, asking students:

> What was the best material for the pigs to use to build a home?
> Why do you think that material was the best choice?

Step Four: Students are shown pictures of five different types of houses. For each picture the teacher asks the students if the example would be a good house or a bad house for the three little pigs to live in. Then the students are given the handout, A House for the Three Little Pigs, and are instructed to design a house for the pigs. They will decide which design will be the best choice so that the house can survive the big bad wolf. The teacher and school librarian will assure the students that in real life a big bad wolf will not come to their house, but rain, snow, sun, and cold weather will come in contact with a house built today.

Completion of Project:

The final project will be the completed drawing on the House for the Three Little Pigs handout.

Student Assessment/Reflection:

The final project is the object of the main student assessment and is based on the rubric for the project. Conversations with the teacher and school librarian throughout the process will also be included in the assessment process.

Professional Reflection—Librarian Notes:

If a computer and projector are available, searching "house" images online or using www.flickr.com is a good way to lead the discussion of the various types of houses.

House Design Rubric

	Excellent	Satisfactory	Unsatisfactory
Step One: House Drawing	Work completed as assigned on time.	Work completed but not on time or extensive assistance was needed.	Work not completed or having several revisions before moving to the next step.
Step Two: Building Justification	Work completed on time and all requirements have been met.	Work not completed on time or missing elements.	Work not completed or missing major elements.
Staying on Task Daily	Student working as assigned and not disengaged or causing a disruption.	Student working well on assignment most days.	Student not on task daily or is a discipline problem.

Student Name:

House Design Grade:

	Excellent	Satisfactory	Unsatisfactory
Step One: House Drawing			
Step Two: Building Justification			
Staying on Task Daily			

SUGGESTED BIBLIOGRAPHY

Barton, B. (1990). *Building a House.* New York, NY: Greenwillow Books.

Bean, J. (2013). *Building Our House.* New York, NY: Farrar, Straus and Giroux.

Gibbons, G. (1996). *How a House Is Built.* New York, NY: Holiday House.

Marshall, J. (2000). *The Three Little Pigs.* New York, NY: Grosset & Dunlap.

Moore, I. (2011). *A House in the Woods.* Somerville, MA: Candlewick.

Ring, S. (2006). *Places We Live.* Mankato, MN: Capstone Classroom.

Yates, V. (2008). *Buildings.* Mankato, MN: Capstone Classroom.

Zimmerman, K. (2013). *Alex Builds a House.* Amazon Digital Services.

SCIENCE   Grade Levels: K–1

Let's Take a Weather Trip

Lesson Summary: The lesson is designed to help students establish an understanding of weather symbols and build background knowledge about weather concepts.

Standards Addressed:

AASL *Standards for the 21st Century Learner*

- Inquire, think critically, and gain knowledge (1.1.1; 1.1.2; 1.1.3; 1.1.4; 1.1.6; 1.4.2)
- Draw conclusions, make informed decisions, apply knowledge to new situations, and create new knowledge (2.1.1; 2.1.3)
- Share knowledge and participate ethically and productively as members of our democratic society (3.1.1; 3.2.1)
- Pursue personal and aesthetic growth (4.1.3)

Common Core State Standards

- CCSS.ELA-Literacy.RI.K.1; RI.K.4; RI.K.5
- CCSS.ELA-Literacy.RL.K.1; RL.K.4; RL.K.7
- CCSS.ELA-Literacy.SL.K.1; SL.K.2; SL.K.3; SL.K.6
- CCSS.ELA-Literacy.RI.1.1; RI.1.2; RI.1.4; RI.1.5; RI.1.6
- CCSS.ELA-Literacy.RL.1.1; RL.1.4
- CCSS.ELA-Literacy.SL.1.1; SL.1.2; SL.1.3; SL.1.6

Instructional Resources:

- *Required*
  - *Thunder Cake* by Patricia Polacco
  - Local newspapers that include the weather section showing the United States map with weather symbols
  - Weather symbols and words on cards
  - United States map
  - Document camera if needed

All handouts are included in the Student Resource site found at http://www.abc-clio.com/Libraries Unlimited/product.aspx?pc=A4367P.

Instructional Roles:

The classroom teacher and school librarian co-teach this lesson and take students on a weather trip. As the students "travel" they will demonstrate that they can identify the words for weather and the related symbols.

Procedure for Completion:

Step One: The students are taken to the periodical area in the school library and shown where the newspapers are located. They sit in an open area so they can see each other. The teachers will show the

Adapted from an SLM learning plan by Karen Scribner. Science: Let's Take a Weather Trip. *School Library Monthly*, Volume XXVII, Number 1, September–October 2010, pp. 18–19.

students a newspaper and demonstrate how each section is organized by alphabet. They will open the newspaper to the section containing the United States map with the weather symbols, utilizing a document camera for magnification if needed.

Step Two: Each student will be handed a flashcard with a weather symbol and instructed to raise their weather flashcard when they hear their weather word as the teachers make statements like, "It's raining," "Now there is ice falling from the sky," "Oh no, we're having a thunderstorm."

The teachers tell the students that they are going on a weather trip and are directed to lift their symbol when they hear their weather word. Ask them to get ready to pretend that they are all on a bus together and are going to many wonderful places that will be great fun to visit. However, there will be some kind of weather taking place at each stop of their trip and it will be their job to help you know the symbols that match the weather along the route. The teachers will create a trip that begins in their hometown, circles the United States, and ends back where it began. A United States map could be posted as a way to track the trip.

Step Three—Completion: The school librarian and classroom teacher check for understanding by having the students trade their weather card with another student, then discuss how some people are afraid of thunderstorms or other severe weather. The school librarian reads aloud *Thunder Cake* by Patricia Polacco and leads a discussion on fear of severe weather and what we can do to ease that fear. After the story the classroom teacher will call out the name of each type of weather as the students hand in their cards.

Student Assessment/Reflection:

Understanding of the weather symbols is the object of the main student assessment and is based on observations and conversations with the teacher and school librarian throughout the lesson.

Professional Reflection—Librarian Notes:

Other weather-themed stories and activities can be read to further enhance the students' knowledge of their weather vocabulary. A suggestion to the classroom teacher may be to include weather words and symbols in their classroom calendars throughout the year.

Weather Trip Rubric			
	Excellent	Satisfactory	Unsatisfactory
Symbol Identification	Student correctly identified the weather symbol.	Student had to be encouraged to identify their weather symbol correctly.	Student did not participate in the activity.
Weather Trip Participation	Student actively participated in the activity.	Student minimally participated in the activity.	Student did not participate in the activity.
Staying on Task	Student contributing to the activity and not disengaged or causing a disruption.	Student contributing to the activity most of the time.	Student not on task or is a discipline problem.

Student Name:

Weather Trip Grade:

	Excellent	Satisfactory	Unsatisfactory
Symbol Identification			
Weather Trip Participation			
Staying on Task			

SUGGESTED BIBLIOGRAPHY

Branley, F. M. (1999). *Flash, Crash, Rumble, and Roll.* New York, NY: HarperCollins.

Dean, J. (2013). *Freddy the Frogcaster.* Washington, DC: Regnery Kids.

Dean, J. (2014). *Freddy the Frogcaster and the Big Blizzard.* Washington, DC: Regnery Kids.

Gibbins, G. (1992). *Weather Words and What They Mean.* New York, NY: Holiday House.

Martin, B. (1988). *Listen to the Rain.* New York, NY: Henry Holt.

Polacco, P. (1997). *Thunder Cake.* New York, NY: Puffin.

Rabe, T. (2004). *Oh Say Can You Say What's the Weather Today?: All About Weather.* New York, NY: Random House Books for Young Readers.

Simon, S. (2006). *Weather.* New York, NY: HarperCollins.

Snedeker, J. (2012). *The Everything KIDS' Weather Book: From Tornadoes to Snowstorms, Puzzles, Games, and Facts That Make Weather for Kids Fun!* Fort Collins, CO: Adams Media.

Online Resource:

Weather Symbols: http://prognoza.hr/wsymbols.html

SCIENCE   **Grade Levels:** K–2

Animals

Lesson Summary: This lesson is designed to enhance the teaching of animals in the early elementary curriculum. Students will investigate and understand that animals have life needs and specific physical characteristics. They will be guided to research a particular animal and learn about key elements such as habitat, diet, physical characteristics, and location.

Standards Addressed:

AASL *Standards for the 21st Century Learner*

- Inquire, think critically, and gain knowledge (1.1.1–1.1.6; 1.2.1–1.2.7; 1.3.1–1.3.5)
- Draw conclusions, make informed decisions, apply knowledge to new situations, and create new knowledge (2.1.2; 2.1.4; 2.1.5; 2.1.6; 2.2.4; 2.4.3)
- Share knowledge and participate ethically and productively as members of our democratic society (3.1.2; 3.1.3; 3.1.6; 3.2.1)
- Pursue personal and aesthetic growth (4.1.8; 4.2.1; 4.2.3; 4.3.3; 4.3.4; 4.4.1–4.4.3)

Common Core State Standards

- CCSS.ELA-Literacy.RI.K.1; RI.K.2; RI.K.3; RI.K.4; RI.K.8; RI.K.9
- CCSS.ELA-Literacy.RF.K.1; RF.K.2; RF.K.3; RF.K.4
- CCSS.ELA-Literacy.L.K.1; L.K.2; L.K.4; L.K.5; L.K.6
- CCSS.ELA-Literacy.SL.K.1; SL.K.2; SL.K.3; SL.K.4; SL.K.5; SL.K.6
- CCSS.ELA-Literacy.RI.1.1; RI.1.2; RI.1.3; RI.1.4; RI.1.5; RI.1.6; RI.1.7; RI.1.8; RI.1.9; RI.1.10
- CCSS.ELA-Literacy.RF.1.1; RF.1.2; RF.1.3; RF.1.4
- CCSS.ELA-Literacy.L.1.1; L.1.2; L.1.4; L.1.5; L.1.6
- CCSS.ELA-Literacy.SL.1.1; SL.1.2; SL.1.3; SL.1.4; SL.1.5; SL.1.6
- CCSS.ELA-Literacy.RI.2.1; RI.2.2; RI.2.3; RI.2.4; RI.2.5; RI.2.6; RI.2.7; RI.2.8; RI.2.9; RI.2.10
- CCSS.ELA-Literacy.RF.2.3; RF.2.4
- CCSS.ELA-Literacy.L.2.1; L.2.2; L.2.3; L.2.4; L.2.5; L.2.6
- CCSS.ELA-Literacy.SL.2.1; SL.2.2; SL.2.3; SL.2.4; SL.2.5; SL.2.6

Instructional Resources:

- *Required*
  - Access to research materials such as encyclopedias, books, magazines, and online resources
  - Organizational handout for students to complete
  - Poster board, pencils, markers, crayons, paper

All handouts are included in the Student Resource site found at http://www.abc-clio.com/Libraries Unlimited/product.aspx?pc=A4367P.

Instructional Roles:

The classroom teacher will introduce animals as a unit. The school librarian will introduce beginning research skills that include encyclopedias, books, magazines, and online resources.

Procedure for Completion:

Day One: The teacher introduces the animal unit and both teacher and school librarian will work with the class in completing the organizational handout with a sample animal.

Day Two: The school librarian teaches basic research skills and provides students the opportunity to research their animal using a variety of sources that may be available in their school library.

Day Three: Students return to the library to continue research and completion of organizational handout.

Day Four: Students are provided time and supplies to complete the poster.

Day Five—Completion: Students will present their research to the class utilizing the poster as a resource.

Completion of Project:

The result will be completion of a poster that includes the information required on an organizational handout, a drawing or picture of the animal, and presentation of their work to the class. These will be displayed in the school library or classroom.

Student Assessment/Reflection:

The final project and presentation is the object of the main student assessment and is based on the rubric for the project. Conversations with the teacher and school librarian throughout the process will also be included in the assessment process.

Professional Reflection—Librarian Notes:

The Common Core State Standards align well with the collection development of nonfiction materials. Each school library will have a variety of resources specific to their school, but lessons such as this provide an opportunity to expand the collection.

Animal Rubric

	Excellent	Satisfactory	Unsatisfactory
Step One: Choose an Animal to Research	Work completed as assigned on time.	Work completed but not on time or extensive assistance was needed.	Work not completed or having several revisions before moving to the next step.
Step Two: Completion of the Organizational Handout	Work completed on time and all requirements have been met.	Work not completed on time or missing elements.	Work not completed or missing major elements.
Step Three: Completed Poster and Presentation	Work completed on time, presentation understandable, and all elements included.	Work completed but not on time or missing elements.	Work not completed or needing several revisions.
Staying on Task Daily	Student working as assigned and not disengaged or causing a disruption.	Student working well on assignment most days.	Student not on task daily or is a discipline problem.

Student Name:

Animal Grade:

	Excellent	Satisfactory	Unsatisfactory
Step One: Choose an Animal to Research			
Step Two: Completion of the Organizational Handout			
Step Three: Completed Poster and Presentation			
Staying on Task Daily			

SUGGESTED BIBLIOGRAPHY

Arctic Animals. (2015). LEAP (Little Books with Attitude). Mankato, MN: Capstone Classroom.

Flamingo Features. (2015). LEAP (Little Books with Attitude). Mankato, MN: Capstone Classroom.

Flying Disks. (2015). LEAP (Little Books with Attitude). Mankato, MN: Capstone Classroom.

Frog Features. (2015). LEAP (Little Books with Attitude). Mankato, MN: Capstone Classroom.

Martin, I. (2015). *Amphibians: A Question and Answer Book.* Mankato, MN: Capstone Classroom.

Martin, I. (2015). *Birds: A Question and Answer Book.* Mankato, MN: Capstone Classroom.

Martin, I. (2015). *Fish: A Question and Answer Book.* Mankato, MN: Capstone Classroom.

Martin, I. (2015). *Insects: A Question and Answer Book.* Mankato, MN: Capstone Classroom.

Martin, I. (2015). *Mammals: A Question and Answer Book.* Mankato, MN: Capstone Classroom.

Martin, I. (2015). *Reptiles: A Question and Answer Book.* Mankato, MN: Capstone Classroom.

Rissman, R. (2015). *Barn Owls: Nocturnal Hunters.* Mankato, MN: Capstone Classroom.

Rissman, R. (2015). *Bats: Nocturnal Flyers.* Mankato, MN: Capstone Classroom.

Rissman, R. (2015). *Hedgehogs: Nocturnal Foragers.* Mankato, MN: Capstone Classroom.

Rissman, R. (2015). *Mice: Nocturnal Explorers.* Mankato, MN: Capstone Classroom.

Rissman, R. (2015). *Red Foxes: Nocturnal Predators.* Mankato, MN: Capstone Classroom.

South American Animals. (2015). LEAP (Little Books with Attitude). Mankato, MN: Capstone Classroom.

Tiger Features. (2015). LEAP (Little Books with Attitude). Mankato, MN: Capstone Classroom.

SCIENCE   **Grade Levels:** 2–3

Everyday Weather

Lesson Summary: This lesson is designed to allow students to conduct investigations and use appropriate tools to build an understanding of the changes in weather throughout the year.

Standards Addressed:

AASL *Standards for the 21st Century Learner*

- Inquire, think critically, and gain knowledge (1.1.1–1.1.6; 1.1.8; 1.2.1; 1.3.3; 1.3.5; 1.4.2; 1.4.4)
- Draw conclusions, make informed decisions, apply knowledge to new situations, and create new knowledge (2.2.1; 2.1.2; 2.1.3; 2.2.3; 2.2.4; 2.3.1)
- Share knowledge and participate ethically and productively as members of our democratic society (3.1.1; 3.3.4)
- Pursue personal and aesthetic growth (4.1.4; 4.1.6; 4.1.8; 4.3.2)

Common Core State Standards

- CCSS.ELA-Literacy.RI.2.1; RI.2.2; RI.2.3; RI.2.4; RI.2.5; RI.2.6; RI.2.7; RI.2.8; RI.2.9; RI.2.10
- CCSS.ELA-Literacy.RF.2.3; RF.2.4
- CCSS.ELA-Literacy.W.2.2; W.2.8
- CCSS.ELA-Literacy.RI.3.1; RI.3.2; RI.3.3; RI.3.4; RI.3.5; RI.3.7; RI.3.8; RI.3.9; RI.3.10
- CCSS.ELA-Literacy.RF.3.3; RF.3.4
- CCSS.ELA-Literacy.W.3.2; W.3.4; W.3.8

Instructional Resources:

- *Required*
  - o KWL Everyday Weather Chart handout
  - o Illustrated Weather Chart handout
  - o Access to online climate databases

All handouts are included in the Student Resource site found at http://www.abc-clio.com/Libraries Unlimited/product.aspx?pc=A4367P.

Instructional Roles:

The classroom teacher will introduce weather vocabulary, concepts, and tools. The school librarian works with the teacher to engage students in developing the KWL chart on weather and directs the students in accessing and using a variety of resources.

Procedure for Completion:

Step One: The classroom teacher instructs students in the use of weather tools such as thermometers, wind vanes, anemometers, and rain gauges. The school librarian introduces search strategies for weather-related resources in print, nonprint, and digital formats, demonstrates the use of weather databases, and provides weather data from a variety of seasons to allow for comparison of student-collected data to changes throughout the year.

Adapted from an SLM learning plan by Sandra Andrews & Linda Gann. Science: EverydayWeather. *School Library Monthly*, Volume 28, Number 2, November 2011, pp. 52–53.

Step Two: The co-teachers assist students in constructing a KWL chart using previous knowledge and research tools to complete the "What do I know?" column. Students generate questions based on their data in the K column to complete the "What do I want to know?" column.

Step Three: Students use a variety of resources to discover answers to their questions and complete illustrated charts of the differences in weather during each of the four seasons. Illustrations should show appropriate clothing for the weather, seasonal activities, and accurate representation of the outdoors. Their charts should include descriptions of temperature, precipitation, and wind.

Step Four—Completion: Students will individually complete the KWL and Illustrated Weather charts comparing the differences in weather data among seasons.

Student Assessment/Reflection:

The KWL and Illustrated Weather charts will be assessed based on the project rubric. The teacher and the school librarian will also focus on the process based on observations and conversations with the student throughout the lesson.

Professional Reflection—Librarian Notes:

This unit can be expanded beyond the science area to include social studies by exploring famous weather-related events or language arts through creative writing, poetry, and fictional accounts of weather events.

Everyday Weather Rubric

	Excellent	Satisfactory	Unsatisfactory
KWL Weather Chart	Student completed the chart with thoughtful questions.	Chart not filled in completely or with superficial questions.	Student did not complete the chart.
Illustrated Weather Chart	Student completed the chart correctly, neatly, and creatively.	Student completed the chart but it was messy or inaccurate.	Student did not complete the chart.
Staying on Task	Student contributing to the activity and not disengaged or causing a disruption.	Student contributing to the activity most of the time.	Student not on task or was a discipline problem.

Student Name:
Everyday Weather Grade:

	Excellent	Satisfactory	Unsatisfactory
KWL Weather Chart			
Illustrated Weather Chart			
Staying on Task			

SUGGESTED BIBLIOGRAPHY

Barraclough, S. (2009). *Weather and Seasons*. Mankato, MN: Heinemann.

Branley, F. M. (1999). *Flash, Crash, Rumble, and Roll*. New York, NY: HarperCollins.

Cassino, M., & Nelson, J. (2009). *The Story of Snow: The Science of Winter's Wonder*. San Francisco, CA: Chronicle Books.

Gibbins, G. (1992). *Weather Words and What They Mean*. New York, NY: Holiday House.

Goin, M. B. (2009). *Storms*. Washington, DC: National Geographic.

Rockwell, A. (2008). *Clouds*. New York, NY: Collins.

Royston, A. (2008). *Looking at Weather and Seasons: How Do They Change?* Berkeley Heights, NJ: Enslow.

Sievert, T. (2005). *Weather Forecasting*. Mankato, MN: Capstone Classroom.

Stille, D. R. (2012). *The Science Behind Weather*. Mankato, MN: Raintree.

Williams, J. (2004). *Searching for Stormy Weather with a Scientist*. Berkeley Heights, NJ: Enslow.

Online Resources:

National Climatic Data Center: http://www.ncdc.noaa.gov/oa/ncdc.html

Weather Channel: http://www.weather.com/

State or Regional Databases for Weather Information:

Florida Climate Center: http://climatecenter.fsu.edu/

Indiana State Climate Office: http://iclimate.org/index.asp

New Hampshire State Climate Office: http://www.unh.edu/stateclimatologist/

North Carolina State Climate Office: http://www.nc-climate.ncsu.edu/cronos

North Dakota State Climate Office: http://www.ndsu.edu/ndsco/

State Climate Offices Director: http://www.hprcc.unl.edu/stateoffices.php

Wisconsin State Climate Office: http://www.aos.wisc.edu/~sco/

Wyoming State Climate Office: http://www.wrds.uwyo.edu/sco/climate_office.html

SCIENCE   Grade Levels: 2–3
"Getting Buggy"

Lesson Summary: This lesson utilizes fiction stories by David Biedrzycki and nonfiction books to review research and technology skills while exploring insects.

Standards Addressed:

AASL *Standards for the 21st Century Learner*

- Inquire, think critically, and gain knowledge (1.1.1–1.1.6; 1.1.9; 1.2.3; 1.2.4; 1.2.6; 1.3.5; 1.4.2; 1.4.4)
- Draw conclusions, make informed decisions, apply knowledge to new situations, and create new knowledge (2.1.1–2.1.4; 2.1.6; 2.3.1)
- Share knowledge and participate ethically and productively as members of our democratic society (3.1.1; 3.1.3; 3.3.4)
- Pursue personal and aesthetic growth (4.1.1; 4.1.2; 4.1.3; 4.1.6; 4.1.8; 4.2.1; 4.3.2; 4.4.1)

Common Core State Standards

- CCSS.ELA-Literacy.RI.2.1; RI.2.2; RI.2.3; RI.2.4; RI.2.5; RI.2.6; RI.2.7; RI.2.9; RI.2.10
- CCSS.ELA-Literacy.RL.2.1; RL.2.4; RL.2.5; RL.2.6; RL.2.10
- CCSS.ELA-Literacy.SL.2.1; SL.2.2; SL.2.3
- CCSS.ELA-Literacy.RI.3.1; RI.3.2; RI.3.3; RI.3.4; RI.3.5; RI.3.6; RI.3.7; RI.3.8; RI.3.9; RI.3.10
- CCSS.ELA-Literacy.RL.3.1; RL.3.3; RL.3.4; RL.3.6; RL.3.7; RL.3.10
- CCSS.ELA-Literacy.SL.3.1; SL.3.2; SL.3.3

Instructional Resources:

- *Required*
  - *Ace Lacewing, Bug Detective* by David Biedrzycki
  - Computer access to online instructional databases and the author's website
  - Insect Information Organizer handout
  - Pencil, markers, colored pencils, crayons
  - Access to books and resources about insects

All handouts are included in the Student Resource site found at http://www.abc-clio.com/Libraries Unlimited/product.aspx?pc=A4367P.

- *Recommended*
  - Document camera, projector, Smartboard, whiteboard

Instructional Roles:

The classroom teacher and the school librarian will co-teach this lesson by dividing the activities in the manner best suited to their strengths as teachers.

Adapted from an SLM learning plan by Pamela Cassel. Science/Language Arts: "Getting Buggy" with David Biedrzycki. *School Library Monthly*, Volume 28, Number 8, May–June 2012, pp. 53–55.

Procedure for Completion:

Day One: The school librarian introduces author David Biedrzcky to the students by sharing background information from his website and blog, including an overview of the books he has illustrated and authored. The three *Ace Lacewing* books, *The Beetle Alphabet Book, The Icky Bug Colors,* and *The Icky Bug Numbers* should be available for the students to look through and ask what they notice about his possible interests (bugs).

The school librarian guides the students and points out the author's picture in the back of *Ace Lacewing, Bug Detective, Bad Bugs are My Business* and points out that he chose to use a photo from when he was a young boy (about their age). The school librarian may want to ask the students what is unusual about the photo (he has antennae on top of his head) and share the information below his photo to discuss why he uses words such as "larvae," "pupa," and "nest," in his author biography. The end papers of *Ace Lacewing, Bad Bugs Are My Business* showing the map of the City of Motham may be of particular interest as the names of the locations shown on the map relate to the names of insects that are referred to on the map.

The school librarian will read *Ace Lacewing, Bad Bugs Are My Business* to the class, projecting the illustrations if possible so they can see the many details that have been included and pausing as needed to list insects that are mentioned in the story.

Day Two—Completion: The co-teachers will review the list of insects that the students generated the previous day. Share the information that David Biedrzycki used the facts he had gathered about insects to write the book. Even though *Ace Lacewing, Bad Bugs Are My Business* is a fiction story, there are many details that are factual about the insect characters. For instance, baby boll weevils grow up inside the cotton bolls and do not emerge until they are adults.

The students are informed that they will become experts in an insect, will be given an Insect Information Organizer handout, and are to choose an insect to research. The co-teachers will guide the students to the appropriate resources and check their handouts as they work. If the notes are complete the students will be given markers, crayons, or colored pencils to create an illustration of their insect.

Completion of Project:

Students will complete the notes and illustration on the Insect Information Organizer.

Student Assessment/Reflection:

The Insect Information Organizer will be assessed based on the project rubric. The teacher and the school librarian will also focus on the process based on observations and conversations with the students throughout the lesson.

Professional Reflection—Librarian Notes:

The original lesson was a precursor for an author visit by David Biedrzycki by familiarizing the students with his books and incorporating the science lesson. The school librarian may want to investigate the possibility of bringing the author to the school or have a local expert on the subject visit.

Getting Buggy Rubric

	Excellent	Satisfactory	Unsatisfactory
Student Contribution to Group Lesson	Student contributed to the group discussion with thoughtful responses.	Student contributed minimally to the group discussion or was prompted to participate.	Student did not contribute to the discussion.
Insect Information Organizer	Student completed the chart correctly, neatly, and creatively.	Student completed the chart but it was messy or inaccurate.	Student did not complete the chart.
Staying on Task	Student contributing to the activity and not disengaged or causing a disruption.	Student contributing to the activity most of the time.	Student not on task or was a discipline problem.

Student Name:
Getting Buggy Grade:

	Excellent	Satisfactory	Unsatisfactory
Student Contribution to Group Lesson			
Insect Information Organizer			
Staying on Task			

From *The Common Core in Action: Ready-to-Use Lesson Plans for K–6 Librarians* by Deborah J. Jesseman. Santa Barbara, CA: Libraries Unlimited. Copyright © 2015.

SUGGESTED BIBLIOGRAPHY

Ashley, S. (2011). *Incredible Ants.* New York, NY: Gareth Stevens.

Ashley, S. (2011). *Incredible Grasshoppers.* New York, NY: Gareth Stevens.

Ashley, S. (2011). *Incredible Ladybugs.* New York, NY: Gareth Stevens.

Ashley, S. (2011). *Incredible World of Insects.* New York, NY: Gareth Stevens.

Biedrzycki, D. (2008). *Ace Lacewing: Bug Detective.* Watertown, MA: Charlesbridge.

Biedrzycki, D. (2011). *Ace Lacewing, Bug Detective: Bad Bugs Are My Business.* Watertown, MA: Charlesbridge.

Biedrzycki, D. (2010). *Ace Lacewing, Bug Detective: The Big Swat.* Watertown, MA: Charlesbridge.

Biedrzycki, D., & Pallotta, J. (2004). *The Beetle Alphabet Book.* Watertown, MA: Charlesbridge.

Hall, M. (2006). *Dragonflies.* Mankato, MN: Capstone Press.

Hall, M. (2006). *Fireflies.* Mankato, MN: Capstone Press.

Hall, M. (2004). *Praying Mantises.* Mankato, MN: Capstone Press.

Howard, F. (2005). *Walkingsticks.* Mankato, MN: Capstone Press.

Miller, C. C. (2011). *The Creepiest Animals.* Mankato, MN: Capstone Press.

Miller, C. C. (2007). *Disgusting Bugs.* Mankato, MN: Capstone Press.

Pallotta, J., & Biedrzycki, D. (illus.) (2004). *The Icky Bug Colors.* New York, NY: Scholastic.

Pallotta, J., & Biedrzycki, D. (illus.) (2004). *The Icky Bug Numbers.* New York, NY: Scholastic.

Sexton, C. A. (2009). *Aphids.* Minneapolis, MN: Bellweather Media.

Online Resources:

David Biedrzycki's blog: http://davidbiedrzycki.com/sandbox/davids-blog/

David Biedrzycki's website: http://www.davidbiedrzycki.com/Its_All_About_Me.html

SCIENCE   **Grade Levels:** 3–4

Volcanoes

Lesson Summary: This lesson is included as the culminating activity during the study of volcanoes. The lesson will include facts about the formation of volcanoes, research on the modern-day eruption of Mount St. Helens and the recent eruption in Hawaii, and conclude with the students creating and "erupting" a volcano.

Standards Addressed:

AASL *Standards for the 21st Century Learner*

- Inquire, think critically, and gain knowledge (1.1.1–1.1.9; 1.2.1; 1.3.4; 1.3.5)
- Draw conclusions, make informed decisions, apply knowledge to new situations, and create new knowledge (2.1.1–2.1.5; 2.3.1–2.3.3; 2.4.1–2.4.4)
- Share knowledge and participate ethically and productively as members of our democratic society (3.1.1; 3.1.2; 3.1.5; 3.1.6; 3.3.3; 3.3.4; 3.4.3)
- Pursue personal and aesthetic growth (4.1.6–4.1.8; 4.2.1; 4.3.1–4.3.4; 4.4.1–4.4.6)

Common Core State Standards

- CCSS.ELA-Literacy.RI.3.1; RI.3.2; RI.3.3; RI.3.4; RI.3.5; RI.3.6; RI.3.7; RI.3.8; RI.3.9; RI.3.10
- CCSS.ELA-Literacy.RF.3.3; RF.3.4
- CCSS.ELA-Literacy.RI.4.1; RI.4.2; RI.4.3; RI.4.4; RI.4.5; RI.4.6; RI.4.7; RI.4.8; RI.4.9; RI.4.10
- CCSS.ELA-Literacy.RF.4.3; RF.4.4

Instructional Resources:

- *Required*
  - Each group will be provided:
    - A jar for the ingredients
    - A dishpan to protect surfaces and collect the mess
    - Measuring cups
    - Water
    - Baking soda
    - Dish soap
    - Vinegar
    - Food coloring
- *Recommended*
  - Access to a computer, presentation hardware, and TeacherTube videos

Instructional Roles:

The teacher will provide the scientific facts about volcanoes and the school librarian will share and guide the research on volcanic eruptions and their aftermath. The instructors will co-teach with the culminating activity of a volcanic eruption.

Procedure for Completion:

Day One: The classroom teacher and school librarian will co-teach to provide background and instruction on the cross-section of the volcano. If possible, a computer display of this information should be utilized.

Day Two: The co-teachers will present information and stories on the eruption of Mount St. Helens and in Hawaii. Online access will provide additional visual information. The school librarian may include the reading of a picture book on the topic.

Day Three—Completion: Students will work in groups to construct a "volcano" and "erupt" it.

Completion of Project:

The successful eruption of the volcano in each group.

Student Assessment/Reflection:

The successful eruption of the group volcano and conversations with the teacher and school librarian throughout the process will also be included in the assessment process. The teacher may include a quiz or test on the facts and research.

Professional Reflection—Librarian Notes:

This is an opportunity for the school librarian to work with the teacher in presenting the lesson by providing online resources as well as fiction and nonfiction books on the subject. The recent volcanic eruptions in Iceland and the disruption of air travel in the United Kingdom and Scandinavia may be topics to explore further with the students.

Volcanoes Rubric

	Excellent	Satisfactory	Unsatisfactory
Step One: Building the Volcano	Work completed as assigned on time.	Work completed but not on time or extensive corrections needed before eruption.	Work not completed.
Step Two: Volcanic Eruption	A successful eruption!	The result was not as expected or the group needed to redo the mixture.	Did not follow directions and the reaction did not work.
Staying on Task Daily	Student working as assigned and not disengaged or causing a disruption	Student working well on assignment most days.	Student not on task daily or is a discipline problem.

Student Name:

Volcanoes Grade:

	Excellent	Satisfactory	Unsatisfactory
Step One: Building the Volcano			
Step Two: Volcanic Eruption			
Staying on Task Daily			

SUGGESTED BIBLIOGRAPHY

Griffey, H. (1998). *DK Readers: Volcanoes and Other Natural Disasters.* (1998). New York, NY: DK Children.

Jenner, C. (2014). *DK Adventures: In the Shadow of the Volcano.* New York, NY: DK Children.

Kehret, P. (1998). *The Volcano Disaster.* New York, NY: Aladdin.

Lauber, P. (1993). *Volcano: The Eruption and Healing of Mount St. Helens.* New York, NY: Turtleback Books.

Rusch, E., & Uhlman, T. (2013). *Eruption: Volcanoes and the Science of Saving Lives.* Boston: Houghton Mifflin Books for Children.

Schreiber, A. (2008). *Volcanoes!* Washington, DC: National Geographic Children's Books.

Thomsen, P. (1997). *Mountain of Fire: The Daring Rescue from Mount St. Helens.* Dallas, TX: Institute for Creation Research.

Website and TeacherTube Examples:

http://www.teachertube.com/video/how-volcanoes-work-188551Volcano (3 minutes)

http://www.teachertube.com/video/mt-st-helens-eruption-explosion-280127 (4 minutes)

http://www.teachertube.com/video/rp-volcanoes-230989 (43 minutes)

http://www.teachertube.com/video/volcano-interactive-lesson-19611 (6 minutes)

http://www.wikihow.com/Make-a-Volcano

SCIENCE

Solar System

Grade Levels: 3–4

Lesson Summary: This lesson takes students on an out-of-this-world field trip that helps them understand the solar system and the planets within. It also provides a creative way to gather and share information.

Standards Addressed:

AASL *Standards for the 21st Century Learner*

- Inquire, think critically, and gain knowledge (1.1.1–1.1.6; 1.1.8; 1.2.3; 1.2.6; 1.2.7; 1.3.1; 1.3.3; 1.3.5; 1.4.2; 1.4.4)
- Draw conclusions, make informed decisions, apply knowledge to new situations, and create new knowledge (2.1.2; 2.1.3; 2.1.4; 2.1.6; 2.2.1; 2.2.3; 2.2.4; 2.3.1; 2.4.1; 2.4.4)
- Share knowledge and participate ethically and productively as members of our democratic society (3.1.1; 3.1.3; 3.1.4; 3.1.6; 3.3.4)
- Pursue personal and aesthetic growth (4.1.4; 4.1.6; 4.1.8; 4.3.4)

Common Core State Standards

- CCSS.ELA-Literacy.RI.3.1; RI.3.3; RI.3.4; RI.3.5; RI.3.7; RI.3.9; RI.3.10
- CCSS.ELA-Literacy.W.3.2; W.3.3; W.3.4; W.3.5; W.3.6; W.3.7; W.3.10
- CCSS.ELA-Literacy.RI.4.1; RI.4.3; RI.4.4; RI.4.5; RI.4.7; RI.4.9; RI.4.10
- CCSS.ELA-Literacy.W.4.2; W.4.3; W.4.4; W.4.5; W.4.6; W.4.7; W.4.9; W.4.10

Instructional Resources:

- *Required*
  - *Postcards from Pluto: A Tour of the Solar System* by Loreen Leedy
  - Access to information websites such as Enchanted Learning, Fact Monster, or an online encyclopedia
  - Nonfiction books about planets
  - Planet Facts worksheet
  - Access to Microsoft Word, Pages software, or other word processing software
  - Pencils, markers, pens, glue, scissors

All handouts are included in the Student Resource site found at http://www.abc-clio.com/Libraries Unlimited/product.aspx?pc=A4367P.

Instructional Roles:

The school librarian and the classroom teachers determine the aspects of the planets that need to be covered or reinforced during a unit on the solar system.

Adapted from an SLM learning plan by Ann O'Keefe. Science: Postcards from the Solar System. *School Library Monthly,* Volume 28, Number 4, January 2012, pp. 50–51.

Procedure for Completion:

Day One: The school librarian introduces the idea of a very special field trip around the solar system. Prior knowledge about the planets should be solicited and a review or introduction of the planetary order may be needed. Discuss Pluto and the fact that it is no longer considered a planet but will still be a stop on this imaginary field trip. The school librarian will read *Postcards from Pluto* followed by class discussion about the story.

The students will be informed that they will each be "dropped off" on a planet and it will be their job to research it and send home a postcard based on one of the models in *Postcards from Pluto*. They will each be assigned a planet and guided in their research by the question: "Since we really cannot visit these planets, where can we find information?"

Day Two: The students will research their particular planet, completing the Planet Facts worksheet.

Day Three: The co-teachers will discuss postcards in general and bring in some real ones to show the students. The lesson begins with the message portion of the postcard, referring to examples in *Postcards from Pluto* such as a clever note, a mini-quiz, and a poem. The students will prepare a draft of their postcard to include some of the information gathered in the research about their planet. The co-teachers will check the drafts prior to completion of the project.

Day Four: Students create a postcard, beginning with the message portion, by typing into a 5" x 7" text box in a Word document or utilizing a "Cards and Invitations" template in Pages software. The picture portion of the postcard will be created by having the students search for and insert a good image into the template. The school librarian will remind students of copyright and guide them to free images websites. The co-teachers will guide the students throughout this process.

Day Five—Completion: The two-page postcards are printed and the students will assemble them to hand in.

Completion of Project:

The Planet Facts worksheet and the completed postcard are the final products of this lesson.

Student Assessment/Reflection:

The Planet Facts worksheet and the completion of a neat and creative postcard are the major assessments of this lesson and are based on the project rubric. Conversations with the teacher and school librarian throughout the process will also be included in the assessment process.

Professional Reflection—Librarian Notes:

This lesson may also include the address portion of the postcard that utilizes class time for filling in the students' real home address, apart from the science lesson. The school librarian may expand the lesson to the creation of a postage stamp for the postcard, which may include books and websites about stamp collections, the value of stamps, and the variety produced around the world.

Solar System Rubric			
	Excellent	Satisfactory	Unsatisfactory
Planet Facts	Work completed as assigned, accurate and on time.	Work completed but not on time or contains inaccuracies.	Work not completed or handed in.
Postcard	The postcard is factual, neat, creative, and on time.	The postcard is inaccurate or messy or not handed in on time.	Work not completed.
Staying on Task Daily	Student working as assigned and not disengaged or causing a disruption.	Student working well on assignment most days.	Student not on task daily or is a discipline problem.

Student Name:

Solar System Grade:

	Excellent	Satisfactory	Unsatisfactory
Planet Facts			
Postcard			
Staying on Task Daily			

SUGGESTED BIBLIOGRAPHY

Ballard, C. (2010). *Earth and the Solar System.* Mankato, MN: Raintree.

Best, C. (2001). *Shrinking Violet.* New York, NY: Farrar, Straus and Giroux.

Florian, D. (2007). *Comets, Stars, the Moon and Mars: Space Poems and Paintings.* New York, NY: Harcourt Children's Books.

Graham, I. (2012). *What Do We Know about the Solar System?* Mankato, MN: Raintree.

Hoena, B. A. (2008). *The Puzzling Pluto Plot: Eek & Ack.* Mankato, MN: Stone Arch Books.

Kortenkamp, S. (2011). *The Planets of Our Solar System.* Mankato, MN: Capstone Classroom.

Leedy, L. (1996). *Postcards from Pluto: A Tour of the Solar System.* New York, NY: Holiday House.

Mills. C. (2009). *How Oliver Olson Changed the World.* New York, NY: Farrar, Straus and Giroux.

Other nonfiction books on planets and the solar system.

Sayre, A. P. (2005). *Stars Beneath Your Bed: The Surprising Story of Dust.* New York, NY: Greenwillow.

Shedden, R., Morris, N., Solway, A. Graham, I., & Farndon, J. (2011). *Earth, Space, & Beyond.* Mankato, MN: Raintree.

Online Resource:

Fact Monster: http://www.factmonster.com/

SCIENCE
Grade Levels: 3–5
Endangered Animals

Lesson Summary: The lesson is designed to enhance the understanding of how humans can influence the animal population in the upper elementary curriculum. Students will investigate and understand that animals have life needs and specific physical characteristics. They will be guided to research a particular animal that is on the endangered or extinct list and learn about key elements such as habitat, diet, physical characteristics, and location.

Standards Addressed:

AASL *Standards for the 21st Century Learner*

- Inquire, think critically, and gain knowledge (1.1.1–1.1.9; 1.2.1–1.2.7; 1.3.1–1.3.5; 1.4.1–1.4.4)
- Draw conclusions, make informed decisions, apply knowledge to new situations, and create new knowledge (2.1.2–2.1.6; 2.2.1–2.2.4; 2.3.1–2.3.2; 2.4.1; 2.4.3)
- Share knowledge and participate ethically and productively as members of our democratic society (3.1.1–3.1.3; 3.1.5–3.1.6; 3.2.1; 3.3.3; 3.3.4)
- Pursue personal and aesthetic growth (4.1.5–4.1.6; 4.1.8; 4.2.2; 4.3.2; 4.4.2; 4.4.3; 4.4.4)

Common Core State Standards

- CCSS.ELA-Literacy.RI.3.1; RI.3.2; RI.3.3; RI.3.4; RI.3.5; RI.3.6; RI.3.7; RI.3.8; RI.3.9; RI.3.10
- CCSS.ELA-Literacy.RF.3.3; RF.3.4
- CCSS.ELA-Literacy.L.3.1; L.3.2; L.3.3; L.3.4; L.3.6
- CCSS.ELA-Literacy.SL.3.1; SL.3.4; SL.3.5; SL.3.6
- CCSS.ELA-Literacy.RI.4.1; RI.4.2; RI.4.3; RI.4.4; RI.4.5; RI.4.7; RI.4.8; RI.4.9; RI.4.10
- CCSS.ELA-Literacy.RF.4.3; RF.4.4
- CCSS.ELA-Literacy.L.4.1; L.4.2; L.4.3; L.4.4; L.4.6
- CCSS.ELA-Literacy.SL.4.1; SL.4.2; SL.4.4; SL.4.5; SL.4.6
- CCSS.ELA-Literacy.RI.5.1; RI.5.2; RI.5.3; RI.5.4; RI.5.5; RI.5.6; RI.5.7; RI.5.8; RI.5.9; RI.5.10
- CCSS.ELA-Literacy.RF.5.3; RF.5.4
- CCSS.ELA-Literacy.L.5.1; L.5.3; L.5.4; L.5.6
- CCSS.ELA-Literacy.SL.5.1; SL.5.2; SL.5.4; SL.5.6

Instructional Resources:

- *Required*
  - Access to research materials and online resources
  - Animal Research Chart for students to complete
  - Poster board, pencils, markers, crayons, paper

All handouts are included in the Student Resource site found at http://www.abc-clio.com/Libraries Unlimited/product.aspx?pc=A4367P.

Instructional Roles:

The classroom teacher and school librarian will co-teach this lesson, with the classroom teacher providing the basic scientific information relating to endangered and extinct animals. The school librarian will assist with research resources that include encyclopedias, books, magazines, and online resources.

Procedure for Completion:

Day One: The teacher introduces the unit by providing background information on endangered and extinct animals. The school librarian will introduce library and online resources for the students to use during their research project. Both instructors will assist the class in completing the Organizational Handout with a sample animal.

Days Two–Three: Students are provided the opportunity to research their animal using a variety of sources as they complete the Animal Research Chart. Both the classroom teacher and the school librarian will assist the students as needed.

Day Four: Students are provided time and supplies to complete the poster.

Day Five—Completion: Students will present their research to the class utilizing the poster as a resource.

Completion of Project:

The final project will be completion of a poster that includes the information required on an organizational handout, a drawing or picture of the animal, and presentation of their work to the class.

Student Assessment/Reflection:

The final project and presentation is the object of the main student assessment and is based on the rubric for the project. Conversations with the teacher and school librarian throughout the process will also be included in the assessment process.

Professional Reflection—Librarian Notes:

The Common Core State Standards aligns well with the collection development of nonfiction materials. Each school library will have a variety of resources specific to their school, but lessons such as this provide an opportunity to expand the collection.

Animal Rubric

	Excellent	Satisfactory	Unsatisfactory
Step One: Choose an Animal to Research	Work completed as assigned on time.	Work completed but not on time or extensive assistance was needed.	Work not completed or having several revisions before moving to the next step.
Step Two: Completion of the Animal Research Chart	Work completed on time and all requirements have been met.	Work not completed on time or missing elements.	Work not completed or missing major elements.
Step Three: Completed Poster and Presentation	Work completed on time, presentation understandable, and all elements included	Work completed but not on time or missing elements.	Work not completed or needing several revisions.
Staying on Task Daily	Student working as assigned and not disengaged or causing a disruption.	Student working well on assignment most days.	Student not on task daily or is a discipline problem.

Student Name:

Animal Grade:

	Excellent	Satisfactory	Unsatisfactory
Step One: Choose an Animal to Research			
Step Two: Completion of the Animal Research Chart			
Step Three: Completed Poster and Presentation			
Staying on Task Daily			

SUGGESTED BIBLIOGRAPHY

Arctic Animals. (2015). LEAP (Little Books with Attitude). Mankato, MN: Capstone Classroom.

Flamingo Features. (2015). LEAP (Little Books with Attitude). Mankato, MN: Capstone Classroom.

Flying Disks. (2015). LEAP (Little Books with Attitude). Mankato, MN: Capstone Classroom.

Frog Features. (2015). LEAP (Little Books with Attitude). Mankato, MN: Capstone Classroom.

Martin, I. (2015). *Amphibians: A Question and Answer Book.* Mankato, MN: Capstone Classroom.

Martin, I. (2015). *Birds: A Question and Answer Book.* Mankato, MN: Capstone Classroom.

Martin, I. (2015). *Fish: A Question and Answer Book.* Mankato, MN: Capstone Classroom.

Martin, I. (2015). *Insects: A Question and Answer Book.* Mankato, MN: Capstone Classroom.

Martin, I. (2015). *Mammals: A Question and Answer Book.* Mankato, MN: Capstone Classroom.

Martin, I. (2015). *Reptiles: A Question and Answer Book.* Mankato, MN: Capstone Classroom.

Rissman, R. (2015). *Barn Owls: Nocturnal Hunters.* Mankato, MN: Capstone Classroom.

Rissman, R. (2015). *Bats: Nocturnal Flyers.* Mankato, MN: Capstone Classroom.

Rissman, R. (2015). *Hedgehogs: Nocturnal Foragers.* Mankato, MN: Capstone Classroom.

Rissman, R. (2015). *Mice: Nocturnal Explorers.* Mankato, MN: Capstone Classroom.

Rissman, R. (2015). *Red Foxes: Nocturnal Predators.* Mankato, MN: Capstone Classroom.

South American Animals. (2015). LEAP (Little Books with Attitude). Mankato, MN: Capstone Classroom.

Tiger Features. (2015). LEAP (Little Books with Attitude). Mankato, MN: Capstone Classroom.

SCIENCE   Grade Levels: 4–6

Butterflies

Lesson Summary: Butterflies are an essential part of our ecosystem. In this lesson students will explore the types of butterflies that can be found in their area of the country, butterfly habitats, what they need to survive, and how they contribute to the environment.

Standards Addressed:

AASL *Standards for the 21st Century Learner*

- Inquire, think critically, and gain knowledge (1.1.1–1.1.9; 1.2.1–1.2.7; 1.3.4; 1.3.5; 1.4.1–1.4.4)
- Draw conclusions, make informed decisions, apply knowledge to new situations, and create new knowledge (2.1.1–2.1.6; 2.2.1–2.2.4; 2.3.1–2.3.3; 2.4.1–2.4.4)
- Share knowledge and participate ethically and productively as members of our democratic society (3.1.1–3.1.6; 3.2.3; 3.3.1–3.3.5; 3.4.3)
- Pursue personal and aesthetic growth (4.1.6–4.1.8; 4.2.1; 4.2.3; 4.3.1–4.3.4; 4.4.1–4.4.6)

Common Core State Standards

- CCSS.ELA-Literacy.RI.4.1; RI.4.2; RI.4.3; RI.4.4; RI.4.5; RI.4.6; RI.4.7; RI.4.8; RI.4.9; RI.4.10
- CCSS.ELA-Literacy.RF.4.3; RF.4.4
- CCSS.ELA-Literacy.RI.5.1; RI.5.2; RI.5.3; RI.5.4; RI.5.5; RI.5.6; RI.5.7; RI.5.8; RI.5.9; RI.5.10
- CCSS.ELA-Literacy.RF.5.3; RF.5.4
- CCSS.ELA-Literacy.RI.6.1; RI.6.2; RI.6.3; RI.6.4; RI.6.5; RI.6.6; RI.6.7; RI.6.8; RI.6.9; RI.6.10
- CCSS.ELA-Literacy.RST.6-8.1; RST.6-8.2; RST.6-8.3; RST.6-8.4; RST.6-8.5; RST.6-8.6; RST.6-8.7; RST.6-8.8; RST.6-8.9; RST.6-8.10

Instructional Resources:

- *Required*
  - Butterfly Notes Chart handout
  - *The Prince of Butterflies* by Bruce Coville
  - Poster board, pencils, markers, scissors
  - Computer access and presentation hardware

All handouts are included in the Student Resource site found at http://www.abc-clio.com/Libraries Unlimited/product.aspx?pc=A4367P.

- *Recommended*
  - Raise Your Own Butterflies Kit

Instructional Roles:

The classroom teacher will lead the basic science lesson, and the school librarian will facilitate exploration of resources for the research portion of the project.

Procedure for Completion:

Day One: The school librarian will read *The Prince of Butterflies* by Bruce Coville to the students and use one of the websites in the bibliography to explore the migration path of the monarch butterfly.

Day Two: Working in pairs, students will choose a particular butterfly species found in their geographic area to research in depth.

Day Three—Completion: Students will conduct research in the library to develop either a poster or a booklet on the life cycle of a specific butterfly species. The Butterfly Notes Chart handout will assist in gathering information.

Completion of Project:

The final project will be a poster or booklet on the life cycle of the particular butterfly species. The research will include migration patterns, habitat, and any other pertinent information. The final projects will be displayed in the school library or classroom.

Student Assessment/Reflection:

The final project is the object of the main student assessment and is based on the rubric for the project. Conversations with the teacher and school librarian throughout the process will also be included in the assessment process.

Professional Reflection—Librarian Notes:

If it is possible, purchase Butterfly Hatching Kits, usually available at a reasonable fee for painted ladies. This is a wonderful way for students to view the life cycle of the typical butterfly and release them after they have evolved. Further information that can be shared by the instructors may include butterfly farms and the depletion of the monarch habitat.

Butterfly Project Rubric

	Excellent	Satisfactory	Unsatisfactory
Step One: Choose a Butterfly Species to Research	Work completed as assigned on time.	Work completed but not on time or extensive assistance was needed.	Work not completed or having several revisions before moving to the next step.
Step Two: Development and Completion of the Research	Work completed on time and all requirements have been met.	Work not completed on time or missing elements.	Work not completed or missing major elements.
Step Three: Completed Report	Work completed on time, presentation understandable, and all elements included.	Work completed but not on time or missing elements.	Work not completed or needing several revisions.
Staying on Task Daily	Student working as assigned and not disengaged or causing a disruption.	Student working well on assignment most days.	Student not on task daily or is a discipline problem.

Student Name:
Butterfly Project Grade:

	Excellent	Satisfactory	Unsatisfactory
Step One: Choose a Butterfly Species to Research			
Step Two: Development and Completion of the Research			
Step Three: Completed Report			
Staying on Task Daily			

SUGGESTED BIBLIOGRAPHY

Aston, D. H., & Long, S. (2011). *A Butterfly Is Patient*. San Francisco, CA: Chronicle Books.

Bender, M. (2006). *Butterfly Mother: Miao (Hmong) Creation Epics from Guizhou, China*. Cambridge, MA: Hackett.

Brock, J., & Kaufman, K. (2006). *Butterflies of North America (Kaufman Field Guides)*. New York, NY: Houghton Mifflin Harcourt.

Coville, B. (2007). *The Prince of Butterflies*. New York, NY: Voyager Books.

Holmes, K. J. (1998). *Butterflies*. Mankato, MN: Capstone Classroom.

Jo, E. (2012). *The Mystery of Monarch Metamorphosis*. Mankato, MN: MN Heritage Press.

Manos-Jones, M. (2000). *The Spirit of Butterflies: Myth, Magic, and Art*. New York, NY: Harry N. Abrams.

Marsh, L. (2011). *National Geographic Readers: Great Migrations Butterflies*. Washington, DC: National Geographic Children's Books.

Melton, K. (2013). *The Butterfly and the Rock*. Lantern Hollow Press.com.

Pasternak, C. (2012). *How to Raise Monarch Butterflies: A Step-by-Step Guide for Kids*, Richmond Hill, ON, Canada: Firefly Books.

Schaffer, D. (1999). *Painted Lady Butterflies*. Mankato, MN: Capstone Classroom.

Simon, S. (2011). *Butterflies*. New York, NY: HarperCollins.

Online Resources:

http://www.learner.org/jnorth/monarch/

http://www.monarch-butterfly.com/monarch-migration.html

http://www.monarchbutterflyusa.com/Migration.htm

http://www.monarchlab.org/Lab/Research/Topics/Migration/WhereToGo.aspx

http://monarchwatch.org/tagmig/index.htm

http://video.nationalgeographic.com/video/butterfly_monarch

http://www.vrml.k12.la.us/k/k_trophy/k/themes/theme7/th7wk1/stories/theme7wkstories.htm

SCIENCE   **Grade Levels:** 4–6
Weather or Not?

Lesson Summary: The lesson is designed to allow students to conduct investigations and use appropriate technology to build an understanding of weather and climate and to determine how temperature, wind direction and speed, precipitation, cloud cover, and air pressure are predictable patterns.

Standards Addressed:

AASL *Standards for the 21st Century Learner*

- Inquire, think critically, and gain knowledge (1.1.1–1.1.9; 1.2.1–1.2.7; 1.3.1–1.3.5; 1.4.1–1.4.3)
- Draw conclusions, make informed decisions, apply knowledge to new situations, and create new knowledge (2.1.1–2.1.6; 2.2.1–2.2.4; 2.3.1–2.3.3)
- Share knowledge and participate ethically and productively as members of our democratic society (3.1.1–3.1.6; 3.2.1–3.2.3; 3.3.1–3.3.4)
- Pursue personal and aesthetic growth (4.1.6; 4.1.7; 4.1.8)

Common Core State Standards

- CCSS.ELA-Literacy.RL.4.1; RL.4.2; RL.4.9; RL.4.10
- CCSS.ELA-Literacy.RI.4.1; RI.4.2; RI.4.3; RI.4.4; RI.4.5; RI.4.6; RI.4.7; RI.4.8; RI.4.9; RI.4.10
- CCSS.ELA-Literacy.SL.4.1; SL.4.2; SL.4.3; SL.4.5
- CCSS.ELA-Literacy.RL.5.1; RL.5.2; RL.5.9; RL.5.10
- CCSS.ELA-Literacy.RI.5.1; RI.5.2; RI.5.3; RI.5.4; RI.5.5; RI.5.6; RI.5.7; RI.5.8; RI.5.9; RI.5.10
- CCSS.ELA-Literacy.SL.5.1; SL.5.2; SL.5.4; SL.5.5
- CCSS.ELA-Literacy.RL.6.1; RL.6.2; RL.6.9; RL.6.10
- CCSS.ELA-Literacy.RI.6.1; RI.6.2; RI.6.3; RI.6.4; RI.6.5; RI.6.6; RI.6.7; RI.6.8; RI.6.9; RI.6.10
- CCSS.ELA-Literacy.SL.6.1; SL.6.2; SL.6.3; SL.6.4; SL.6.5

Instructional Resources:

- *Required*
  - Access to encyclopedias and online reference resources
  - A variety of nonfiction books as suggested in the Bibliography list
  - Weather or Not? Checklist handout
  - You Be the Mythbuster! handout

All handouts are included in the Student Resource site found at http://www.abc-clio.com/Libraries Unlimited/product.aspx?pc=A4367P.

- *Recommended*
  - Presentation by a local meteorologist
  - TeacherTube meteorology video

Instructional Roles:

The classroom teacher and school librarian will co-teach this lesson. They will arrange for a visit by a meteorologist or explore and identify an appropriate TeacherTube video to share with students. The

Adapted from an SLM learning plan by Sandra Andrews & Linda Gann. Science: Weather or Not? *School Library Monthly*, Volume 28, Number 2, November 2011, pp. 53–55.

classroom teacher will review the concepts of weather and the tools for measuring weather, and the school librarian will guide the students in understanding and researching weather-related proverbs and folktales.

Procedure for Completion:

Day One: The classroom teacher reviews the concepts of weather and tools for measuring weather, including thermometers, anemometer, wine vane, rain gauge, and barometer. A local meteorologist visits the class to discuss the science of predicting the weather. Students ask the meteorologist previously created questions focusing on how weather can be predicted. If a meteorologist is not available, the co-teachers should find a video that will explore the science of weather prediction at the appropriate grade level. After the visit or video the co-teachers lead a discussion on how people predict the weather in their everyday lives.

Day Two: The co-teachers discuss the program *MythBusters*, focusing on how the MythBusters try to prove or disprove an urban legend or common belief. The school librarian introduces the concept of weather proverbs and folklore as a means for predicting weather, stressing the fact that weather proverbs and folklore have been around long before tools were created to measure the weather.

Day Three: The school librarian uses an example of a proverb or folklore to model the research process with the class, using reference materials to determine the accuracy of the proverb and utilizing the format from *MythBusters*. Some examples of a proverb or folklore may include:

- Thunder in the morning, all day storming/Thunder at night is the traveler's delight.
- When chairs squeak, of rain they speak.
- A ring around the sun or moon means rain or snow coming soon.
- When leaves show their undersides, be very sure that rain betides.
- Cold is the night when the stars shine bright.
- Wide brown bands on a wooly bear caterpillar mean a mild winter.

Day Four: Students will be divided into groups of three. Each group will find a total of three examples of proverbs or folklore for the weather elements: temperature, wind direction and speed, precipitation, cloud cover, and air pressure. After identifying the proverb or folklore, the students will analyze the scientific accuracy of each proverb by utilizing reference materials, books, and selected online resources while completing the You Be the Mythbuster! handout.

Day Five—Completion: The group will present their research and conclusion to the class. The multimedia presentation will include the original proverb or folklore, the scientific principle regarding what is true or not true about the proverb or folklore, and their conclusion following the Weather or Not Checklist and the You Be the Mythbuster handouts.

Student Assessment/Reflection:

The group presentation and the handouts will be the major assessments for this project. The teacher and the school librarian will also focus on the process based on observations and conversations with the students throughout the lesson.

Professional Reflection—Librarian Notes:

Showing a portion of a *MythBusters* episode may generate student interest and give them an understanding of the process to follow while researching. Other ways to present the research are to have the student groups act out the proverb or tale or develop a podcast.

Weather or Not? Rubric

	Excellent	Satisfactory	Unsatisfactory
Weather or Not! Handout	Work completed on time and all requirements have been met.	Work completed but not on time or extensive assistance was needed.	Student did not complete the work or hand it in.
You Be the Mythbuster Handout	Work completed on time and all requirements have been met.	Work completed but not on time or extensive assistance was needed.	Student did not complete the work or hand it in.
Group Presentation	Work completed on time, contributed to the presentation, and all elements included.	Work completed but student did not contribute effectively to the project.	Student did not contribute to the presentation.
Staying on Task	Student contributing to the activity and not disengaged or causing a disruption.	Student contributing to the activity most of the time.	Student not on task or was a discipline problem.

Student Name:

Weather or Not? Grade:

	Excellent	Satisfactory	Unsatisfactory
Weather or Not! Handout			
You Be the Mythbuster Handout			
Group Presentation			
Staying on Task			

SUGGESTED BIBLIOGRAPHY

Breen, M. (2008). *The Kids' Book of Weather Forecasting: Build a Weather Station, "Read" the Sky, & Make Predictions*. Charlotte, VA: Williamson Publishing.

Cosgrove, B. (2007). *Weather*. New York, NY: DK Publishing.

Fleishner, P. (2011). *Doppler Radar, Satellites, and Computer Models: The Science of Weather Forecasting*. Minneapolis, MN: Lerner Publishing.

Freier, G. D. (1992). *Weather Proverbs: How 600 Proverbs, Sayings, and Poems Accurately Explain Our Weather*. Jackson, TN: Da Capo Press.

Koehler, S. (2008). *Weather*. Vero Beach, FL: Rourke.

Lockhart, G. (1988). *The Weather Companion: An Album of Meteorological History, Science, Legend, and Folklore*. Hoboken, NJ: Wiley Press.

Miller, P. (2004). *Yankee Weather Proverbs*. Colbyville, VT: Silver Print Press.

Pierce, T. (2007). *Forecasting Fun: Weather Nursery Rhymes*. Mankato, MN: Picture Window Books.

Rodgers, A. (2007). *Forecasting the Weather*. Mankato, MN: Heinemann.

Sanna, E. (2003). *Folk Customs*. Birmingham, AL: Crest.

Sloane, E. (2005). *Eric Sloane's Weather Book*. Mineola, NY: Dover Publications.

Vogel, C. G. (2001). *Weather Legends, Native American Lore, and the Science of Weather*. Minneapolis, MN: Millbrook Press.

Online Resources:

Climatologists' Toolbox: http://whyfiles.org/021climate/

Miami Museum of Science Weather Tools: http://www.miamisci.org/hurricane/weathertools.html

MythBusters: http://www.discovery.com/tv-shows/mythbusters/games-and-more/brain-teasers.htm

TLC Family—Weather Folktales: http://lifestyle.howstuffworks.com/crafts/other-arts-crafts/science-projects-for-kids-weather-and-seasons9.htm

Weather Wiz Kids: http://www.weatherwizkids.com/

Chapter 3

Social Studies

SOCIAL STUDIES   **Grade Levels:** K–2
Family History

Lesson Summary: In this lesson students will create a book that records their personal history.

Standards Addressed:

AASL *Standards for the 21st Century Learner*

- Inquire, think critically, and gain knowledge (1.1.1–1.1.3; 1.1.9; 1.2.1; 1.2.3; 1.4.2; 1.4.4)
- Draw conclusions, make informed decisions, apply knowledge to new situations, and create new knowledge (2.1.2; 2.2.4; 2.3.1)
- Share knowledge and participate ethically and productively as members of our democratic society (3.1.3; 3.3.4)
- Pursue personal and aesthetic growth (4.1.6; 4.1.8)

Common Core State Standards

- CCSS.ELA-Literacy.RL.K.1; RL.K.2; RL.K.3; RL.K.4; RL.K.7; RL.K.9; RL.K.10
- CCSS.ELA-Literacy.RI.K.1; RI.K.2; RI.K.3; RI.K.4; RI.K.5; RI.K.6; RI.K.7; RI.K.8; RI.K.9; RI.K.10
- CCSS.ELA-Literacy.RF.K.1; RF.K.2; RF.K.3; RF.K.4
- CCSS.ELA-Literacy.L.K.1; L.K.2; L.K.4; L.K.5; L.K.6
- CCSS.ELA-Literacy.SL.K.1; SL.K.2; SL.K.3; SL.K.4; SL.K.5; SL.K.6
- CCSS.ELA-Literacy.W.K.2; W.K.3; W.K.5; W.K.6; W.K.8
- CCSS.ELA-Literacy.RL.1.1; RL.1.2; RL.1.3; RL.1.5; RL.1.6; RL.1.7; RL.1.9; RL.1.10
- CCSS.ELA-Literacy.RI.1.1; RI.1.2; RI.1.3; RI.1.4; RI.1.5; RI.1.6; RI.1.7; RI.1.8; RI.1.9; RI.1.10
- CCSS.ELA-Literacy.RF.1.1; RF.1.2; RF.1.3; RF.1.4
- CCSS.ELA-Literacy.L.1.1; L.1.2; L.1.4; L.1.5; L.1.6
- CCSS.ELA-Literacy.SL.1.1; SL.1.2; SL.1.3; SL.1.4; SL.1.5; SL.1.6
- CCSS.ELA-LiteracyW.1.2; W.1.3; W.1.5; W.1.6; W.1.8
- CCSS.ELA-Literacy.RL.2.1; RL.2.3; RL.2.5; RL.2.6; RL.2.7; RL.2.10
- CCSS.ELA-Literacy.RI.2.1; RI.2.2; RI.2.4; RI.2.5; RI.2.6; RI.2.7; RI.2.9; RI.2.10
- CCSS.ELA-Literacy.RF.2.3; RF.2.4
- CCSS.ELA-Literacy.L.2.1; L.2.2; L.2.3; L.2.4; L.2.5; L.2.6
- CCSS.ELA-Literacy.SL.2.1; SL.2.2; SL.2.3; SL.2.4; SL.2.6
- CCSS.ELA-LiteracyW.2.2; W.2.3; W.2.5; W.2.6; W.2.7; W.2.8

Instructional Resources:

- *Required*
  - o Photographs of the student and their family
  - o Paper, markers, pencils, crayons
  - o Family Tree handout
  - o *Me and My Family Tree* by J. Sweeney

All handouts are included in the Student Resource site found at http://www.abc-clio.com/Libraries Unlimited/product.aspx?pc=A4367P.

- *Recommended*
  - o Computer access
  - o Microsoft Word or other word processing program
  - o Comic Life—a fun program for students to make their book into a comic book–style product
  - o Digital cameras

Instructional Roles:

The classroom teacher and the school librarian will co-teach the lesson. The instructional roles include reading books on families to the students, guiding them to create their own book or scrapbook, uploading photos into a document, and utilizing the various tools within the program.

Procedure for Completion:

Day One: Prior to the unit students should have access to photos of themselves to be used for the project. The school librarian will read *Me and My Family Tree* by J. Sweeney to teach them about the basic family tree. There are many free Family Tree templates online, but a simple one is reproduced here and for students to begin to complete.

Day Two: The school librarian will read one of the selection of "Families" books to the students and the co-teachers will promote a discussion of what makes up a family. The students will start writing about themselves and their families.

Day Three—Completion: Students will continue to work on their books until completion, with the co-teachers assisting as necessary and taking turns reading stories about families.

Completion of Project:

Students will write and illustrate, either by hand or with pictures inserted in a Word document, a history of themselves and their family with the inclusion of a family tree. The completed student books should be bound in some fashion.

Student Assessment/Reflection:

The final project is the object of the main student assessment and is based on the rubric for the project. Conversations with the teacher and school librarian throughout the process will also be included in the assessment process.

Professional Reflection—Librarian Notes:

This lesson can easily be utilized for all levels of elementary school students. Using a program such as Kidspiration, the student writing and organization of thoughts can be a focus of the lesson. Comic Life is another tool that can follow the student writing process as well as promote creativity.

Family History Rubric

	Excellent	Satisfactory	Unsatisfactory
Complete a Family Tree	The tree was neat and complete.	The result was not complete or messy.	Work not completed.
Complete the Book	Work completed as assigned on time.	Work completed but not on time or extensive corrections needed before completed.	Work not completed.
Staying on Task Daily	Student working as assigned and not disengaged or causing a disruption.	Student working well on assignment most days.	Student not on task daily or is a discipline problem.

Student Name:

Family History Grade:

	Excellent	Satisfactory	Unsatisfactory
Complete a Family Tree			
Complete the Book			
Staying on Task Daily			

From *The Common Core in Action: Ready-to-Use Lesson Plans for K–6 Librarians* by Deborah J. Jesseman. Santa Barbara, CA: Libraries Unlimited. Copyright © 2015.

SUGGESTED BIBLIOGRAPHY

Harris, R. (2012). *Who's in My Family?: All About Our Families.* Somerville, MA: Candlewick.

Hoffman, M. (2011). *The Great Big Book of Families.* New York, NY: Dial.

Kuklin, S. (2006). *Families.* New York, NY: Hyperion Books.

Morris, A. (2000). *Families.* New York, NY: HarperCollins.

Parr, T. (2010). *The Family Book.* Boston, MA: Little, Brown Books for Young Readers.

Skutch, R. (1997). *Who's in a Family?* Berkeley, CA: Tricycle Press.

Sweeney, J. (2000). *Me and My Family Tree.* Decorah, IA: Dragonfly Books.

Online Resource:

Family Tree handout: http://family-tree-template.org/family-tree-chart/

SOCIAL STUDIES/TECHNOLOGY   Grade Levels: 1–2
Information Detectives

Lesson Summary: The lesson is designed to emphasize the integration of technology in connection with students' research. Students are studying a foreign country, Mexico, for example, and become Information Detectives by searching an online encyclopedia seeking answers to a question posed for them about the country.

Standards Addressed:

AASL *Standards for the 21st Century Learner*

- Inquire, think critically, and gain knowledge (1.1.1–1.1.3; 1.1.8–1.1.9; 1.3.5; 1.4.2; 1.4.4)
- Draw conclusions, make informed decisions, apply knowledge to new situations, and create new knowledge (2.1.1–2.1.5; 2.3.1; 2.4.1; 2.4.2; 2.4.3)
- Share knowledge and participate ethically and productively as members of our democratic society (3.1.1; 3.1.3; 3.2.3; 3.4.2)
- Pursue personal and aesthetic growth (4.3.2)

Common Core State Standards

- CCSS.ELA-Literacy.RI.1.1; RI.1.2; RI.1.3; RI.1.4; RI.1.5; RI.1.6; RI.1.7; RI.1.8; RI.1.9; RI.1.10
- CCSS.ELA-Literacy.SL.1.1; SL.1.2; SL.1.3; SL.1.4; SL.1.6
- CCSS.ELA-Literacy.W.1.2; W.1.8
- CCSS.ELA-Literacy.RI.2.1; RI.2.2; RI.2.3; RI.2.4; RI.2.5; RI.2.6; RI.2.7; RI.2.8; RI.2.9; RI.2.10
- CCSS.ELA-Literacy.SL.2.1; SL.2.2; SL.2.3; SL.2.4; SL.2.6
- CCSS.ELA-Literacy.W.2.2; W.2.8

Instructional Resources:

- *Required*
  - Access to computers, presentation hardware, and an online encyclopedia such as *Worldbook.com*
  - Magnifying glass
  - Student Question handout
  - Question/Answer Skit handout
  - Teacher-Directed Questions Example handout
  - Paper, pencils, pens

All handouts are included in the Student Resource site found at http://www.abc-clio.com/Libraries Unlimited/product.aspx?pc=A4367P.

Instructional Roles:

The classroom teacher and the school librarian will co-teach this lesson. They will develop a skit to identify the roles of each and expectations for the lesson and share the information presentation and assessment.

Adapted from an SLM learning plan by Rae Ciciora. Social Studies: Information Detectives. *School Library Monthly,* Volume XXVII, Number 2, November 2010, pp. 18–20.

Procedure for Completion:

Day One: The school librarian and classroom teacher perform a question/answer skit about how to find information. Utilizing a computer and projector or Smartboard, an entry about Mexico is accessed on the online encyclopedia following the guidelines in the Teacher-Directed Questions Example handout. This is a group-directed lesson in preparation for the paired activity.

Day Two—Completion: Students will work in pairs to research a prepared question by finding the answer using the online encyclopedia. After finding the information, they will return to the large group to review the process, determine how they were Information Detectives, and share the information they learned.

Completion of Project:

The final project will be a written answer on the Student Question handout and sharing of the information in the large group.

Student Assessment/Reflection:

The written answer on the Student Question handout and presentation of the information to the class are the objects of the main student assessment and are based on the rubric for the project. Conversations with the teacher and school librarian throughout the process will also be included in the assessment process.

Professional Reflection—Librarian Notes:

In this lesson it is best that resources are prepared and set up before the students arrive. The pairing may be intentional with a high reader matched with a lower reader.

Information Detective Rubric

	Excellent	Satisfactory	Unsatisfactory
Conduct Research	Work completed on time and all requirements have been met.	Work not completed on time or missing elements.	Work not completed.
Share Research with Group	Work completed on time, presentation understandable, and all elements included.	Work completed but not on time or missing elements.	Work not completed.
Staying on Task Daily	Student working as assigned and not disengaged or causing a disruption.	Student working well on assignment most days.	Student not on task daily or is a discipline problem.

Student Name:

Information Detective Grade:

	Excellent	Satisfactory	Unsatisfactory
Conduct Research			
Share Research with Group			
Staying on Task Daily			

SUGGESTED BIBLIOGRAPHY

Alcraft, R. (2009). *A Visit to France.* Mankato, MN: Capstone Classroom.

Alcraft, R. (2009). *A Visit to Mexico.* Mankato, MN: Capstone Classroom.

Bell, R. (2009). *A Visit to Italy.* Mankato, MN: Capstone Classroom.

Bell, R. (2009). *A Visit to Ireland.* Mankato, MN: Capstone Classroom.

Cane, E. (2014). *My World Series.* Mankato, MN: Capstone Classroom.

Cooper, S. K. (2006). *France ABCs: A Book about the People and Places of France.* Mankato, MN: Capstone Classroom.

Dahl, M. (1999). *China* (Countries of the World). Mankato, MN: Bridgestone Books.

Frost, H. (2005). *Our World Series.* Mankato, MN: Capstone Classroom.

Heiman, S. (2003). *Mexico ABCs: A Book about the People and Places of Mexico.* Mankato, MN: Capstone Classroom.

Juarez, C. (2014). *Countries Series.* Mankato, MN: Capstone Classroom.

National Geographic Kids (2011). *Beginner's World Atlas.* Washington, DC: Geographic Children's Books.

Roop, P. (2009). *A Visit to Egypt.* Mankato, MN: Capstone Classroom.

Roop, P. (2009). *A Visit to India.* Mankato, MN: Capstone Classroom.

Roop, P. (2009). *A Visit to Japan.* Mankato, MN: Capstone Classroom.

Roop, P. (2009). *A Visit to Vietnam.* Mankato, MN: Capstone Classroom.

Sexton, C. (2010). *Japan.* Minneapolis, MN: Bellwether Media.

Yesh, J. (2004). *China ABCs: A Book about the People and Places of China.* Mankato, MN: Capstone Classroom.

SOCIAL STUDIES   Grade Levels: 2–3

Cinderella Stories and Geography

Lesson Summary: Nearly every culture has a version of the story of Cinderella, and this lesson explores the story, culture, and aspects of life in different countries. The lesson is a group project where students will choose a country to research and the corresponding Cinderella story to read. The group project will be included in an International Festival set in the school library.

Standards Addressed:

AASL *Standards for the 21st Century Learner*

- Inquire, think critically, and gain knowledge (1.1.1–1.1.9; 1.2.1–1.2.7; 1.3.1–1.3.5; 1.4.1–1.4.4)
- Draw conclusions, make informed decisions, apply knowledge to new situations, and create new knowledge (2.1.1–2.1.6; 2.2.1–2.2.4; 2.3.1–2.3.3; 2.4.1–2.4.4)
- Share knowledge and participate ethically and productively as members of our democratic society (3.1.1–3.1.5; 3.2.1–3.2.3; 3.3.1–3.3.5; 3.3.7; 3.4.1–3.4.3)
- Pursue personal and aesthetic growth (4.1.1–4.1.8; 4.2.1–4.2.3; 4.3.1–4.3.4; 4.4.1–4.4.6)

Common Core State Standards

- CCSS.ELA-Literacy.RL.2.1; RL.2.2; RL.2.3; RL.2.4; RL.2.5; RL.2.6; RL.2.7; RL.2.9; RL.2.10
- CCSS.ELA-Literacy.RI.2.1; RI.2.2; RI.2.3; RI.2.4; RI.2.5; RI.2.6; RI.2.7; RI.2.8; RI.2.9; RI.2.10
- CCSS.ELA-Literacy.RF.2.3; RF.2.4
- CCSS.ELA-Literacy.L.2.1; L.2.2; L.2.3; L.2.4; L.2.5; L.2.6
- CCSS.ELA-Literacy.SL.2.1; SL.2.2; SL.2.3; SL.2.4; SL.2.6
- CCSS.ELA-Literacy.RL.3.1; RL.3.2; RL.3.3; RL.3.4; RL.3.5; RL.3.6; RL.3.7; RL.3.9; RL.3.10
- CCSS.ELA-Literacy.RI.3.1; RI.3.2; RI.3.4; RI.3.5; RI.3.6; RI.3.7; RI.3.8; RI.3.9; RI.3.10
- CCSS.ELA-Literacy.RF.3.3; RF.3.4
- CCSS.ELA-Literacy.L.3.1; L.3.2; L.3.3; L.3.4; L.3.5; L.3.6
- CCSS.ELA-Literacy.SL.3.1; SL.3.2; SL.3.3; SL.3.4; SL.3.6

Instructional Resources:

- *Required*
  - Cinderella stories from around the world
  - Poster board, art supplies
  - The Charles Perrault version of *Cinderella*

Instructional Roles:

The school librarian and classroom teacher will coordinate the project and the culminating International Festival, with the school librarian facilitating reference and resource assistance.

Procedure for Completion:

Day One: This unit begins with a read-aloud of the traditional *Cinderella* by Charles Perrault. The co-teachers will lead a discussion about various cultures around the world and how many have a version of a Cinderella story.

Day Two—Completion: Students will work in groups and are assigned a Cinderella book to read and a country to explore. They will research the country and develop a project to be displayed or presented at an International Festival in the school library.

Completion of Project:

The display will be set up for an International Festival Day in the school library, with invitations to visit the festival sent to all classes in the school. Students will stand by each display to answer questions and share the facts about their chosen country and their project.

Student Assessment/Reflection:

The final project is the object of the main student assessment and is based on the rubric for the project. Questions asked during the oral presentation as well as conversations with the teacher and school librarian throughout the process will also be included in the assessment.

Professional Reflection—Librarian Notes:

If the school does not already participate in an international festival or celebration of some sort, the school librarian can set the stage and organize an event that may grow with schoolwide activities and participation.

A short lesson that is fun would be to research and share various foods from the countries that students have researched

---

Cinderella Stories and Geography
Rubric

	Excellent	Satisfactory	Unsatisfactory
Group Participation	Work completed on time; it was accurate, pleasing to view, and the student participated significantly in the final product.	Work may have been late, evidence of some inaccuracies in background research, or the student did not participate significantly in the final product.	Work was not completed or missing major elements. The student did not participate in the group effort.
Formal Presentation	Work completed on time; it was accurate, pleasing to view, and the student participated significantly in the final product.	Work may have been late, evidence of some inaccuracies in background research, or the student did not participate significantly in the final product.	Work was not completed or missing major elements. The student did not participate in the presentation.
Staying on Task Daily	Student working as assigned and not disengaged or causing a disruption.	Student not on task daily.	Student not on task daily and/or was a discipline problem.

Student Name:
Cinderella Stories and Geography Grade:

	Excellent	Satisfactory	Unsatisfactory
Group Participation			
Formal Presentation			
Staying on Task Daily			

Suggested Bibliography

Canada: Martin, R. (1998). *The Rough-Face Girl.* New York, NY: Puffin Books.

Caribbean: San Souci, R. (2002). *Cendrillon, a Cajun Cinderella.* New York, NY: Aladdin.

China: Louie, Ai-Ling (1996). *Yeh-Shen: A Cinderella Story.* New York, NY: Puffin Books.

Climo, S. (1996). *The Korean Cinderella.* New York, NY: Trophy Picture Books.

Egypt: Climo, S. (1992). *The Egyptian Cinderella.* New York, NY: HarperCollins.

France: Perrault, C., & Craft, K. Y. (illus.), (2000). *Cinderella.* San Francisco, CA: Chronicle Books.

Germany: Huck, C. (1994). *Princess Furball.* New York, NY: Greenwillow Books.

Hollenbeck, K. M. (2003). *Teaching with Cinderella Stories from Around the World.* Teaching Resources. Also available in eBook from Scholastic.com.

India: Brucker, M. B. (2002). *Anklet for a Princess: A Cinderella Story from India.* New York, NY: Shen's Books and Supplies.

Ireland: Climo, S. (2000). *The Irish Cinderlad.* New York, NY: HarperCollins.

Korea: Plunkett, S. (1996). *Kongi and Potgi.* New York, NY: Dial Books.

Meister, C. (2015). *Cinderella Stories Around the World.* Mankato, MN: Capstone Classroom.

Persia (now Iran): Climo, S. (2001). *The Persian Cinderella.* New York, NH: HarperCollins.

Southern Africa: Steptoe, J. (1986). *Mufaro's Beautiful Daughters.* Boston, MA: Lothrop, Lee & Shepard.

Southwestern United States (Zuni): Pollock, P. (1996). *The Turkey Girl: A Zuni Cinderella Story.* Boston, MA: Little, Brown Books for Young Readers.

SOCIAL STUDIES
Global Tooth Fairies

Grade Levels: 2–4

Lesson Summary: Children around the world have different backgrounds, cultures, and religions but one thing they have in common is that they all lose teeth. This lesson combines global studies with different traditions concerning losing teeth.

Standards Addressed:

AASL *Standards for the 21st Century Learner*

- Inquire, think critically, and gain knowledge (1.1.1; 1.1.2; 1.1.4; 1.1.6; 1.4.2; 1.4.4)
- Draw conclusions, make informed decisions, apply knowledge to new situations, and create new knowledge (2.1.2; 2.1.3; 2.1.4; 2.1.6; 2.2.4; 2.3.1; 2.3.2; 2.4.3)
- Share knowledge and participate ethically and productively as members of our democratic society (3.1.3)
- Pursue personal and aesthetic growth (4.1.1; 4.1.2; 4.1.4; 4.1.6; 4.1.8)

Common Core State Standards

- CCSS.ELA-Literacy.RL.2.1; RL.2.2; RL.2.3; RL.2.6; RL.2.7; RL.2.9; RL.2.10
- CCSS.ELA-Literacy.W.2.2; W.2.5
- CCSS.ELA-Literacy.SL.2.1; SL.2.2; SL.2.3; SL.2.4; SL.2.6
- CCSS.ELA-Literacy.RL.3.2; RL.3.3; RL.3.4; RL.3.5; RL.3.6; RL.3.7; RL.3.10
- CCSS.ELA-Literacy.W.3.3; W.3.4; W.3.5; W.3.10
- CCSS.ELA-Literacy.SL.3.1; SL.3.2; SL.3.3; SL.3.4; SL.3.6
- CCSS.ELA-Literacy.RL.4.1; RL.4.2; RL.4.3; RL.4.4; RL.4.7; RL.4.9; RL.4.10
- CCSS.ELA-Literacy.W.4.3; W.4.4; W.4.5; W.4.10
- CCSS.ELA-Literacy.SL.4.1; SL.4.2; SL.4.3; SL.4.4

Instructional Resources:

- *Required*
  - Drawing paper, writing paper, art supplies
  - Access to a globe, world map, or online map sites
  - *Throw Your Tooth on the Roof: Tooth Traditions from Around the World* by Selby Beeler
  - *Tooth Tales from Around the World* by Marlene Brill
  - *I Lost My Tooth in Africa* by Penda Diakite
  - New Tooth Fairy Custom Outline handout

All handouts are included in the Student Resource site found at http://www.abc-clio.com/Libraries Unlimited/product.aspx?pc=A4367P.

Instructional Roles:

The school librarian and classroom teacher will co-teach the lesson. The instructional roles include reading books to the students, facilitating the activities, and guiding the students in their research.

Adapted from an SLM learning plan by Virginia Case. Social Studies: Global Tooth Fairies. *School Library Monthly*, Volume XXVIII, No. 5, February 2012, pp. 54–55.

Procedure for Completion:

Step One: The co-teachers will invite students to share any information they may have about losing a tooth and the Tooth Fairy. Some questions may include:

- What experiences have they had with the Tooth Fairy?
- Where does the Tooth Fairy come from?
- How did she get the job?
- Do any students come from another country or have relatives outside the United States?
- What do they know about the tooth customs that are followed in those countries?

The co-teachers will share information from Marlene Targ Brill's *Tooth Tales from Around the World.* This author explored how various customs began and wrote that teeth were a sign of strength to people in Asia and Africa, dating back thousands of years. These people believed that everyone had a spirit that lived on after death and they saved the teeth to keep the body whole and so the spirit could live forever. Eventually they began to hide the teeth so evil spirits could not find them.

The teachers will then share information about what children around the world do with their baby teeth, as included in Selby B. Beeler's *Throw Your Tooth on the Roof: Tooth Traditions from Around the World.*

The students will select a few countries they would like to know about. The classroom teacher will find the countries on a map or globe, and the school librarian will read the tooth customs that take place in that country.

Step Two—Completion: The students will create a tooth custom for a country they will invent. The Tooth Fairy Custom Outline will guide the students as they make up a name for the new nation, write a paragraph about the tooth customs practiced there, and complement the description by drawing a picture of this custom. The co-teachers will check the handout before students write up and illustrate the final project.

Completion of Project:

The final project is the written and illustrated new Tooth Fairy Custom.

Student Assessment/Reflection:

The final project is the object of the main student assessment and is based on the rubric for the project. Observations and conversations with the teacher and school librarian throughout the process will also be included in the assessment.

Professional Reflection—Librarian Notes:

This lesson may be expanded as part of a thematic unit across the curriculum. As a Social Studies extension the students could research the various countries that have the Tooth Fairy tradition and include capital, population, typography, climate, or sites of interest.

A discussion of the qualifications for the job of Tooth Fairy could lead older elementary students to employment opportunities in the newspaper. This could be expanded to writing a want ad or developing a simple resume and cover letter.

Global Tooth Fairies Rubric			
	Excellent	Satisfactory	Unsatisfactory
New Custom Paragraph	Work was completed on time; it was creative and neat.	Work was not completed on time; it was not unique or it was messy.	Work was not completed or missing major elements.
New Custom Illustration	Work completed on time, pleasing to view, and neat.	Work was not completed on time or it was messy.	Work was not completed.
Staying on Task Daily	Student working as assigned and not disengaged or causing a disruption.	Student not on task daily.	Student not on task daily and/or was a discipline problem.

Student Name:

Global Tooth Fairies Grade:

	Excellent	Satisfactory	Unsatisfactory
New Custom Paragraph			
New Custom Illustration			
Staying on Task Daily			

SUGGESTED BIBLIOGRAPHY

Beeler, S. B. (1998). *Throw Your Tooth on the Roof: Tooth Traditions from Around the World.* New York: Houghton Mifflin.
Brill, M. T. (1998). *Tooth Tales from Around the World.* Watertown, MA: Charlesbridge.
Diakite, P. (2006). *I Lost My Tooth in Africa.* New York, NY: Scholastic.
Schwartz, A. (1985). *In a Dark, Dark Room and Other Scary Stories.* New York, NY: HarperCollins.

Online Resource:

Google Maps: http://maps.google.com/

SOCIAL STUDIES   **Grade Levels:** 3–4

Famous Americans

Lesson Summary: In this lesson students will use reference and technology skills to research the contributions of famous Americans. The project will include the KWL format of questioning and completion of a Bio Cube of facts.

Standards Addressed:

AASL *Standards for the 21st Century Learner*

- Inquire, think critically, and gain knowledge (1.1.1–1.1.8; 1.2.3; 1.2.4; 1.2.6; 1.2.7; 1.3.1; 1.3.5; 1.4.2; 1.4.4)
- Draw conclusions, make informed decisions, apply knowledge to new situations, and create new knowledge (2.1.1–2.1.4; 2.1.6; 2.2.4; 2.3.1; 2.4.1)
- Share knowledge and participate ethically and productively as members of our democratic society (3.1.1; 3.1.3; 3.1.4; 3.1.6; 3.3.4)
- Pursue personal and aesthetic growth (4.1.6; 4.2.1; 4.3.2)

Common Core State Standards

- CCSS.ELA-Literacy.RI.3.3; RI.3.4; RI.3.5; RI.3.7; RI.3.10
- CCSS.ELA-Literacy.L.3.1; L.3.2; L.3.3; L.3.4; L.3.6
- CCSS.ELA-Literacy.W.3.2; W.3.4; W.3.5; W.3.6; W.3.7; W.3.8; W.3.10
- CCSS.ELA-Literacy.RI.4.3; RI.4.4; RI.4.5; RI.4.6; RI.4.7; RI.4.10
- CCSS.ELA-Literacy.L.4.1; L.4.2; L.4.3; L.4.6
- CCSS.ELA-Literacy.W.4.2; W.4.4; W.4.5; W.4.6; W.4.7; W.4.8; W.4.10

Instructional Resources:

- *Required*
  - Computer and Internet access
  - KWL handout
  - BioChart handout

All handouts are included in the Student Resource site found at http://www.abc-clio.com/Libraries Unlimited/product.aspx?pc=A4367P.

Instructional Roles:

The school librarian and classroom teacher will coordinate and co-teach the project, with the school librarian facilitating reference and resource assistance.

Procedure for Completion:

Day One: This unit begins with the instructors introducing some examples of famous Americans that contributed to history in a variety of ways. These examples may include Helen Keller, Pocahontas, and Susan B. Anthony. The school librarian and classroom teacher will choose an individual to demonstrate the Bio Cube interactive website and other online resources.

Adapted from an SLM learning plan by Jennifer M. Rascoe. Social Studies: Women Who Paved the Way. *School Library Monthly*, Volume XXIV, Number 6, February 2008, pp. 18–23.

Day Two: The students will choose an individual to research and will be provided access to materials, books, and websites to assist in completing the KWL handout. The co-teacher will be available to assist students having difficulties completing the handout.

Day Three: Students will continue to research their subject and complete a Bio Cube from the online website or the BioChart handout.

Day Four—Completion: Students will complete a Flipbook about their subject to include information gathered for the KWL and BioChart handouts. The Flipbook instructions are included on the Bio Cube website.

Completion of Project:

Students will complete a Flipbook on their choice of a famous American.

Student Assessment/Reflection:

The final project is the object of the main student assessment and is based on the rubric that includes the steps in gathering information. Questions and conversations with the teacher and school librarian throughout the process will be included in the assessment.

Professional Reflection—Librarian Notes:

The original lesson from which this one is adapted focused on famous American women and may be a good lesson to present during Women's History Month or focus on African Americans during Black History or African Americans Month.

Famous Americans
Rubric

	Excellent	Satisfactory	Unsatisfactory
KWL Chart	Work completed on time and accurately.	Work not completed on time; evidence of some inaccuracies.	Work was not completed or missing major elements.
BioChart or Bio Cube	Work completed on time and accurately.	Work not completed on time; evidence of some inaccuracies.	Work was not completed or missing major elements.
Flipbook	Work completed on time and accurately.	Work not completed on time; evidence of some inaccuracies.	Work was not completed or missing major elements.
Staying on Task Daily	Student working as assigned and not disengaged or causing a disruption.	Student not on task daily.	Student not on task daily and/or was a discipline problem.

Student Name:

Famous Americans Grade:

	Excellent	Satisfactory	Unsatisfactory
KWL Chart			
BioChart or Bio Cube			
Flipbook			
Staying on Task Daily			

SUGGESTED BIBLIOGRAPHY

Books from the Biography collection on famous Americans

Online Resources:

BBC: www.bbc.co.uk/schools/primaryhistory/famouspeople
Cube Creator: http://www.readwritethink.org/files/resources/interactives/cube_creator/
Flipbook: http://www.readwritethink.org/files/resources/interactives/flipbook/
Helen Keller Birthplace: http://www.helenkellerbirthplace.org/
Incwell.com—Canadian Blog: http://www.incwell.com/Biographies/
Library of Congress: http://www.americaslibrary.gov/aa/index.php
New York Public Library: http://digitalgallery.nypl.org/ (for digital searches)

SOCIAL STUDIES   Grade Levels: 3–4
Almanacs

Lesson Summary: In this lesson students learn the basics of using an almanac. This information will allow them to move beyond basic fact finding to higher level thinking by interpreting information and learning to navigate a reference source.

Standards Addressed:

AASL *Standards for the 21st Century Learner*

- Inquire, think critically, and gain knowledge (1.1.1–1.1.5; 1.1.9)
- Draw conclusions, make informed decisions, apply knowledge to new situations, and create new knowledge (2.1.2; 2.1.3; 2.1.5; 2.1.6; 2.2.4; 2.3.1)
- Share knowledge and participate ethically and productively as members of our democratic society (3.1.1; 3.1.2; 3.2.3; 3.3.4)
- Pursue personal and aesthetic growth (4.3.1; 4.3.2)

Common Core State Standards

- CCSS.ELA-Literacy.RI.3.1; RI.3.4; RI.3.5; RI.3.7; RI.3.10
- CCSS.ELA-Literacy.SL.3.1; SL.3.2; SL.3.3
- CCSS.ELA-Literacy.RI.4.1; RI.4.4; RI.4.5; RI.4.7; RI.4.10
- CCSS.ELA-Literacy.SL.4.1; SL.4.2

Instructional Resources:

- *Required*
    - *World Almanac for Kids*, latest edition
    - Large chart paper
    - 3 markers of different colors
    - Copies of outline maps of the United States
    - Almanac Search worksheet
    - Student Research Journals

All handouts are included in the Student Resource site found at http://www.abc-clio.com/Libraries Unlimited/product.aspx?pc=A4367P.

Instructional Roles:

The school librarian will show students how to use the table of contents of the almanac to look up the origins of state names, the classroom teacher will facilitate the written Research Journal reflections, and they will co-ordinate organization of the origin of state names and facilitation of color-coding a map of the United States.

Procedure for Completion:

Step One: The school librarian begins by introducing students to *The World Almanac for Kids*. As a large group, students will develop a working definition of an almanac, including various types of information

Adapted from an SLM learning plan by Holly Taylor-Fox & Dana Rose. Social Studies: Almanacs Reveal State Secrets. *School Library Monthly*, Volume 28, Number 3, December 2011, pp. 52–53.

found in the resource. They will individually record the definition in a Research Journal. Students will be prompted to think about the different tools they use to find information in books with the questions located on the Almanac Search worksheet.

Step Two: The school librarian will direct students to the table of contents, lead groups to find the location of state information, and model using the information to find the date upon which a specific state entered the union. As a group they will find where the state information is located and note the information found through the table of contents.

In pairs, students will use the table of contents to research the origin of the names of four states and record the information in their Research Journals. The class as a whole will cover all 50 states.

Step Three—Completion: The classroom teacher will create a chart with the students, based on their findings, to classify the origin of every state. For this lesson, the classifications are Native American Languages, British Influences, and Other Influences. Students will work in small groups to color-code a map according to the three classifications of origin of state name.

Completion of Project:

The lesson is complete when the students have finalized their Research Journal entries, Almanac Search worksheet, the class chart, and the color-coded map.

Student Assessment/Reflection:

The classroom teacher and the school librarian will assess the students based on the accuracy of the research recorded in their Research Journals, Almanac Search worksheet, the class chart, and the color-coded maps. Questions and conversations with the teacher and school librarian throughout the process will be included in the assessment.

Professional Reflection—Librarian Notes:

As an extension of the lesson, students may be urged to further explore fun facts about each state, such as the way in which states with similar name origins are clustered regionally or how different states obtained their motto.

Almanac Rubric			
	Excellent	Satisfactory	Unsatisfactory
Research Journal	Work completed on time, accurate, and well written.	Work not completed on time, may include some inaccuracies in research or errors in writing.	Work was not completed or missing major elements.
Almanac Search Worksheet	Work completed on time and accurate.	Work not completed on time or evidence of inaccuracies in research.	Work was not completed or missing major elements.
Group Work—Class Chart and Map	Student contributed in a positive manner to the group work.	Student contributed to the group work but needed to be encouraged or provided inaccurate responses.	The student did not participate in the group effort.
Staying on Task Daily	Student working as assigned and not disengaged or causing a disruption.	Student not on task daily.	Student not on task daily or was a discipline problem.

Student Name:

Almanac Grade:

	Excellent	Satisfactory	Unsatisfactory
Research Journal			
Almanac Search Worksheet			
Group Work—Class Chart and Map			
Staying on Task Daily			

From *The Common Core in Action: Ready-to-Use Lesson Plans for K–6 Librarians* by Deborah J. Jesseman. Santa Barbara, CA: Libraries Unlimited. Copyright © 2015.

SUGGESTED BIBLIOGRAPHY

The World Almanac for Kids (2014). New York, NY: Simon & Schuster.

Online Resource:

The World Almanac: http://www.worldalmanac.com/learning-resources.aspx

Images for United States Maps:

http://www.clker.com/clipart-united-states-map.html
http://www.free-coloring-pages.com/pages/usa-map.html
http://www.freeusandworldmaps.com/html/USAandCanada/USPrintable.html

SOCIAL STUDIES

Grade Levels: 3–5

American Revolution—The Freedom Trail

Lesson Summary: This lesson explores Boston's Freedom Trail and is included in a unit on the Revolutionary War. Utilizing a variety of resources, students will search for pieces of information about the Revolutionary War.

Standards Addressed:

AASL *Standards for the 21st Century Learner*

- Inquire, think critically, and gain knowledge (1.1.1–1.1.9; 1.2.1–1.2.7; 1.3.1–1.3.5; 1.4.1–1.4.4)
- Draw conclusions, make informed decisions, apply knowledge to new situations, and create new knowledge (2.1.1–2.1.6; 2.2.1–2.2.4; 2.3.1–2.3.3; 2.4.1–2.4.4)
- Share knowledge and participate ethically and productively as members of our democratic society (3.1.1; 3.1.3; 3.1.6; 3.3.4; 3.3.7; 3.4.1–3.4.2)
- Pursue personal and aesthetic growth (4.1.1–4.1.8; 4.2.1–4.2.3; 4.3.1–4.3.4; 4.4.1–4.4.6)

Common Core State Standards

- CCSS.ELA-Literacy.RL.3.1; RL.3.3; RL.3.4; RL.3.5; RL.3.6; RL.3.7; RL.3.9; RL.3.10
- CCSS.ELA-Literacy.RI.3.1; RI.3.2; RI.3.4; RI.3.5; RI.3.6; RI.3.7; RI.3.8; RI.3.9; RI.3.10
- CCSS.ELA-Literacy.RF.3.3; RF.3.4
- CCSS.ELA-Literacy.L.3.1; L.3.2; L.3.3; L.3.4; L.3.5; L.3.6
- CCSS.ELA-Literacy.SL.3.1; SL.3.2; SL.3.3; SL.3.4; SL.3.6
- CCSS.ELA-Literacy.W.3.2; W.3.4; W.3.5; W.3.6; W.3.7; W.3.8; W.3.10
- CCSS.ELA-Literacy.RL.4.1; RL.4.3; RL.4.4; RL.4.5; RL.4.6; RL.4.7; RL.4.9; RL.4.10
- CCSS.ELA-Literacy.RI.4.1; RI.4.2; RI.4.4; RI.4.5; RI.4.6; RI.4.7; RI.4.8; RI.4.9; RI.4.10
- CCSS.ELA-Literacy.RF.4.3; RF.4.4
- CCSS.ELA-Literacy.L.4.1; L.4.2; L.4.3; L.4.4; L.4.5; L.4.6
- CCSS.ELA-Literacy.SL.4.1; SL.4.2; SL.4.3; SL.4.4; SL.4.6
- CCSS.ELA-Literacy.W.4.2; W.4.4; W.4.5; W.4.6; W.4.7; W.4.8; W.4.9; W.4.10
- CCSS.ELA-Literacy.RL.5.1; RL.5.2; RL.5.3; RL.5.4; RL.5.5; RL.5.6; RL.5.7; RL.5.8; RL.5.10
- CCSS.ELA-Literacy.RI.5.1; RI.5.2; RI.5.3; RI.5.4; RI.5.5; RI.5.6; RI.5.7; RI.5.8; RI.5.9; RI.5.10
- CCSS.ELA-Literacy.RF.5.3; RF.5.4
- CCSS.ELA-Literacy.L.5.1; L.5.2; L.5.3; L.5.4; L.5.5; L.5.6
- CCSS.ELA-Literacy.SL.5.1; SL.5.2; SL.5.3; SL.5.4; SL.5.6
- CCSS.ELA-Literacy.W.5.2; W.5.4; W.5.5; W.5.6; W.5.7; W.5.8; W.5.9; W.5.10

Instructional Resources:

- *Required*
  - Computer access
  - *Paul Revere's Ride* by Henry Wadsworth Longfellow
  - Scavenger Hunt Questions handout
  - Writing materials

All handouts are included in the Student Resource site found at http://www.abc-clio.com/Libraries Unlimited/product.aspx?pc=A4367P.

Instructional Roles:

The classroom teacher and the school librarian will co-teach the lesson and guide the students through the online resources and research and writing process.

Procedure for Completion:

Day One: The school librarian will read the poem *Paul Revere's Ride* by Henry Wadsworth Longfellow to the students and have them explore the various sites on the Interactive Map of the Freedom Trail at http://www.iboston.org/pap/freedom.htm.

Day Two: Students continue to research and explore the Freedom Trail and discover the items on the scavenger hunt. The class will come together as a group and share the scavenger hunt responses. Students will select a topic from the Revolutionary War era for additional research. The topics must be approved by the teacher and school librarian.

Day Three—Completion: Students will conduct research on their topics and submit a written report for assessment.

Completion of Project:

Written report about the Revolutionary War era.

Student Assessment/Reflection:

The final report is the object of the main student assessment and is based on the rubric for the report. Conversations with the teacher and school librarian throughout the process will also be included in the assessment process.

Professional Reflection—Librarian Notes:

It is suggested that this activity coincide with a novel study about this period such as *My Brother Sam Is Dead* or *Johnny Tremain*.

The school librarian has the opportunity to provide extra resources for the Revolutionary War unit. There are many online resources, teacher-specific resources, and resources that may be obtained directly from the City of Boston and the surrounding area such as Concord and Lexington.

American Revolution Rubric

	Excellent	Satisfactory	Unsatisfactory
Step One: Choose a Topic to Research	Work completed as assigned on time.	Work completed but not on time or the student needed extensive assistance.	Work not completed or needing several revisions before moving to the next step.
Step Two: Development and Completion of the Research	Work completed on time and all requirements met.	Work not completed on time or missing major elements.	Work not completed.
Step Three: Completed Report	Work completed on time, presentation understandable, and all elements were included,	Work completed but not on time or missing elements.	Work not completed.
Staying on Task Daily	Student working as assigned and not disengaged or causing a disruption.	Student working well on assignment most days.	Student not on task daily or is a discipline problem.

Student Name:

American Revolution Grade:

	Excellent	Satisfactory	Unsatisfactory
Step One: Choose a Topic to Research			
Step Two: Development and Completion of the Research			
Step Three: Completed Report			
Staying on Task Daily			

SUGGESTED BIBLIOGRAPHY

Benchley, N. (1969). *Sam the Minuteman.* New York, NY: HarperCollins.

Borden, L. (2000). *Sleds on Boston Common: A Story from the American Revolution.* New York, NY: Margaret K. McElderry Books.

Forest, C. (2013). *The Biggest Battles of the Revolutionary War.* Mankato, MN: Capstone Classroom.

Forest, C. (2013). *The Rebellious Colonists and the Causes of the American Revolution.* Mankato, MN: Capstone Classroom.

Fradin, D., & Day, L. (2009). *Let It Begin Here!: Lexington & Concord: First Battles of the American Revolution.* London, UK: Walker Children's Books.

Hall, B. (2013). *Great Women of the American Revolution.* Mankato, MN: Capstone Classroom.

Jerome, K. B. (2011). *Boston and the State of Massachusetts: Cool Stuff Every Kid Should Know.* Mount Pleasant, SC: Arcadia.

Kimmel, H. (2007). *The Battles of Lexington and Concord.* Danbury, CT: Children's Press.

Longfellow, H. W. (1996). *Paul Revere's Ride.* New York, NY: Puffin.

Marsh, C. (2003). *The Mystery on the Freedom Trail* (Real Kids, Real Places). Peachtree City, GA: Gallopade International.

Raum, E. (2009). *The Revolutionary War: An Interactive History Adventure.* Mankato, MN: Capstone Young Readers.

Raum, E. (2013). *The Stories of the Revolutionary War.* Mankato, MN: Capstone Classroom.

Scarbrough, M. H. (2013). *Heroes of the American Revolution.* Mankato, MN: Capstone Classroom.

Schanzer, R. (2007). *George vs. George: The American Revolution as Seen from Both Sides.* Washington, DC: National Geographic Children's Books.

Online Resources:

http://www.cityofboston.gov/freedomtrail/
http://www.iboston.org/pap/freedom.htm
http://www.thefreedomtrail.org/index.html

SOCIAL STUDIES   Grade Levels: 5–6
Dinotopia and a New Society

Lesson Summary: In this lesson students will create their own idea of an ideal "Society" utilizing a fictional world created by artist and author James Gurney in *Dinotopia* as an example and to demonstrate the interconnectedness of life.

Standards Addressed:

AASL *Standards for the 21st Century Learner:*

- Inquire, think critically, and gain knowledge (1.1.1–1.1.9; 1.2.1–1.2.7; 1.3.1–1.3.5; 1.4.1–1.4.4)
- Draw conclusions, make informed decisions, apply knowledge to new situations, and create new knowledge (2.1.1–2.1.6; 2.2.1–2.2.4; 2.3.1–2.3.3; 2.4.1–2.4.4)
- Share knowledge and participate ethically and productively as members of our democratic society (3.1.1–3.1.5; 3.2.1–3.2.3; 3.3.1–3.3.5; 3.3.6; 3.4.1–3.4.3)
- Pursue personal and aesthetic growth (4.1.1–4.1.8; 4.2.1–4.2.3; 4.3.1–4.3.4; 4.4.1–4.4.6)

Common Core State Standards

- CCSS.ELA-Literacy.RF.5.3; RF.5.4
- CCSS.ELA-Literacy.RI.5.1; RI.5.2; RI.5.3; RI.5.4; RI.5.5; RI.5.7; RI.5.8; RI.5.9; RI.5.10
- CCSS.ELA-Literacy.RL.5.1; RL.5.2; RL.5.3; RL.5.4; RL.5.5; RL.5.6; RL.5.7; RL.5.8; RL.5.10
- CCSS.ELA-Literacy.SL.5.1; SL.5.2; SL.5.3; SL.5.4; SL.5.6
- CCSS.ELA-Literacy.L.5.1; L.5.2; L.5.3; L.5.4; L.5.5; L.5.6
- CCSS.ELA-Literacy.RI.6.1; RI.6.2; RI.6.3; RI.6.4; RI.6.5; RI.6.6; RI.6.7; RI.6.8; RI.6.9; RI.6.10
- CCSS.ELA-Literacy.RL.6.1; RL.6.2; RL.6.3; RL.6.4; RL.6.5; RL.6.6; RL.6.7; RL.6.9; RL.6.10
- CCSS.ELA-Literacy.RH.6-8.3; RH.6-8.4; RH.6-8.5; RH.6-8.6; RH.6-8.7; RH.6-8.8; RH.6-8.9
- CCSS.ELA-Literacy.SL.6.1; SL.6.2; SL.6.3; SL.6.4; SL.6.5; SL.6.6
- CCSS.ELA-Literacy.L.6.1; L.6.2; L.6.3; L.6.4; L.6.5; L.6.6

Instructional Resources:

- *Required*
  - Computer access, art supplies as necessary
  - *Dinotopia* by James Gurney

Instructional Roles:

The classroom teacher and the school librarian will co-teach this unit. The classroom teacher will provide prior learning instruction for measurement, use of rulers and compasses, and shapes. The school librarian is the facilitator and guide in the research and resources.

Procedure for Completion:

Week One: The school librarian will begin the unit by reading *Dinotopia* by James Gurney to the students and expand the story by promoting a discussion of the many roles the citizens of Dinotopia have on the

Adapted from an SLM learning plan by Deborah Jesseman. *Dinotopia* and a New Society. *School Library Monthly*, Volume 30, March 2014, pp. 53–54.

island, how the two species interact, the geography, and economics. The teacher will parallel the story while teaching about societal roles, geography, economics, and bartering.

Week Two: The students will be separated into groups with each group given the responsibility of developing some aspect of their ideal society. Examples of groups would include Government, Economics, Geography, Professions or Careers, Biology, and Plant and Animal Life.

Week Three—Completion: Over the course the project, the students will:

- Choose roles within the group.
- Research their aspect of the society.
- Brainstorm to come up with their project.
- Provide a written outline of what they have developed.

Completion of Project:

The group will formally present what they have created. The presentation options may be artwork, video, PowerPoint, or a trifold poster. Any physical project may be displayed in the classroom or media center.

Student Assessment/Reflection:

Assessment is based on the rubric for the project and conversations between the teacher and school librarian throughout the process.

Professional Reflection—Librarian Notes:

The school librarian may encourage further reading and exploration of the spin-off books from this series as well as the TV movie, and how different or similar it is to the books. Books and materials on dinosaurs and fossils should be available as well as websites for archeology. There is a series of *Dinotopia* spin-off novels written by a variety of authors for students who would like to delve further into the society and their imagination.

This is a lesson that could be expanded to be included in a thematic unit across the curriculum since the possibilities of collaboration between the school librarian, Math, English, Science, Economics, Art, and Social Studies teachers are extensive.

Dinotopia and a New Society Rubric

	Excellent	Satisfactory	Unsatisfactory
Outline of Project	Outline was completed as assigned on time.	Outline was completed but not on time or corrections were needed before moving on to the next step.	The work was not completed or needed several revisions before moving to next step.
Group Participation	Work was completed on time, cooperatively, and the student fully participated in the group discussion.	The student participated in the project but with a minimal effort or was marginally cooperative.	The student did not participate cooperatively with the group or gave minimal effort.
Formal Presentation	Work completed on time; it was accurate, pleasing to view, and the student participated significantly in the final product.	Work not completed on time, included some inaccuracies in background research, or the student did not participate significantly in the final product.	Work was not completed or missing major elements. The student did not participate in the group effort.
Staying on Task Daily	Student working as assigned and not disengaged or causing a disruption.	Student not on task daily.	Student not on task daily or was a discipline problem.

Student Name:
Dinotopia and a New Society Grade:

	Excellent	Satisfactory	Unsatisfactory
Outline of Project			
Group Participation			
Formal Presentation			
Staying on Task Daily			

SUGGESTED BIBLIOGRAPHY

Faulkner, R. (2008). *Fossils.* Mankato, MN: Capstone Classroom.

Gurney, J. (1994). *Dinotopia.* Atlanta, GA: Turner.

Gurney, J. (1998). *Dinotopia: The World Beneath.* New York, NY: HarperCollins.

Gurney, J. (2007). *Dinotopia: Journey to Chandara.* Riverside, NJ: Andrews McMeel.

Wooster, P. (2012). *An Illustrated Timeline of Dinosaurs.* Mankato, MN: Capstone Classroom.

Online Resources:

Dinotopia website: http://www.dinotopia.com/

James Gurney website: http://jamesgurney.com/site/

SOCIAL STUDIES
Segregation and Change

Grade Levels: 5–6

Lesson Summary: In this lesson students will compare and contract an historical fiction picture book with a nonfiction book about segregation. They will create a recipe for their future.

Standards Addressed:

AASL *Standards for the 21st Century Learner:*

- Inquire, think critically, and gain knowledge (1.1.1–1.1.9; 1.2.1–1.2.5; 1.3.2; 1.3.4; 1.3.5; 1.4.2; 1.4.3; 1.4.4)
- Draw conclusions, make informed decisions, apply knowledge to new situations, and create new knowledge (2.1.1–2.1.6; 2.2.1–2.2.4; 2.3.1; 2.4.1)
- Share knowledge and participate ethically and productively as members of our democratic society (3.1.1–3.1.6; 3.2.2; 3.2.3; 3.3.4; 3.4.1–3.4.3)
- Pursue personal and aesthetic growth (4.1.5; 4.1.6; 4.1.8; 4.4.4)

Common Core State Standards

- CCSS.ELA-Literacy.RI.5.1; RI.5.2; RI.5.3; RI.5.4; RI.5.5; RI.5.6; RI.5.7; RI.5.8; RI.5.9; RI.5.10
- CCSS.ELA-Literacy.W.5.3; W.5.4; W.5.5; W.5.7; W.5.9; W.5.10
- CCSS.ELA-Literacy.RI.6.1; RI.6.2; RI.6.3; RI.6.4; RI.6.5; RI.6.6; RI.6.7; RI.6.8; RI.6.9; RI.6.10
- CCSS.ELA-Literacy.W.5.3; W.5.4; W.5.5; W.5.9; W.5.10

Instructional Resources:

- *Required*
  - *Sit In: How Four Friends Stood Up by Sitting Down* by Andrea Pinkney
  - *The Gold Cadillac* by Mildred Taylor
  - Smartboard or projector
  - Conflict Diagram example for instructor projection
  - Venn Diagram handout
  - Student Checklist handout
  - Access to websites in the Online Resources
  - Photos of the Greensboro Four

All handouts are included in the Student Resource site found at http://www.abc-clio.com/Libraries Unlimited/product.aspx?pc=A4367P.

Instructional Roles:

The school librarian and the classroom teacher will co-teach this unit by collaboratively planning the activities to accommodate diverse learners.

Procedure for Completion:

Step One: The school librarian reads *The Gold Cadillac* to the students while they are learning about the civil rights era in the classroom. At the conclusion of the book, the co-teachers ask the students what they learned from *The Gold Cadillac* and promote discussion about segregation.

Adapted from an SLM learning plan by Mary Creekmore. English/Social Studies: A Sweet Recipe for Change. *School Library Monthly*, Volume 28, No. 6, March 2012, pp. 52–55.

Step Two: The co-teachers promote discussion to review what the students learned about segregation from *The Gold Cadillac* and are asked if they are familiar with the Greensboro Four. The school librarian reads the class *Sit-In: How Four Friends Stood Up by Sitting Down.* Students view pictures from the story, then real pictures of the Greensboro Four. The Plot Diagram is displayed to convey the events that led to the conflict.

Step Three: The students are grouped in pairs and given a Venn Diagram handout to complete. The diagram will compare and contrast the events in *The Gold Cadillac* and *Sit-In: How Four Friends Stood Up by Sitting Down.* The co-teachers assist by projecting the Venn Diagram on the screen, suggesting facts to include, and modeling completion of the diagram. The students should include one similarity and one difference in the setting of the books, identify similar messages they convey, and work cooperatively with a partner.

Step Four—Completion: The Recipe for Integration is a poignant ending to the story and should be displayed through the projector. The co-teachers review the recipe and the Student Checklist. Students must write a recipe for their bright future, to include at least six ingredients, and decorate or illustrate the page.

Completion of Project:

The individual student Recipe for a Bright Future is the final product.

Student Assessment/Reflection:

Assessment is based on the rubric for the project, the Venn Diagram, and conversations between the teacher and school librarian throughout the process.

Professional Reflection—Librarian Notes:

The students' final recipes can be compiled into one recipe book for the class.

Bright Future Recipe Rubric

	Excellent	Satisfactory	Unsatisfactory
Venn Diagram	Completed as assigned, on time, and working collaboratively.	Completed but not on time or corrections were needed before moving on.	The work was not completed or needed several revisions before moving to next step.
Title and 6 or More Ingredients	Student included a title that is relevant and creative and included 6 or more ingredients.	The student included 3 to 5 ingredients and a title.	The student did not include a title or included 2 or fewer ingredients.
Colorful, Creative, and Neat	Student included colorful illustrations and the product was neat and legible.	Student included illustrations but they were not relevant or the product was messy or illegible.	Student did not include illustrations or did not hand in a finished product.
Staying on Task Daily	Student working as assigned and not disengaged or causing a disruption.	Student not on task daily.	Student not on task daily or was a discipline problem.

Student Name:

Bright Future Recipe Grade:

	Excellent	Satisfactory	Unsatisfactory
Venn Diagram			
Title and 6 or More Ingredients			
Colorful, Creative, and Neat			
Staying on Task Daily			

SUGGESTED BIBLIOGRAPHY

Adamson, H. (2014). *The Civil Rights Movement.* Mankato, MN: Capstone Press.

Fitzgerald, S. (2006). *Struggling for Civil Rights. Mankato,* MN: Raintree Press.

Higgins, N. (2014). *The Split History of the Civil Rights Movement.* Mankato, MN: Compass Point Books.

Landau, E. (2003). *The Civil Rights Movement in America.* New York, NY: Children's Press.

Levine, E. (2000). *Freedom's Children: Young Civil Rights Activists Tell Their Own Stories.* New York: Puffin.

Osborne, L. B. (2012). *Miles to Go for Freedom: Segregation and Civil Rights in the Jim Crow Years.* New York, NY: Harry N. Abrams.

Parks, R., & Haskins, J. (1999). *Rosa Parks: My Story.* New York, NY: Puffin.

Pinkney, A. (2010). *Sit-In: How Four Friends Stood Up by Sitting Down.* New York, NY: Little, Brown.

Rubin, S. G. (2014). *Freedom Summer: The 1964 Struggle for Civil Rights in Mississippi.* New York, NY: Holiday House.

Taylor, M. D. (1998). *The Gold Cadillac.* New York, NY: Puffin Books.

Tougas, S. (2011). *Birmingham 1963: How a Photograph Rallied Civil Rights.* Mankato, MN: Compass Point Books.

Tougas, S. (2012). *Little Rock Girl 1957: How a Photograph Changed the Fight for Integration.* Mankato, MN: Compass Point Books.

Turck, M. C. (2000). *The Civil Rights Movement for Kids.* Chicago, IL: Chicago Review Press.

Online Resources:

Greensboro Four: http://www.infoplease.com/ipa/A0900073.html

International Civil Rights Center & Museum: http://www.sitinmovement.org/

Sit-ins: http://www.sitins.com/index.shtml

SOCIAL STUDIES

Grade Level: 6

Primary and Secondary Sources

Lesson Summary: In this lesson students will use letters from a historical fiction novel for context while searching for information relevant to World War I, formulating questions, and locating answers in primary and secondary sources.

Standards Addressed:

AASL *Standards for the 21st Century Learner:*

- Inquire, think critically, and gain knowledge (1.1.1–1.1.9; 1.3.1–1.3.5; 1.4.2; 1.4.4)
- Draw conclusions, make informed decisions, apply knowledge to new situations, and create new knowledge (2.1.1; 2.1.2; 2.1.5; 2.3.1; 2.4.1–2.4.4)
- Share knowledge and participate ethically and productively as members of our democratic society (3.1.6; 3.2.1–3.2.3; 3.4.1; 3.4.2)
- Pursue personal and aesthetic growth (4.1.4; 4.1.6)

Common Core State Standards

- CCSS.ELA-Literacy.RI.6.1; RI.6.3; RI.6.4; RI.6.5; RI.6.6; RI.6.7; RI.6.9; RI.6.10

Instructional Resources:

- *Required*
  - ○ Computer access to Library of Congress and other historical databases
  - ○ Multiple copies of *Moon over Manifest* by Clare Vanderpool
  - ○ Books about World War I
  - ○ *Moon over Manifest* booktalk
  - ○ Copies of Ned's letters in *Moon over Manifest*, pp. 37, 107, 116, 156, 179, 205, 228, 251
  - ○ Graphic Organizer handout
  - ○ Primary/Secondary Sources game such as "Classroom Feud"

All handouts are included in the Student Resource site found at http://www.abc-clio.com/Libraries Unlimited/product.aspx?pc=A4367P.

Instructional Roles:

The classroom teacher will be responsible for teaching the World War I content and supporting new knowledge gained through the lesson. The school librarian will introduce the fiction book and teach primary and secondary sources. Both the teacher and the school librarian will guide students in their research efforts.

Procedure for Completion:

Day One: The school librarian booktalks *Moon over Manifest* by Clare Vanderpool, covering key points:

- *Moon over Manifest* won the 2011 Newbery Medal.
- She is a first-time author.

Adapted from an SLM learning plan by Lisa Chilcoat. Social Studies: WWI Primary and Secondary Sources and a Novel. *School Library Monthly*, Volume 28, Number 7, April 2012, pp. 55–57.

- It is set in 1936 when 12-year-old Abilene Tucker is sent to her father's hometown, Manifest, Kansas, to spend the summer.
- Abilene stays with a friend of her father, Pastor Shady, in his church/saloon.
- In her room she locates a cigar box full of mementos from someone's past.

The students are shown a cigar box with a stack of letters inside and are told, "I can't tell you everything that was in that cigar box, but I will tell you about the letters. Abilene found a stack of letters written by Ned Gillen, a World War I soldier, to his friend Jinx. Ned mentions some usual things in his letters and Abilene is eager to know more. She will enlist the help of a diviner (seer or psychic) to figure out the mysteries in the cigar box."

The co-teachers will distribute copies of Ned's letters to student pair groups and project a copy as a model. The school librarian will read one letter and demonstrate weeding out irrelevant information and finding details relating to World War I, highlighting each and instructing students to do the same.

The teachers will model how to turn the information from the letter into a question. For example, in the letter on page 156, Ned writes, "If President Wilson comes to visit again, which he probably won't, tell him Ned Gillen says hey and us boys overseas could use some warm blankets and better food." This detail could form the question: "Why were the soldiers lacking supplies and food?" The students will do the same and write their question on the Graphic Organizer.

Day Two: The co-teachers will create and introduce the students to a game, such as *Jeopardy* or *Family Feud*, as a fun way to reveal what they know about primary and secondary sources. The students will record the knowledge gained from the game on their Graphic Organizer.

Day Three—Completion: The students will continue their partnerships and search for information related to their question from Day One with the goal of using at least one primary source and one secondary source.

Completion of Project:

Students will submit their Graphic Organizer handout and include a reflection on the back that describes the difference between a primary and secondary source and how they would search for each one.

Student Assessment/Reflection:

Assessment is based on the rubric for the project and conversations and observations by the teacher and school librarian throughout the process.

Professional Reflection—Librarian Notes:

This lesson is specific to the instruction of primary and secondary sources. However, it may be a starting point for expanding collaboration with the classroom teacher on culminating research projects.

Primary and Secondary Sources Rubric

	Excellent	Satisfactory	Unsatisfactory
Group Participation	The student participated fully and worked cooperatively.	The student participated minimally or was marginally cooperative.	The student did not participate cooperatively or gave minimal effort.
Graphic Organizer	Work completed on time and accurately.	Work was late or was inaccurate.	Work was not completed or missing major elements.
Reflection	Work was completed and included all elements.	Work was completed but may have been late or missing elements.	Work was not turned in.
Staying on Task Daily	Student working as assigned and not disengaged or causing a disruption.	Student not on task daily.	Student not on task daily or was a discipline problem.

Student Name:
Primary and Secondary Sources Grade:

	Excellent	Satisfactory	Unsatisfactory
Group Participation			
Graphic Organizer			
Reflection			
Staying on Task Daily			

From *The Common Core in Action: Ready-to-Use Lesson Plans for K–6 Librarians* by Deborah J. Jesseman. Santa Barbara, CA: Libraries Unlimited. Copyright © 2015.

SUGGESTED BIBLIOGRAPHY

Adams, S. (2007). *DK Eyewitness Books: World War I*. New York, NY: DK Children.

Allan, T. (2003). *The Causes of World War I*. Mankato, MN: Heinemann.

Burgan, M. (2014). *The Split History of World War I: A Perspectives Flip Book*. Mankato, MN: Compass Point Books.

Connolly, S. (2003). *World War I*. Mankato, MN: Heinemann.

Dell, P. (2014). *A World War I Timeline*. Mankato, MN: Capstone Press.

Freedman, R. (2013). *The War to End All Wars: World War I*. New York, NY: HMH Books for Young Readers.

Hale, N. (2014). *Treaties, Trenches, Mud, and Blood (A World War I Tale)*. New York, NY: Harry N. Abrams.

Hunter, N. (2014). *The Home Fronts in World War I*. Mankato, MN: Heinemann.

Hunter, N. (2014). *Remembering World War I*. Mankato, MN: Heinemann.

Kenney, K. L. (2014). *National Geographic Kids Everything World War I: Dig In with Thrilling Photos and Fascinating Facts*. Washington, DC: National Geographic Children's Books.

Maybury, R. J. (2003). *World War I: The Rest of the Story and How It Affects You Today, 1870 to 1935*. Placerville, CA : Bluestocking Press.

Swain, G. (2012). *World War I: An Interactive History Adventure*. Mankato, MN: Capstone Press.

Vanderpool, C. (2010). *Moon over Manifest*. New York, NY: Delacorte Books for Young Readers.

Online Resources:

Library of Congress: http://www.loc.gov/index.html

PowerPoint Games Templates: http://powerpointgames.wikispaces.com/PowerPoint+Game+Templates

Chapter 4

Math

MATH

Number Poetry

Grade Level: K

Lesson Summary: In this early kindergarten lesson the students will learn to identify sequences of numbers from 1 to 10 and count to 20 in play situations or while reading number books.

AASL *Standards for the 21st Century Learner*

- Inquire, think critically, and gain knowledge (1.1.1; 1.1.2; 1.1.6; 1.1.9)
- Draw conclusions, make informed decisions, apply knowledge to new situations, and create new knowledge (2.1.1; 2.1.3; 2.1.5; 2.2.4; 2.3.1)
- Share knowledge and participate ethically and productively as members of our democratic society (3.1.1; 3.3.4; 3.4.2)
- Pursue personal and aesthetic growth (4.1.1; 4.1.3; 4.1.5; 4.1.8)

Common Core State Standards

- CCSS.Math.Content.K.MD.B.3

Instructional Resources:

- *Required*
  - ○ *Ten Little Monkeys Jumping on the Bed* by T. Freeman
  - ○ Felt board with numbers 1 to 20
  - ○ *How Many Bugs in a Box?* by D. A. Carter
  - ○ Access to the song "Counting 1 to 20" by Jack Hartmann, http://www.songsforteaching.com /jackhartmann/counting1to20.htm
- *Recommended*
  - ○ A wide assortment of counting and poetry books and resources, suggestions included in the Bibliography
  - ○ Access to Internet sites, suggestions included in the Bibliography

Instructional Roles:

The school librarian and the classroom teacher work together to assist the students in identifying resources to use and learning activities included in the lesson.

Adapted from an SLM learning plan by Amanda Bell. Language Arts/Science/Math: Animal and Number Poetry. *School Library Media Activities Monthly*, Volume XXIII, Number 8, April 2007, pp. 11–12.

Procedure for Completion:

Day One: The school librarian begins the lesson by reading *Ten Little Monkeys Jumping on the Bed* by T. Freeman, the classroom teacher incorporates the use of numbers with a felt board while demonstrating the rules of counting, and the students are encouraged to chime in during the parts of the story that are appropriate. After the story, the co-teachers teach the students the poetry song "Counting 1 to 20" by Jack Hartmann while incorporating the numbers on a felt board.

Day Two—Completion: The co-teacher will review the lesson from the previous day and have the students sing the "Counting 1 to 20" song. The school librarian will read the students another counting storybook such as *How Many Bugs in a Box?* by D. A. Carter. A document reader or Smartboard may be used to enlarge the book so the students can actively engage in the counting exercise.

The students will choose number and poetry books to check out from the library and count from 1 to 20 during the checkout process.

Completion of Project:

Students will become familiar with the song "Counting 1 to 20," know how to find the counting books in the school library, and be able to count from 1 to 20.

Student Assessment/Reflection:

The co-teachers will listen to the students during the song "Counting 1 to 20" to observe participation in the activity. The students will choose number and poetry books to check out from the library and count from 1 to 20 during the checkout process.

Professional Reflection—Librarian Notes:

This lesson can be easily revised to accommodate the various counting and rhyming books in the school library. A similar lesson can be used to reinforce alphabet lessons.

Number Poetry Rubric

	Excellent	Satisfactory	Unsatisfactory
Recite the Numbers 1 to 20	Student recited the numbers 1 to 20 with ease.	Student made some errors while counting from 1 to 20.	Student could not count from 1 to 20.
Participate in the Singing	Student participated in the singing part of the lesson	Student was reluctant to participate but did so with encouragement.	Student did not participate.
Staying on Task Daily	Student was engaged and well behaved throughout the lesson.	Student behaved well most days.	Student not on task daily or was a discipline problem.

Student Name:
Number Poetry Grade:

	Excellent	Satisfactory	Unsatisfactory
Recite the Numbers 1 to 20			
Participate in the Singing			
Staying on Task Daily			

SUGGESTED BIBLIOGRAPHY

Alaina, M. (2012). *You Can Count!* Mankato, MN: Capstone Press.

Bingham, K., & Zelinsky, P. (2012). *Z Is for Moose.* New York, NY: Greenwillow Books.

Carter, D. A. (2006). *How Many Bugs in a Box?* New York, NY: Little Simon.

Freeman, T. (2003). *Ten Little Monkeys Jumping on the Bed.* Wiltshire: Childs Play Intl.

Geisel, T. S. (1960). *One Fish Two Fish Red Fish Blue Fish.* New York, NY: Random House Books for Young Readers.

Giganti, P. (1994). *How Many Snails?: A Counting Book.* New York, NY: Greenwillow Books.

Hopkins, L. B. (2001). *Marvelous Math: A Book of Poems.* New York, NY: Simon & Schuster Books for Young Readers.

Martin, B. (2011). *Chicka Chicka Boom Boom.* New York, NY: Simon & Schuster Books for Young Readers.

Penn, M. W. (2012). *Pebble Math.* Mankato, MN: Capstone Press.

Scarry, R. (2010). *Richard Scarry's Best Counting Book Ever.* New York, NY: Sterling Press.

Sidman, J. (2006). *Meow Ruff: A Story in Concrete Poetry.* New York, NY: Houghton Mifflin.

Williams, R. L. (2001). *The Coin Counting Book.* Watertown, MA: Charlesbridge.

Online Resources:

"Counting 1 to 20": http://www.songsforteaching.com/jackhartmann/counting1to20.htm

Giggle Poetry: http://www.gigglepoetry.com/index.aspx

MATH/SCIENCE   **Grade Levels:** K–1
Got the Time?

Lesson Summary: This lesson incorporates stories and activities with learning to tell time.

Standards Addressed:

AASL *Standards for the 21st Century Learner*

- Inquire, think critically, and gain knowledge (1.1.1; 1.1.2; 1.1.9; 1.4.2; 1.4.4)
- Draw conclusions, make informed decisions, apply knowledge to new situations, and create new knowledge (2.1.1; 2.1.2; 2.1.5; 2.2.4; 2.3.1)
- Share knowledge and participate ethically and productively as members of our democratic society (3.1.2; 3.1.3; 3.2.3; 3.3.4)
- Pursue personal and aesthetic growth (4.1.1.; 4.1.2; 4.1.6; 4.1.8; 4.3.1)

Common Core State Standards

- CCSS.ELA-Literacy.RL.K.1; RL.K.2; RL.K.3; RL.K.4; RL.K.5; RL.K.6; RL.K.7; RL.K.10
- CCSS.ELA-Literacy.RL.1.1; RL.1.2; RL.1.3; RL.1.4; RL.1.5; RL.1.6; RL.1.7; RL.1.9; RL.1.10
- CCSS.ELA-Math.Content.1.MD.C.4

Instructional Resources:

- *Required*
  - *The Grouchy Ladybug* by Eric Carle
  - *Time to …* by Bruce McMillan
  - Computer access to websites
  - Smartboard or projector and laptop
  - Dice
  - Paper and pencils
  - Supplies to make Ladybug Clocks:
    – Paper plates
    – Red and black construction paper
    – Markers
    – Big and little hands made from poster board
    – Brass fasteners
    – Googly eyes
    – Scissors
    – Glue sticks

All handouts are included in the Student Resource site found at http://www.abc-clio.com/Libraries Unlimited/product.aspx?pc=A4367P.

- *Recommended*
  - A real ladybug in a jar
  - A ladybug puppet

Adapted from an SLM learning plan by Elizabeth Labaire. Science: Our Class Pet: A Dinosaur? *School Library Media Activities Monthly*, Volume XXV, No. 10, June 2009, pp. 12–13.

Instructional Roles:

The librarian and the classroom teacher work together to plan, teach, and assess the unit in which students learn how to tell time to the hour.

Procedure for Completion:

Day One: The co-teachers introduce the lesson by showing students a clock, naming the various parts of the clock, and demonstrating the hands moving around the clock face. The school librarian will read *The Grouchy Ladybug*, with assistance from a ladybug puppet and a real ladybug in a jar if possible.

Day Two: The co-teachers will utilize BrainPop, an animated educational site for kids, to introduce students to the parts of a clock. Students will view a video on parts of a clock and telling time, utilizing one of the websites listed in the Bibliography or a purchased video. If the co-teachers are using a Smartboard, they should stop the video and have students individually identify the parts of the clock. Following this activity the students will make their own Ladybug Clock.

Day Three: The school librarian will read the story *Time to ...* by Bruce McMillan. After listening to the story the students are grouped into threes and take turns rolling dice to form times on the clocks they made in the previous lesson. There is a three-child rotation for this activity: Child A rolls the dice, Child B writes the time, and Child C makes the hands on the clock reflect the corresponding time. This rotation continues until each child has had two turns at all three rotations.

Completion: The school librarian will reread *The Grouchy Ladybug* and the students will each move the hands on their individual clocks while the classroom teacher circulates to correct as necessary.

Completion of Project:

The students will complete the Telling Time handout for assessment.

Student Assessment/Reflection:

The main student assessment is through observation by the co-teachers and student completion of the Telling Time handout and the Ladybug Clock.

Professional Reflection—Librarian Notes:

The lesson can be expanded to include the study of the animals mentioned in *The Grouchy Ladybug*. The addition of puppets allows the students to relate to the characters in a fun way.

Time Rubric

	Excellent	Satisfactory	Unsatisfactory
Ladybug Clock	Student neatly completed the activity.	Student had to be encouraged to complete the activity or it was missing some element and messy.	Student did not complete the activity.
Telling Time Handout	Student completed the assignment correctly and on time.	Student only partially completed the assignment or did not complete it on time.	Student did not complete the assignment.
Staying on Task	Student was not disengaged or causing a disruption.	Student was engaged in the activity most of the time.	Student not on task or was a discipline problem.

Student Name:

Time Grade:

	Excellent	Satisfactory	Unsatisfactory
Ladybug Clock			
Telling Time Handout			
Staying on Task			

From *The Common Core in Action: Ready-to-Use Lesson Plans for K–6 Librarians* by Deborah J. Jesseman. Santa Barbara, CA: Libraries Unlimited. Copyright © 2015.

SUGGESTED BIBLIOGRAPHY

Carle, E. (1999). *The Grouchy Ladybug.* New York, NY: HarperCollins

Harper, D., & Moser, B. (1998). *Telling Time with Big Mama Cat.* New York, NY: HMH Books for Young Readers.

Harris, T. (2009). *The Clock Struck One: A Time-telling Tale* (Math Is Fun!). Minneapolis, MN: Millbrook Press.

McMillan, B. (1989). *Time to …* New York, NY: Scholastic.

Older, J. (2000). *Telling Time: How to Tell Time on Digital and Analog Clocks.* Watertown, MA: Charlesbridge.

Steffora, T. (2011). *Times of the Day.* Mankato, MN: Heinemann.

Online Resources:

Ambleside Primary School on the Web: http://www.amblesideprimary.com/ambleweb/mentalmaths/clock.html

Brain Pop Jr.: http://www.brainpop.com/educators/community/bp-jr-topic/parts-of-a-clock/

Eric Carle: http://www.eric-carle.com/home.html

Time Monsters: http://www.timemonsters.com/

MATH

Grade Levels: K–1

Patterns

Lesson Summary: Through the use of literature, students will learn about the concept of patterns and apply that understanding by locating patterns in their school library environment.

Standards Addressed:

AASL *Standards for the 21st Century Learner*

- Inquire, think critically, and gain knowledge (1.1.1; 1.1.2; 1.1.6; 1.4.4)
- Draw conclusions, make informed decisions, apply knowledge to new situations, and create new knowledge (2.1.1; 2.1.2; 2.1.3; 2.1.5; 2.1.6; 2.4.3)
- Share knowledge and participate ethically and productively as members of our democratic society (3.1.1; 3.1.2; 3.1.3)

Common Core State Standards

- CCSS.ELA-Literacy.RL.K.1; RL.K.3; RL.K.4; RL.K.7; RL.K.10
- CCSS.ELA-Literacy.SL.K.1; SL.K.2; SL.K.3; SL.K.5; SL.K.6
- CCSS.ELA-Math.Content.K.G.A.1; K.G.A.2; K.G.A.3; K.G.A.4; K.G.A.5; K.G.A.6
- CCSS.ELA-Literacy.RL.1.1; RL.1.2; RL.1.3; RL.1.5
- CCSS.ELA-Literacy.SL.1.1; SL.1.2; SL.1.3; SL.1.5; SL.1.6
- CCSS.ELA-Math.Content.1.G.A.1; 1.G.A.2; 1.G.A.3

Instructional Resources:

- *Required*
  - Paper
  - Crayons, markers, and pencils
  - Stickers and miscellaneous craft supplies
  - *Max Found Two Sticks* by Brian Pinkney
- *Recommended*
  - *Two Sticks* by Orel Protopopscu for sound patterns
  - *Over in the Ocean* by Marianne Berkes for rhythmical patterns
  - *Jonathan and His Mommy* by Irene Small for feet patterns/movement

Instructional Roles:

The librarian and the classroom teacher work together to support the curriculum and student learning in this lesson. Prior discussion about math patterns may include collecting different objects to be sorted into patterns.

Procedure for Completion:

Step One: The school librarian reads aloud *Max Found Two Sticks* by Brian Pinkney and asks the students to clap the beat (pattern) on their laps. When the story is completed they are asked if they can think of any other patterns. These responses may be written on the board or chart paper.

Adapted from an SLM learning plan by Kim Bautz. Math/Science: Pattern Storytime. *School Library Monthly*, Volume 28, No. 8, May–June 2012, p. 50.

Step Two—Completion: The students will be given paper and pencil and directed to look around the library to find patterns. Examples of these can be ceiling tiles, carpet squares, furniture, or the arrangement of books. They can write or draw the patterns initially as a "rough draft." The final product will be the creation of a pattern picture using different shapes, letters, stickers, and miscellaneous craft supplies.

Completion of Project:

Pattern pictures are the final project to be displayed in the library or the classroom.

Student Assessment/Reflection:

The main student assessment is the rough draft of pattern observations and the final pattern picture. Throughout the process the teacher and school librarian will engage the students in discussions about what will be included in the assessment process.

Professional Reflection—Librarian Notes:

To reinforce this lesson and patterns, the school librarian may choose to read other pattern-related books such as some suggested in the Bibliography.

Patterns Rubric

	Excellent	Satisfactory	Unsatisfactory
Rough Draft Observations	Student correctly identified multiple patterns.	Student had to be encouraged to complete the assignment.	Student did not participate in the activity.
Pattern Picture	Student completed the assignment neatly and creatively.	Student minimally participated in the activity or only partially completed the assignment.	Student did not participate in the activity and did not complete the assignment.
Staying on Task	Student was not disengaged or causing a disruption.	Student was engaged in the activity most of the time.	Student not on task or was a discipline problem.

Student Name:

Patterns Grade:

	Excellent	Satisfactory	Unsatisfactory
Rough Draft Observations			
Pattern Picture			
Staying on Task			

From *The Common Core in Action: Ready-to-Use Lesson Plans for K–6 Librarians* by Deborah J. Jesseman. Santa Barbara, CA: Libraries Unlimited. Copyright © 2015.

SUGGESTED BIBLIOGRAPHY

Berkes, M. (2004). *Over in the Ocean.* Nevada City, CA: Dawn Publications.

Hall, M. (2007). *Patterns in Nature.* Mankato, MN: Capstone Classroom.

Jocelyn, M. (2004). *Hannah's Collections.* Plattsburgh, NY: Tundra Books.

Olson, N. (2007). *Finding Patterns.* Mankato, MN: Capstone Classroom.

Pinkney, B. (1997). *Max Found Two Sticks.* New York, NY: Aladdin.

Protopopscu, O. (2007). *Two Sticks.* New York, NY: Farrar, Straus and Giroux.

Small, I. (1994). *Jonathan and His Mommy.* Boston, MA: Little Brown.

MATH/SCIENCE
Measurement/Dinosaurs

Grade Levels: K–1

Lesson Summary: Students engage in active learning as they investigate the needs of a pet dinosaur. They will learn about graphs as they investigate the concept of growing, measurement, and comparisons.

Standards Addressed:

AASL *Standards for the 21st Century Learner*

- Inquire, think critically, and gain knowledge (1.1.1–1.1.4; 1.1.6; 1.4.2; 1.4.4)
- Draw conclusions, make informed decisions, apply knowledge to new situations, and create new knowledge (2.1.4; 2.1.5; 2.3.1)
- Share knowledge and participate ethically and productively as members of our democratic society (3.2.2; 3.2.3; 3.3.4)
- Pursue personal and aesthetic growth (4.1.3; 4.1.6; 4.1.8; 4.3.1)

Common Core State Standards

- CCSS.ELA-Math.Content.K.MD.A.1; K.MD.A.2; K.MD.A.3
- CCSS.ELA-Math.Content.K.G.A.3
- CCSS.ELA-Literacy.RL.K.1; RL.K.3; RL.K.4; RL.K.5; RL.K.7; RL.K.10
- CCSS.ELA-Literacy.RI.K.1; RI.K.2; RI.K.4; RI.K.5; RI.K.7; RI.K.10
- CCSS.ELA-Math.Content.1.MD.A.1; 1.MD.A.2
- CCSS.ELA-Literacy.RL.1.1; RL.1.5; RL.1.7
- CCSS.ELA-Literacy.RI.1.1; RI.1.2; RI.1.4; RI.1.6; RI.1.7; RI.1.9; RI.K.10

Instructional Resources:

- *Required*
  - *Buying, Training and Caring for Your Dinosaur* by Laura Joy Rennert
  - *Verdi* by Janell Cannon
  - Nonfiction dinosaur and pet books
  - Laminated dinosaur images in at least three sizes
  - Computer graphing program
  - Graph handouts
  - Crayons, markers, construction paper

All handouts are included in the Student Resource site found at http://www.abc-clio.com/Libraries Unlimited/product.aspx?pc=A4367P.

- *Recommended*
  - Whiteboard with projector for display
  - Smartboard

Instructional Roles:

The librarian and the classroom teacher will work together to support the curriculum and student learning in this lesson.

Adapted from an SLM learning plan by Ann O'Keefe. Science: Our Class Pet: A Dinosaur? *School Library Monthly*, Volume 28, No. 1, September–October 2011, p. 55.

Procedure for Completion:

Step One: The school librarian reads aloud *Buying, Training and Caring for Your Dinosaur* by Laura Joy Rennert and asks the students about getting a dinosaur for the library. Could we? Why or why not? The co-teachers discuss terms such as "extinct," "tame vs. wild," and "learning through make-believe."

Make a dinosaur image and laminate it. Start with one 5 inches tall and place it in a mailing box addressed to the students at the school. The return address can be "The Pretend Pet Company" to develop the pretend vs. real concept. The school librarian measures the new arrival and writes the result on the board or easel chart. Have the students choose a name for this new pet.

Step Two: The co-teachers ask students questions to promote a discussion about living things:

- What do living things need to live and grow?
- How can they find out what a dinosaur needs?
- Will the needs of a dinosaur be the same as a pet dog or wild snake?
- Where should we look for information?

The co-teachers will record prior knowledge offered about dinosaurs on a whiteboard or easel chart, offer a selection of nonfiction dinosaur books for the students' perusal in groups, and collect information about a dinosaur's needs and habitat requirements based on what the group has discovered. The students will create construction paper food (such as leaves and berries) and habitat materials (such as branches, puddles, and streams) to arrange in the Dino home.

Step Three: The school librarian will replace the first dinosaur image with a 10-inch version. The new dinosaur is measured and growth is calculated. The school librarian will read *Verdi* by Janell Cannon and the co-teachers will guide a discussion of growing things:

- What changes did Verdi go through?
- What other things grow?
- Can an ice cream cone grow?
- Can a dog grow?

Step Four—Completion: The school librarian will replace the second dinosaur image with a 15-inch version. The newest dinosaur is measured and growth is calculated. Review the observed measurements, recording the three different heights. Demonstrate graphing software to the class by creating a simple three-bar graph with the measurements, then print the graph for display or project it on a whiteboard/Smartboard. Students are provided a graph format on paper to color that matches the computer-generated graph.

Completion of Project:

Completed colored graphs are the final project to be submitted.

Student Assessment/Reflection:

The main student assessment is ongoing through student contribution to the discussion, observations of group interaction, and completion of the dinosaur measurement graph.

Professional Reflection—Librarian Notes:

Use an aquarium for the dinosaur's "home" and have the students decorate it or fill it with the dinosaur's "needs." This lesson can be expanded to include more scientific facts about dinosaurs, their habitat, or the Mesozoic era.

Measurement Rubric

	Excellent	Satisfactory	Unsatisfactory
Group Contribution	Student contributed constructively to the discussion.	Student had to be encouraged to contribute or was off topic during contribution.	Student did not participate in the group activity.
Graph Handout	Student completed the assignment neatly and accurately.	Student only partially completed the assignment or the work was messy and inaccurate.	Student did not complete the assignment.
Staying on Task	Student was not disengaged or causing a disruption.	Student was engaged in the activity most of the time.	Student not on task or was a discipline problem.

Student Name:

Measurement Grade:

	Excellent	Satisfactory	Unsatisfactory
Group Contribution			
Graph Handout			
Staying on Task			

SUGGESTED BIBLIOGRAPHY

Bennett, K. (2005). *Not Norman: A Goldfish Story*. Somerville, MA: Candlewick Press.

Biedrzyski, D. (2011). *Me and My Dragon*. Watertown, MA: Charlesbridge Publishing.

Cannon, J. (1997). *Verdi*. New York, NY: Harcourt Brace & Company.

DK (1994). *Big Book of Dinosaurs*. New York, NY: DK Publishing.

Dodds, D. A. (2006). *Teacher's Pets*. Somerville, MA: Candlewick Press.

Fraser, M. A. (2003). *I.Q. Goes to the Library*. Somerville, MA: Walker Books.

Fraser, M. A. (2004). *I.Q. Goes to School*. Somerville, MA: Walker Books.

Hughes, C. D. (2011). *National Geographic Little Kids' First Big Book of Dinosaurs*. Washington, DC: National Geographic Children's Books.

Pim, K. (2014). *Dinosaurs—The Grand Tour: Everything Worth Knowing About Dinosaurs from Aardonyx to Zuniceratops*. New York, NY: The Experiment.

Priddy, R. (2011). *My Big Dinosaur Book*. London: Priddy Books.

Rennert, L. J. (2009). *Buying, Training and Caring for Your Dinosaur*. New York, NY: Random House.

Willems, M. (2008). *The Pigeon Wants a Puppy*. New York, NY: Hyperion Books.

Yolen, J. (2011). *How Do Dinosaurs Say Happy Birthday?* Bel Air, CA: Blue Sky Press.

Yolen, J. (2006). *How Do Dinosaurs Play with Their Friends?* Bel Air, CA: Blue Sky Press.

Yolen, J. (2000). *How Do Dinosaurs Say Good Night?* Bel Air, CA: Blue Sky Press.

Dinosaur Images

The following websites are free illustrations that may be used as examples of the "growing" dinosaur:

http://www.coloring.ws/dinosaur.htm

http://www.free-coloring-pages.com/dinosaurs.html

http://www.dinosaur-coloring.com/

MATH

Grade Level: 2

Graph Analysis

Lesson Summary: In this lesson the students will interpret picture graphs, read and interpret bar graphs, and support a conclusion or prediction using information in a table or graph.

Standards Addressed:

AASL *Standards for the 21st Century Learner*

- Inquire, think critically, and gain knowledge (1.1.1; 1.1.2; 1.1.6; 1.1.7; 1.1.8; 1.1.9; 1.2.3; 1.3.5; 1.4.2; 1.4.4)
- Draw conclusions, make informed decisions, apply knowledge to new situations, and create new knowledge (2.1.2; 2.1.3; 2.1.4; 2.1.5; 2.1.6; 2.2.4; 2.3.1)
- Share knowledge and participate ethically and productively as members of our democratic society (3.1.1; 3.1.2; 3.1.3; 3.2.2; 3.2.3; 3.3.2; 3.3.4)
- Pursue personal and aesthetic growth (4.1.4; 4.1.6; 4.3.1)

Common Core State Standards

- CCSS.Math.Content.2.MD.D.9
- CCSS.Math.Content.2.MD.D.10
- CCSS.ELA-Literacy.W.2.2; W.2.5; W.2.6; W.2.7
- CCSS.ELA-Literacy.SL.2.1; SL.2.2; SL.2.6

Instructional Resources:

- *Required*
  - Access to news websites, examples in the Bibliography
  - Newspapers—local, regional, and national
  - Magazines, examples in the Bibliography
  - Computer access to a word processing program such as Microsoft Word
  - Graph Analysis handout

All handouts are included in the Student Resource site found at http://www.abc-clio.com/Libraries Unlimited/product.aspx?pc=A4367P.

Instructional Roles:

The school librarian and the classroom teacher work together to assist the students in identifying resources to use and learning activities included in the lesson. The students will have prior understanding of the purpose of graphs; be able to interpret bar, circle, line, and picture graphs; and make conclusions based on their analysis of the graphs.

Procedure for Completion:

Day One: The students will come to the library where they will be divided into groups of three. The groups will search in magazines, online, and in newspapers to find a circle, bar, line, or picture graph that

Adapted from an SLM learning plan by Amanda Bell. Math/Reading/Language Arts: Writing and Reading and Graphs, Oh My! *School Library Media Activities Monthly,* Volume XXIV, Number 7, March 2008, pp. 11–12.

represents data from each of these sources. Each student in the group will be assigned a different media resource to use and will return to the group once they have found a graph. They will read and discuss the graphs.

Day Two—Completion: The students will return to the library in their groups and, utilizing the Graph Analysis handout, analyze the graphs they found the previous day and make conclusions or predictions from each one. They will write up the overview of their conclusions using computers and a word processing program. Each group will present their graph analysis to the rest of the class.

Completion of Project:

Student written assignments, the Graph Analysis handout, and the group presentation are the culminating activities for this lesson.

Student Assessment/Reflection:

The presentation, written report conclusions, and the Graph Analysis handout are the main student assessments and are based on the rubric for the lesson. Observations and conversations with the teacher and school librarian throughout the process will also be included in the assessment process.

Professional Reflection—Librarian Notes:

This lesson can be used to address Reading and English Language Arts standards by expanding the activity to include a variety of communication techniques such as formal oral presentations and written or multimedia reports.

Graph Analysis Rubric			
	Excellent	Satisfactory	Unsatisfactory
Graph Analysis Handout	The handout was complete and accurate.	The handout was incomplete or late.	The work was not handed in.
Written Conclusions or Predictions	The student completed the conclusion or prediction analysis neatly and thoroughly.	The student did not complete the written conclusion or it was handed in late.	The student did not submit the written assignment.
Presentation	Student actively participated in the group presentation.	Student was reluctant to participate but did so with encouragement.	Student did not participate in the presentation.
Staying on Task Daily	Student was engaged and well behaved throughout the lesson.	Student behaves well most days.	Student not on task daily or was a discipline problem.

Student Name:

Graph Analysis Grade:

	Excellent	Satisfactory	Unsatisfactory
Graph Analysis Handout			
Written Conclusions or Predictions			
Presentation			
Staying on Task Daily			

SUGGESTED BIBLIOGRAPHY

Magazines such as: *Sports Illustrated for Kids, National Geographic Kids, Family Fun, Children's Digest*
Newspapers—local and regional

Online Resources:

AOL home page: http://www.aol.com/?ncid=txtlnkusaolp00001203
BBC home page: http://www.bbc.com/news/
Charter home page: http://www.charter.net/
MSN home page: http://www.msn.com/
Yahoo home page: https://www.yahoo.com/

MATH   Grade Levels: 3–4
Math and Origami

Lesson Summary: This interactive lesson relates to and reinforces the geometry principles of identifying shapes and their attributes to origami paper folding in an interactive lesson.

Standards Addressed:

AASL *Standards for the 21st Century Learner*

- Inquire, think critically, and gain knowledge (1.1.1; 1.1.2; 1.1.6; 1.4.2; 1.4.4)
- Draw conclusions, make informed decisions, apply knowledge to new situations, and create new knowledge (2.1.3)
- Share knowledge and participate ethically and productively as members of our democratic society (3.1.3; 3.2.3)
- Pursue personal and aesthetic growth (4.1.1; 4.4.6)

Common Core State Standards

- CCSS.Math.Content.3.GA.A.1; 3.GA.A.2
- CCSS.ELA-Literacy.RL.3.1; RL.3.3; RL.3.4; RL.3.5; RL.3.6; RL.3.7; RL.3.10
- CCSS.Math.Content.4.GA.A.1; 4.GA.A.2; 4.GA.A.3
- CCSS.ELA-Literacy.RL.4.1; RL.4.2; RL.4.3; RL.4.5; RL.4.6; RL.4.9; RL.4.10

Instructional Resources:

- *Required*
  - Origami paper
  - A Crane handout
  - *Sadako and the Thousand Paper Cranes* by Eleanor Coerr
  - Access to a computer and projection equipment or Smartboard
  - Access to online resources such as TeacherTube
  - Scissors

All handouts are included in the Student Resource site found at http://www.abc-clio.com/Libraries Unlimited/product.aspx?pc=A4367P.

- *Recommended*
  - String or fishing line to hang the cranes from the classroom or library ceiling

Instructional Roles:

The librarian and the classroom teacher work together to support the curriculum and student learning in this lesson. Students should have prior learning about the principles relating to the geometry shapes.

Procedure for Completion:

Step One: The co-teachers will introduce the art of origami to the students, emphasizing the use of geometric shapes in the process. The school librarian will read *Sadako and the Thousand Paper Cranes* followed by teacher-led discussions of the story and tell the students they will make paper cranes to display in the library or classroom.

Step Two: The co-teachers will utilize projection resources to demonstrate how to make a paper crane, pausing at various steps to point out the geometric shapes each fold will make. The students will be given the A Crane handout for a guide, and 8½ x 11 plain white paper to cut into a square and to practice folding into the crane. It may take several attempts with the plain white paper for an acceptable product to be achieved.

Step Three—Completion: The co-teachers will check the white cranes and hand out special origami paper for students to complete their final product.

Completion of Project:

The final product is a folded crane with origami paper.

Student Assessment/Reflection:

The final project is the object of the main student assessment and is based on the rubric for the project. Questions asked during the project and conversations with the teacher and school librarian throughout the process will also be included in the assessment process.

Professional Reflection—Librarian Notes:

The paper cranes should be hung by string or fishing line from the ceiling of the school library and the classroom.

This lesson can be expanded to include Social Studies and the study of Hiroshima, the war, and an Internet exploration of Hiroshima Peace Park. *The Faithful Elephants* by Yukio Tsuchiya may be another story to share with a more mature audience and facilitate further discussion of wars and the harm they do to innocents.

Math and Origami Rubric

	Excellent	Satisfactory	Unsatisfactory
Practice Paper Crane	The student completed the practice crane and is ready for the final.	The student had difficulty with the practice crane and needed significant assistance.	The student did not complete the first step.
Final Paper Crane	The student completed the crane as instructed.	The student had difficulty with the project but completed it with assistance.	Student did not complete the project.
Staying on Task Daily	Student was engaged and well behaved throughout the lesson.	Student behaved well most days.	Student not on task daily or was a discipline problem.

Student Name:

Math and Origami Grade:

	Excellent	Satisfactory	Unsatisfactory
Practice Paper Crane			
Final Paper Crane			
Staying on Task Daily			

 From *The Common Core in Action: Ready-to-Use Lesson Plans for K–6 Librarians* by Deborah J. Jesseman. Santa Barbara, CA: Libraries Unlimited. Copyright © 2015.

SUGGESTED BIBLIOGRAPHY

Coerr, E. (1977). *Sadako and the Thousand Paper Cranes*. New York, NY: G. P. Putnam's Sons.

France, B. (1999). *Unfolding Mathematics with Unit Origami*. Peabody, MA: Key Curriculum Press.

LaFosse, M. G. (2011). *Geometric Origami Kit: The Art of Modular Paper Sculpture*. North Clarendon, VT: Tuttle.

Meinking, M., & Alexander, C. (2010). *Easy Origami: A Step-by-Step Guide for Kids*. Mankato, MN: Capstone Press.

Online Resources:

How to Make an Origami Crane: http://www.monkey.org/~aidan/origami/crane/index.html

Origami Fun: http://www.origami-fun.com/origami-crane.html

TeacherTube Videos: http://www.teachertube.com/video/origami-crane-118344; http://www.teachertube.com/video/origami-crane-50412

WickiHow: http://www.wikihow.com/Fold-a-Paper-Crane

MATH   Grade Levels: 3–4

Golden Rectangle

Lesson Summary: This lesson, an introduction to the ratio also known as the Golden Rectangle, will be provided by the video *Donald in MathMagic Land*. The first 11 minutes is recommended for this lesson as they directly relate to the topic of the Golden Rectangle ratio and how it can be found in real life. Students are guided in discovering the relationship of this ratio to the world around them by expanding the search for the Golden Rectangle to items in architecture, painting, design, music, nature, or the Pyramids.

Standards Addressed:

AASL *Standards for the 21st Century Learner*

- Inquire, think critically, and gain knowledge (1.1.1–1.1.9; 1.2.1–1.2.7; 1.3.1–1.3.5; 1.4.1–1.4.4)
- Draw conclusions, make informed decisions, apply knowledge to new situations, and create new knowledge (2.1.1–2.1.6; 2.2.1–2.2.4; 2.3.1–2.3.3; 2.4.1–2.4.4)
- Share knowledge and participate ethically and productively as members of our democratic society (3.1.2–3.1.6; 3.2.1; 3.2.2; 3.4.2)
- Pursue personal and aesthetic growth (4.1.3–4.1.8; 4.2.1–4.2.3; 4.3.1–4.3.4; 4.4.1–4.4.6)

Common Core State Standards

- CCSS.Math.Content.3.MD.C.5; 3.MD.C.6; 3.MD.C.7
- CCSS.Math.Content.3.MD.D.8
- CCSS.Math.Content.3.G.A.1; 3.G.A.2
- CCSS.Math.Content.4.MD.C.5; 4.MD.C.6; 4.MD.C.7
- CCSS.Math.Content.4.G.A.1; 4.G.A.2; 4.G.A.3
- CCSS.ELA-Literacy.SL.3.1; SL.3.2; SL.3.3; SL.3.4; SL.3.5; SL.3.6
- CCSS.ELA-Literacy.W.3.2; W.3.4; W.3.5; W.3.6; W.3.7; W.3.8; W.3.10
- CCSS.ELA-Literacy.SL.4.1; SL.4.2; SL.4.3; SL.4.4; SL.4.5; SL.4.6
- CCSS.ELA-Literacy.W.4.2; W.4.4; W.4.5; W.4.6; W.4.7; W.4.8; W.4.9; W.4.10

Instructional Resources:

- *Required*
  - *Donald in MathMagic Land* video
  - Ruler or straight-edge, compass, pencils, colored pencils, paper, glue, scissors, poster board
  - Computer access
  - Constructing a Golden Rectangle handout

All handouts are included in the Student Resource site found at http://www.abc-clio.com/Libraries Unlimited/product.aspx?pc=A4367P.

- *Recommended*
  - SmartBoard
  - Trifold poster boards

Instructional Roles:

The teacher and the school librarian will co-teach this lesson. The teacher is the guide for the mathematical content of the lesson, providing prior learning for measurement, use of rulers or straightedges and compasses. The school librarian assists in providing resources for the lesson, access and permission for use of the video, and reference assistance to both the teacher and the students.

Procedure for Completion:

Day One: On the first day of the lesson, the students will be shown the first 11 minutes of the movie *Donald in MathMagic Land*. The movie will be followed by a discussion of examples used in real life, as Donald has indicated in the video. The school librarian will obtain pictures or utilize a document reader or Smartboard to enlarge the examples shown in the movie of the Parthenon, a Greek sculpture, an image of the Cathedral of Notre Dame, and the Mona Lisa.

Day Two: On the second day of the lesson the students will construct a Golden Rectangle using the Constructing a Golden Rectangle handout. The co-teachers will explain the project and students will begin researching their selected subject.

Day Three through Completion: The students will choose their subject, write a brief description of it, print a picture, overlay the Golden Rectangle onto the picture, and glue everything onto a poster. The co-teachers will provide guidance and assistance as needed.

Completion of Project:

The final project will be a poster presentation to the class demonstrating what they have found that illustrates a Golden Rectangle. The completed posters will be displayed around the classroom or library.

Student Assessment/Reflection:

The final project is the object of the main student assessment and is based on the rubric for the project. Questions asked during the oral presentation as well as conversations with the teacher and school librarian throughout the process will also be included in the assessment process.

Professional Reflection—Librarian Notes:

This lesson can become part of a thematic unit that may include the arts, sciences, social studies, and English and may be expanded beyond the initial development of a Golden Rectangle.

Golden Rectangle Rubric

	Excellent	Satisfactory	Unsatisfactory
Step One: Construction of Golden Rectangle	Student completed the project as assigned and on time.	Work was completed but not on time or extensive corrections needed.	Work was not completed or it needed several revisions before moving to the next step.
Step Two: Development and Completion of the Poster	The assignment was completed on time, well designed, and neat.	Work was completed but not on time or the poster was messy or inaccurate.	Work was not completed or needed several revisions.
Step Three: Oral Presentation	The assignment was completed on time, presentation clear and understandable, and questions answered knowledgeably.	Work was not completed on time or the presentation was not understandable.	Work was not completed or missing major elements.
Staying on Task Daily	Student working as assigned and not disengaged or causing a disruption.	Student working well on assignment most days.	Student not on task daily or was a discipline problem.

Student Name:

Golden Rectangle Grade:

	Excellent	Satisfactory	Unsatisfactory
Step One: Construction of Golden Rectangle			
Step Two: Development and Completion of the Poster			
Step Three: Oral Presentation			
Staying on Task Daily			

SUGGESTED BIBLIOGRAPHY

Balliett, B. (2006). *The Wright 3*. New York, NY: Scholastic Press.

Blaisdell, M. (2010). *If You Were a Quadrilateral*. Mankato, MN: Capstone Classroom.

Brezenoff, S. (2010). *The Painting That Wasn't There*. Mankato, MN: Capstone Classroom.

Choisser, J. *Grandpa, Tell Us About Phi, the Golden Number: Explore the Amazing Connection between Nature and Math!* Amazon Digital Services. ASIN: B00IRMVMTQ.

Donald in MathMagic Land (2009). Burbank, CA: Walt Disney Studios Home Entertainment.

Forest, C. (2012). *Pyramids of Ancient Egypt*. Mankato, MN: Capstone Classroom.

Hammel, D. S. (2015). *That Figures!: A Crash Course in Math*. Mankato, MN: Capstone Classroom.

Hart, A. (1997). *Pyramids!: 50 Hands-On Activities to Experience Ancient Egypt*. Charlotte, VT: Williamson.

Krech, B., Birrer, D., & DiLorenzo, S. (2008). *Mini-Lessons, Games, & Activities to Review & Reinforce Essential Math Concepts & Skills*. New York, NY: Scholastic Teaching Resources.

Livio, M. (2002). *The Golden Ratio: The Story of Phi, the World's Most Astonishing Number*. New York: Broadway Books.

Weil, A. (2012). *The World's Most Amazing Pyramids*. Mankato, MN: Capstone Classroom.

MATH/GEOMETRY   **Grade Levels:** 3–5

Quilting and the Underground Railroad

Lesson Summary: This lesson is an enjoyable way for students to learn measurement and explore geometric figures by making paper quilt blocks. It is a lesson that may be utilized as part of a thematic unit across the curriculum to include topics such as slavery and the Underground Railroad, a history of quilts, and the Civil War.

Standards Addressed:

AASL *Standards for the 21st Century Learner*

- Inquire, think critically, and gain knowledge (1.1.1–1.1.9; 1.2.1–1.2.7; 1.3.1–1.3.5; 1.4.1–1.4.4)
- Draw conclusions, make informed decisions, apply knowledge to new situations, and create new knowledge (2.1.1–2.1.6; 2.2.1–2.2.4; 2.3.1–2.3.3; 2.4.1–2.4.4)
- Share knowledge and participate ethically and productively as members of our democratic society (3.1.2–3.1.6; 3.2.1; 3.2.2; 3.4.2)
- Pursue personal and aesthetic growth (4.1.3–4.1.8; 4.2.1–4.2.3; 4.3.1–4.3.4; 4.4.1–4.4.6)

Common Core State Standards

- CCSS.Math.Content.3.MD.B.3; 3.MD.B.4; 3.MD.C.5; 3.MD.C.6; 3.MD.C.7
- CCSS.Math.Content.3.G.A.1; 3.G.A.2
- CCSS.Math.Content.4.MD.A.3; 4.MD.C.5; 4.MD.C.6; 4.MD.C.7
- CCSS.Math.Content.4.G.A.1; 4.G.A.2
- CCSS.Math.Content.5.MD.A.1
- CCSS.Math.Content.5.G.B.3; 5.G.B.4
- CCSS.ELA-Literacy.RL.3.1; RL.3.2; RL.3.3; RL.3.4; RL.3.7
- CCSS.ELA-Literacy.RI.3.1; RI.3.2; RI.3.3; RI.3.4; RI.3.5; RI.3.6; RI.3.7
- CCSS.ELA-Literacy.RL.4.1; RL.4.2; RL.4.3; RL.4.4; RL.4.7
- CCSS.ELA-Literacy.RI.4.1; RI.4.2; RI.4.3; RI.4.4; RI.4.5; RI.4.6; RI.4.7
- CCSS.ELA-Literacy.RL.5.1; RL.5.2; RL.5.3; RL.5.4; RL.5.7
- CCSS.ELA-Literacy.RI.5.1; RI.5.2; RI.5.3; RI.5.4; RI.5.5; RI.5.6; RI.5.7

Instructional Resources:

- *Required*
  - Rulers, compasses, pencils, scissors, glue, newsprint, construction paper (background blocks precut to 12" x 12")
  - Two quilt-related fiction books; a bibliography of suggestions may be found at the end of the lesson
- *Recommended*
  - Access to actual quilts or quilt blocks
  - *Sam Johnson and the Blue Ribbon Quilt* by Lisa Ernst
  - *Sweet Clara and the Freedom Quilt* by Deborah Hopkinson

Adapted from an SLM learning plan by Deborah Jesseman. Math/Geometry Quilting and the Underground Railroad. *School Library Monthly*, Volume 28, No. 8, May–June, pp. 51–53.

Instructional Roles:

The teacher will guide students in the mathematics portion of the lesson by providing prior learning for measurement, use of rulers and compasses, and shapes. The school librarian is the resource for the background research, the reader for sharing of books and stories, and a resource for further student research for the subjects that may include a history of slavery, the underground railroad, and quilting.

Procedure for Completion:

Day One: The school librarian will read *Sweet Clara and the Freedom Quilt* by Deborah Hopkinson to promote a discussion of the value of quilts in history. Quilt books, and if there is access, quilts or fabric quilt blocks will be passed around so the students can see examples up close.

Day Two: The school librarian will read *Sam Johnson and the Blue Ribbon Quilt* by Lisa Ernst. The choice of this book is to demonstrate to boys that it is not a unit "just for girls." The co-teachers will explain the process for developing their own construction paper quilt square.

Day Three through Day Five: Over the course of a week, the students will:

- Choose a quilt block to make in construction paper and receive approval from the co-teachers.
- Draw the chosen block on newsprint, including color choices. For example, the color choices may be a combination of the school colors. The co-teachers will approve the drawing before students move on to the next step.
- Complete the block and submit it for assessment and feedback.

While students are working on their quilt blocks the school librarian will read a variety of quilt- or underground railroad–related stories.

Completion of Project:

The completed construction paper blocks will be submitted and will be used to decorate the classroom or school library. Squares may be set up like a quilt along one wall and some as a border along the top of the walls. This promotes pride in student work and an attractive display in the classroom or library.

Student Assessment/Reflection:

The final quilt block is the object of the main student assessment and is based on the rubric for the project and conversations with the teacher and school librarian throughout the process. Additional student reflection on the topic may include oral or written feedback to the co-teachers about the process, the project, and the historical significance of the era.

Professional Reflection—Librarian Notes:

This unit was completed in a mathematics classroom for several years. It was extremely successful for a number of reasons. It held the students' attention because it was interactive and provided them an opportunity to use some creativity while accomplishing a mathematics requirement. It also provided an opportunity for students to learn more than an isolated geometry concept but also how that concept fit in a real-world situation. The inclusion of stories added to student background knowledge and encouraged them to research more on the topic. Finally, the results provided visual appeal for all classes and administration when the quilt blocks were placed in the classroom and library.

The lesson can be used in an online classroom as well, utilizing a number of technology tools. The simplest is voice-over PowerPoint (see Suggested Bibliography). The instructions and demonstrations of quilts and additional books can be placed on a video or PowerPoint slides with written instructions and voice-over to provide for students with disabilities. The materials are easy to obtain, with most being in every home, school, or home-school environment. If the instructor chooses to use this lesson and does not have the unique knowledge or background in quilting, there are many online and library resources that can be accessed as well as local quilt clubs or shops.

Quilt Block Rubric

	Excellent	Satisfactory	Unsatisfactory
Step One: Choose the Quilt Block Design	Work completed as assigned and on time.	Work completed but not on time or extensive revisions were needed before moving to next step.	Work not completed.
Step Two: Newsprint Template	Work completed on time, well designed, and with colors assigned in appropriate areas of the template.	Work completed but not on time or extensive revisions were needed before moving to next step.	Work not completed.
Step Three: Completed Quilt Block	Work completed on time, design clean, and creative.	Work not completed on time or the project is messy or not accurately measured.	Work not completed or missing major elements.
Staying on Task Daily	Student working as assigned and not disengaged or causing a disruption.	Student working well on assignment most days.	Student not on task daily or is a discipline problem.

Student Name:
Quilt Block Grade:

	Excellent	Satisfactory	Unsatisfactory
Step One: Choose the Quilt Block Design			
Step Two: Newsprint Template			
Step Three: Completed Quilt Block			
Staying on Task Daily			

From *The Common Core in Action: Ready-to-Use Lesson Plans for K–6 Librarians* by Deborah J. Jesseman. Santa Barbara, CA: Libraries Unlimited. Copyright © 2015.

SUGGESTED BIBLIOGRAPHY

Ball, M. (2001). *Creative Quilting with Kids.* Fairfield, OH: Krause.

Benberry, C. R., & Crabb, C. P. (1994). *A Patchwork of Pieces: An Anthology of Early Quilt Stories 1845–1940.* Paducah, KY: Collector Books.

Bial, R. (1999). *The Underground Railroad.* San Anselmo, CA: Sandpiper Press.

Bial, R. (1996). *With Needle and Thread: A Book About Quilts.* New York, NY: Houghton Mifflin Books for Children.

Bourgeois, P. (2001). *Oma's Quilt.* Toronto, ON, Canada: Kids Can Press.

Braddon, K., Hall, N. J., & Taylor, D. (1993). *Math through Children's Literature: Making the NCTM Standards Come Alive.* Santa Barbara, CA: Libraries Unlimited.

Brumbeau, J. (2001). *The Quiltmaker's Gift.* New York, NY: Scholastic.

Brumbeau, J. (2005). *The Quiltmaker's Journey.* Milwaukee, WI: Orchard Press.

Buchberg, W. (1996). *Quilting Activities Across the Curriculum.* New York, NY: Scholastic.

Cigrand, M., & Howard, P. (2000). *Easy Literature-Based Quilts Around the Year.* New York, NY: Scholastic.

Cobb, M. (1995). *The Quilt-Block History of Pioneer Days, with Projects Kids Can Make.* Minneapolis, MN: Millbrook Press.

Cohen, L. S. (1996). *Quilt Design Masters.* Boston, MA: Dale Seymour Publications (Pearson).

Dallas, S. (2013). *The Quilt Walk.* Ann Arbor MI: Sleeping Bear Press.

Erickson, P. (2000). *Daily Life on a Southern Plantation 1853.* New York, NY: Puffin.

Ernst, L. C. *Sam Johnson and the Blue Ribbon Quilt.* New York, NY: HarperCollins.

Flournoy, V. (1985). *The Patchwork Quilt.* New York, NY: Dial Books for Young Readers.

Gibbins, G. (2004). *The Quilting Bee.* New York, NY: Harper Collins.

Greenwood, B. (1998). *The Last Safe House: A Story of the Underground Railroad.* Toronto, ON, Canada: Kids Can Press.

Hines, A. G. (2001). *Pieces: A Year in Poems & Quilts.* New York, NY: Greenwillow Books.

Hopkinson, D. (1995). *Sweet Clara and the Freedom Quilt.* New York, NY: Dragonfly Books.

Hopkinson, D. (2005). *Under the Quilt of Night.* New York, NY: Aladdin.

Howard, E. (1996). *The Log Cabin Quilt.* New York, NY: Holiday House.

Johnston, T., & dePaola, T. (1996). *The Quilt Story.* Amazon Services, FBAPower Setup.

McKissack, P. (2008). *Stitchin' and Pullin': A Gee's Bend Quilt.* New York, NY: Random House Books for Young Readers.

Paul, A. W. (1996). *Eight Hands Round: A Patchwork Alphabet.* New York, NY: HarperCollins.

Polacco, P. (2001). *The Keeping Quilt.* New York, NY: Simon & Schuster for Young Readers.

Smucker, B. (1996). *Selina and the Bear Paw Quilt.* New York, NY: Crown Publishers.

Storms, B. (2001). *Quilting (Kids Can Do It).* Toronto, ON, Canada: Kids Can Press.

Tobin, J. L., & Dobard, R. G. (2000). *Hidden in Plain View: A Secret Story of Quilts and the Underground Railroad.* Rockland, MA: Anchor Press.

Vaughan, M. (2001). *The Secret to Freedom.* New York, NY: Lee & Low Books.

von Olfers, S., & Schoen-Smith, S. (2007). *Mother Earth and Her Children: A Quilted Fairy Tale.* Elmhurst, IL: Breckling Press.

Whittington, M. K. (1991). *The Patchwork Lady.* New York, NY: Harcourt Brace.

Voice-over Powerpoint Resources:

http://www.emergingedtech.com/2012/12/add-voice-over-to-powerpoint-presentations-in-5-easy-steps/

http://www.flippedclassroomworkshop.com/5-easy-steps-for-adding-voice-over-to-powerpoint-presentations/

https://support.office.microsoft.com/en-us/article/Add-narration-to-a-presentation-0b9502c6-5f6c-40ae-b1e7-e47d8741161c?CorrelationId=59e38fc8-2f63-4821-9a3a-d976ddbc8db9&ui=en-US&rs=en-US&ad=US

https://www.youtube.com/watch?v=3uk4CU7uobM

MATH   Grade Levels: 5–6
A Wrinkle in Time and Tesseracts

Lesson Summary: Students will read *A Wrinkle in Time* by Madeline L'Engle and explore the world of mathematical multidimensional shapes that may include: magic tesseract, polytope, simplex, tetrahedrons, and tetrahedral molecular geometry. In this lesson students will build a Polyhedron solid in three dimensions with flat faces, straight edges, and sharp corners.

Standards Addressed:

AASL *Standards for the 21st Century Learner*

- Inquire, think critically, and gain knowledge (1.1.1–1.1.9; 1.2.1–1.2.7; 1.3.5; 1.4.1–1.4.4)
- Draw conclusions, make informed decisions, apply knowledge to new situations, and create new knowledge (2.1.1–2.1.5; 2.2.1–2.2.4; 2.3.1; 2.4.1–2.4.3)
- Share knowledge and participate ethically and productively as members of our democratic society (3.1.1; 3.1.2; 3.1.4; 3.1.6; 3.3.1–3.3.5; 3.4.1; 3.4.2)
- Pursue personal and aesthetic growth (4.1.3–4.1.8; 4.2.1–4.2.4; 4.3.1–4.3.4; 4.4.1–4.4.6)

Common Core State Standards

- CCSS.Math.Content.5.MD.A.1
- CCSS.Math.Content.5.G.A.1; 5.G.A.2; 5.G.B.3; 5.G.B.4
- CCSS.Math.Content.6.RP.A.1; 6.RP.A.2; 6.RP.A.3
- CCSS.Math.Content.6.GA.1; 6.GA.2; 6.GA.3
- CCSS.ELA-Literacy.RL.5.1; RL.5.2; RL.5.3; RL.5.4; RL.5.5; RL.5.6; RL.5.7; RL.5.10
- CCSS.ELA-Literacy.RF.5.3; RF.5.4
- CCSS.ELA-Literacy.RL.6.1; RL.6.2; RL.6.3; RL.6.4; RL.6.5; RL.6.6; RL.6.7; RL.6.10

Instructional Resources:

- *Required*
  - *A Wrinkle in Time* by Madeline L'Engle
  - Heavy paper or poster board, tape, glue, scissors, rulers or straightedges
  - String or fishing line

Instructional Roles:

The school librarian will introduce the story *A Wrinkle in Time* by Madeline L'Engle and share information about the author and the series. The classroom teacher will instruct students in the mathematical concepts of multidimensional figures. Both instructors will guide students in further research of the various figures for them to construct.

Procedure for Completion:

Day One: The classroom teacher will introduce the concepts needed for the development of the multidimensional figures. The school librarian will introduce Madeline L'Engle and her books and read the first chapter of *A Wrinkle in Time.* Students will be assigned the next two chapters for homework.

Day Two: The classroom teacher will continue the background math lessons for the complex figures and students will be assigned chapters 4 and 5 in *A Wrinkle in Time*.

Day Three: Chapter 5 in the book is entitled "The Tesseract" and includes the explanation that "tessering is travel in the fifth dimension: the first dimension is a line; the second is a square; the third is a cube; the fourth is Einstein's concept of time; and the fifth is a tesseract. By adding the tesseract to the other four dimensions, they travel in such a way that the shortest distance between two points is not a straight line." Students will research the concepts of multidimensional figures such as tetrahedrons, polytopes, and simplex figures and begin the project of designing and constructing a figure.

Day Four—Completion: Students are provided time to research and construct their figures.

Completion of Project:

The final project is a multidimensional figure that will be hung by fishing line from the ceiling around the school library and the classroom

Student Assessment/Reflection:

When completed, the figures will be submitted for a grade and will be used to decorate the classroom or school library. This promotes pride in student work and an attractive display in the classroom or library.

Professional Reflection—Librarian Notes:

The school librarian may want to expand the lessons to include the rest of the *Wrinkle in Time* series. Other topics that may relate include the feelings Meg experiences as she grows from a middle school student to high school and the bullying that happens to both her and Charles Wallace.

A Wrinkle in Time and Tesseracts
Rubric

	Excellent	Satisfactory	Unsatisfactory
Step One: Research and Figure Design Choice	Work completed as assigned on time.	Work is completed but not on time or extensive revisions needed before moving to next step.	Work not completed.
Step Two: Daily Readings	Readings completed on time and the student is able to contribute to the discussions.	Readings completed but not on time and the student is not able to add to the discussion.	Readings not completed.
Step Three: Completed Polyhedron Construction	Work completed on time, according to the instructions, and the design is neat and accurate.	Work not completed on time or the project is messy, incomplete, or not accurate.	Work not completed or missing major elements.
Staying on Task Daily	Student working as assigned and not disengaged or causing a disruption.	Student working well on assignment most days.	Student not on task daily or is a discipline problem.

Student Name:
A Wrinkle in Time and Tesseracts Grade:

	Excellent	Satisfactory	Unsatisfactory
Step One: Research and Figure Design Choice			
Step Two: Daily Readings			
Step Three: Completed Polyhedron Construction			
Staying on Task Daily			

From *The Common Core in Action: Ready-to-Use Lesson Plans for K–6 Librarians* by Deborah J. Jesseman. Santa Barbara, CA: Libraries Unlimited. Copyright © 2015.

SUGGESTED BIBLIOGRAPHY

France, B. (1999). *Unfolding Mathematics with Unit Origami*. Emeryville, CA: Key Curriculum Press.

L'Engle, M. (1962). *A Wrinkle in Time*. New York, NY: Farrar, Straus, and Giroux.

L'Engle, M. (1973). *A Wind in the Door*. New York, NY: Farrar, Straus, and Giroux.

L'Engle, M. (1978*). A Swiftly Tilting Planet*. New York, NY: Farrar, Straus, and Giroux.

L'Engle, M. (1986). *Many Waters*. New York, NY: Farrar, Straus, and Giroux.

L'Engle, M. (1989). *An Acceptable Time*. New York, NY: Farrar, Straus, and Giroux.

Serra, M. (2007). *Discovering Geometry: An Investigative Approach*. Dubuque, IA: Kendall Hunt.

Wenninger, M. (2011). *Polyhedron Models for the Classroom*. LAP LAMBERT Academic Publishing: https://www.lap-publishing.com/

Online Resources:

http://www.madeleinelengle.com/

http://www.scholastic.com/browse/lessonplan.jsp?id=1219

MATH   **Grade Levels:** 5–6

Black Friday Sales!

Lesson Summary: In this lesson students will utilize real-life issues to determine price savings and percent of savings. For several weeks prior to November's "Black Friday" sales, stores provide sales flyers in the newspapers and in mass mailings. Students will use these flyers to collect information on what items they might like to purchase during these sales, then compare the prices and determine the percent of savings for each item.

Standards Addressed:

AASL *Standards for the 21st Century Learner*

- Inquire, think critically, and gain knowledge (1.1.1–1.1.9; 1.2.1–1.2.7; 1.3.1–1.3.5; 1.4.1–1.4.4)
- Draw conclusions, make informed decisions, apply knowledge to new situations, and create new knowledge (2.1.1–2.1.6; 2.2.1–2.2.4; 2.3.1–2.3.3; 2.4.1–2.4.4)
- Share knowledge and participate ethically and productively as members of our democratic society (3.1.1–3.1.6; 3.2.1–3.2.2; 3.3.1–3.3.7; 3.4.1–3.4.2)
- Pursue personal and aesthetic growth (4.1.4–4.1.8; 4.2.1–4.2.3; 4.3.1; 4.3.4; 4.4.1–4.4.6)

Common Core State Standards

- CCSS.Math.Content.5.OA.A.1; 5.OA.A.2
- CCSS.Math.Content.5.NBT.A.1; 5.NBT.A.2; 5.NBT.A.3; 5.NBT.A.4; 5.NBT.B.5; 5.NBT.B.6; 5.NBT.B.7
- CCSS.Math.Content.6.RP.A.1; 6.RP.A.2; 6.RP.A.3
- CCSS.Math.Content.6.NS.B.2; 6.NS.B.3; 6.NS.B.4; 6.NS.C.5
- CCSS.Math.Content.6.EE.A.1; 6.EE.A.2; 6.EE.B.6; 6.EE.B.7
- CCSS.ELA-Literacy.RI.5.3; RI.5.4; RI.5.5; RI.5.7; RI.5.9; RI.5.10
- CCSS.ELA-Literacy.SL.5.1; SL.5.2; SL.5.3; SL.5.4; SL.5.5; SL.5.6
- CCSS.ELA-Literacy.RI.6.3; RI.6.4; RI.6.6; RI.6.7; RI.6.8; RI.6.10
- CCSS.ELA-Literacy.SL.6.1; SL.6.2; SL.6.3; SL.6.4; SL.6.5; SL.6.6

Instructional Resources:

- *Required*
  - Sales flyers collected from newspapers, online resources, and stores
  - Pencils, paper, calculators, glue, tape, poster board
  - Computer access

Instructional Roles:

The school librarian and the classroom teacher will co-teach this lesson. The classroom teacher will introduce the mathematical concepts, and the school librarian will introduce and guide students through research on products, consumer reports, and price comparisons.

Procedure for Completion:

Day One: The co-teachers will review the mathematical concepts needed to determine percent of savings. Students are provided sales flyers from stores, with each student choosing five items they would like to purchase, cutting them out of the flyer, and gluing them onto a piece of paper or poster board.

Day Two: Students utilize the school library and computer lab to research each of the selected items. They will decide if the products are a good deal based on comparison specifics, price, and percent of savings. This step must be reviewed by the co-teachers prior to students writing the final report.

Completion of Project:

The final project will be a brief report profiling each item, original price, sale price, percent of savings, and student determination of whether it is a good deal or not.

Student Assessment/Reflection:

The final project is the object of the main student assessment and is based on the rubric for the project. Questions asked about the report as well as conversations with the teacher and school librarian throughout the process will also be included in the assessment process.

Professional Reflection—Librarian Notes:

It is suggested that the school librarian develop a varied collection of sales flyers from newspapers to provide access for each student.

Black Friday Sales Rubric

	Excellent	Satisfactory	Unsatisfactory
Step One: Glued Cutouts of 5 Items from the Sales Flyers	Work completed as assigned on time.	Work completed but not on time or needing extensive revisions before moving to the next step.	Work not completed.
Step Two: Development and Completion of the Research	Work completed on time and all requirements have been met.	Work not completed on time or missing elements.	Work not completed or missing major elements
Step Three: Completed Report	Work completed on time, presentation is understandable, and all elements included.	Work completed but not on time or missing elements.	Work not completed.
Staying on Task Daily	Student working as assigned and not disengaged or causing a disruption.	Student working well on assignment most days.	Student not on task daily or is a discipline problem.

Student Name:
Black Friday Sales Grade:

	Excellent	Satisfactory	Unsatisfactory
Step One: Glued Cutouts of 5 Items from the Sales Flyers			
Step Two: Development and Completion of the Research			
Step Three: Completed Report			
Staying on Task Daily			

From *The Common Core in Action: Ready-to-Use Lesson Plans for K–6 Librarians* by Deborah J. Jesseman. Santa Barbara, CA: Libraries Unlimited. Copyright © 2015.

SUGGESTED BIBLIOGRAPHY

Caron, L., & St. Jacques, P. M. (2000). *Percents and Ratios (Math Success)*. Berkeley Heights, NJ: Enslow.

Hammel, D. S. (2015). *That Figures!: A Crash Course in Math*. Mankato, MN: Capstone Classroom.

Harnadek, A. (1996). *Math Word Problems, Level C: Mixed Concepts, Whole Numbers to Percents*. North Bend, OR: Critical Thinking.

McMullen, C. (2012). *Fractions, Decimals, & Percents Math Workbook*. Amazon.com: CreateSpace Independent Publishing Platform.

Moran, A. M. (1999). *Fractions, Decimals and Percents Homework Booklet, Grade 6*. Cumming, GA: Instructional Fair.

Muschla, E. (2012). *Practice Makes Perfect: Fractions, Decimals, and Percents*. New York, NY: McGraw-Hill.

Shields, C. (2004). *How to Work with Fractions, Decimals, and Percents*. Westminster, CA: Teacher Created Resources.

Slade, S. (2014). *The Kids' Guide to Money in Sports*. Mankato, MN: Capstone Classroom.

Wingard-Nelson, R. (2008). *Ratios and Percents (Math Busters)*. Berkeley Heights, NJ: Enslow.

Chapter 5

Libraries and Technology

LIBRARY

Story Time Ducklings

Grade Levels: K–1

Lesson Summary: In this lesson students will be read *Make Way for Ducklings* by Robert McCloskey and will choose their favorite scene from the book to draw or show in a diorama. Throughout the project they will learn about the author, the illustrations, and the story setting.

Standards Addressed:

AASL *Standards for the 21st Century Learner*

- Inquire, think critically, and gain knowledge (1.1.2; 1.1.9; 1.2.3; 1.3.4; 1.4.2; 1.4.4)
- Draw conclusions, make informed decisions, apply knowledge to new situations, and create new knowledge (2.1.2; 2.1.5; 2.1.6; 2.2.4; 2.3.1)
- Share knowledge and participate ethically and productively as members of our democratic society (3.1.2; 3.2.3; 3.3.2; 3.3.4; 3.4.2)
- Pursue personal and aesthetic growth (4.1.1; 4.1.3; 4.1.8; 4.3.1)

Common Core State Standards

- CCSS.ELA-Literacy.RL.K.1; RL.K.3; RL.K.4; RL.K.6; RL.K.7; RL.K.10
- CCSS.ELA-Literacy.W.K.3
- CCSS.ELA-Literacy.RL.1.1; RL.1.2; RL.1.3; RL.1.4; RL.1.7; RL.1.10

Instructional Resources:

- *Required*
  - *Make Way for Ducklings* by Robert McCloskey
  - Access to a Smartboard or a computer and projector
  - Recycled shoe box
  - Construction paper
  - Colored pencils, markers, or crayons
  - Glue/glue stick
  - Recycled file folders

Adapted from an SLM learning plan by Carolyn S. Brodie. Connect the Book: *Make Way for Ducklings* by Robert McCloskey. *School Library Media Activities Monthly*, Volume XXV, No. 8, April 2009, pp. 33–35.

Instructional Roles:

The classroom teacher and the school librarian may co-teach this lesson, but it can also be a stand-alone in the library. The co-teachers will assist the students with their projects and share additional information about the author, the city, and the book.

Procedure for Completion:

Day One: The school librarian will read *Make Way for Ducklings* by Robert McCloskey to the students. After the story is complete the co-teachers will utilize the Smartboard to display and discuss some details about the book and the author. Some of these details include:

1. *Make Way for Ducklings* received the Caldecott Medal in 1942 as the "Most distinguished American picture book for children."
   Awards: http://www.ala.org/awardsgrants/awards/6/all_years
2. In 2003, a group of third-grade students at the Dean S. Luce Elementary School in Canton, Massachusetts, led the way for *Make Way for Ducklings* to be designated the state's official children's book.
   Massachusetts Symbols: http://www.statesymbolsusa.org/Massachusetts/Book.html
   Does your state have a state book like Massachusetts? If not, students in the school might enjoy making a list of possibilities and then voting on their favorite.
3. Sculptor Nancy Schon was asked to create a bronze sculpture of *Make Way for Ducklings* for the Boston Public Garden. She created another one that is on display in Moscow.
   Nancy Schon website: http://www.schon.com/public/ducklings-boston.php
   Nancy Schon Moscow website: http://www.schon.com/public/ducklings-moscow.php

Day Two—Completion: The students will be grouped in twos or threes, choose their favorite scene from the book, and create a diorama. If construction of a diorama is too complex for students, the assignment can be an individual drawing of their favorite scene. Other books by Robert McCloskey or stories about ducks may be shared while the students are working. A sample and directions for completing a diorama may be found at: http://www.crayola.com/lesson-plans/duckling-parade-lesson-plan/

Completion of Lesson:

The completed dioramas or drawings will be exhibited in the library or the classroom.

Student Assessment/Reflection:

The completed diorama or drawing is the main student assessment and is based on the rubric for the lesson. Observations by the teacher and school librarian throughout the project will be included in the assessment process.

Professional Reflection—Librarian Notes:

This lesson may be expanded to incorporate a science lesson by having the students investigate the lives of mallard ducks, what type of habitats they live in, and what they eat, or a math lesson by having students illustrate how to find a sum of 10, initially using the parents (2) and ducklings (8), then finding other facts with a sum of 10.

The Memphis, Tennessee, Peabody Hotel is famous for its ducks, and resources include an Animal Planet video: http://www.animalplanet.com/tv-shows/animal-planet-presents/videos/most-outrageous-peabody-hotel-ducks.htm

Diorama Rubric

	Excellent	Satisfactory	Unsatisfactory
Working Cooperatively	The student worked well while completing the project.	The student needed assistance or a reminder to stay on task with the group.	The student did not cooperate with the group.
Listening Attentively to the Story	The student was attentive and engaged with the story.	The student needed an occasional reminder to be attentive.	The student was not listening or engaged with the story.
Completed Diorama	The student cooperated to develop a creative project relevant to the subject.	The student needed assistance while working on the project.	The student did not participate in the completion of the project.
Staying on Task Daily	Student working as assigned and not disengaged or causing a disruption.	Student working well on assignment most days.	Student not on task daily or is a discipline problem.

Student Name:

Diorama Grade:

	Excellent	Satisfactory	Unsatisfactory
Working Cooperatively			
Listening Attentively to the Story			
Completed Diorama			
Staying on Task Daily			

SUGGESTED BIBLIOGRAPHY

McCloskey, R. (1948). *Blueberries for Sal.* New York, NY: Viking Press.

McCloskey, R. (1963). *Burt Dow, Deep-Water Man: A Tale of the Sea in Classic Tradition.* New York, NY: Viking Press.

McCloskey, R. (1940). *Lentil.* New York, NY: Viking Press.

McCloskey, R. (1941). *Make Way for Ducklings.* New York, NY: Viking Press.

McCloskey, R. (1952). *One Morning in Maine.* New York, NY: Viking Press.

McCloskey, R. (1957). *Time of Wonder.* New York, NY: Viking Press.

Online Resources:

Audio and photographic tour of the Boston Public Garden: http://www.audisseyguides.com/boston publicgarden/

Diorama example: http://www.crayola.com/lesson-plans/duckling-parade-lesson-plan/

Friends of the Boston Public Garden website: http://friendsofthepublicgarden.org/

Massachusetts State Book website: http://www.statesymbolsusa.org/Massachusetts/Book.html

Nancy Schon's Moscow site: http://www.schon.com/public/ducklings-moscow.php

Nancy Schon's website: http://www.schon.com/public/ducklings-boston.php

Swan Boats website: http://swanboats.com/

Transcript of interview with Robert McCloskey: http://archive.hbook.com/history/radio/mccloskey.asp

LIBRARY
Book Location Game

Grade Levels: K–1

Lesson Summary: This activity serves to reinforce students' ability to locate books for pleasure reading.

Standards Addressed:

AASL *Standards for the 21st Century Learner*

- Inquire, think critically, and gain knowledge (1.1.1–1.1.4; 1.1.9; 1.2.2; 1.2.3; 1.3.4; 1.4.2; 1.4.4)
- Draw conclusions, make informed decisions, apply knowledge to new situations, and create new knowledge (2.1.1; 2.1.2; 2.1.5; 2.3.1; 2.4.3; 2.4.4)
- Share knowledge and participate ethically and productively as members of our democratic society (3.1.3; 3.2.1; 3.2.2; 3.2.3; 3.4.2)
- Pursue personal and aesthetic growth (4.1.1–4.1.6; 4.1.8; 4.2.4; 4.3.1; 4.3.2; 4.4.1; 4.4.6)

Common Core State Standards

- CCSS.ELA-Literacy.RL.K.1; RL.K.2; RL.K.3; RL.K.4; RL.K.5; RL.K.6; RL.K.7; RL.K.9; RL.K.10
- CCSS.ELA-Literacy.RF.K.1; RF.K.2; RF.K.3; RF.K.4
- CCSS.ELA-Literacy.SL.K.1; SL.K.2; SL.K.3; SL.K.4; SL.K.5; SL.K.6
- CCSS.ELA-Literacy.RL.1.1; RL.1.2; RL.1.3; RL.1.4; RL.1.5; RL.1.6; RL.1.7; RL.1.9; RL.1.10
- CCSS.ELA-Literacy.RF.1.1; RF.1.2; RF.1.3; RF.1.4
- CCSS.ELA-Literacy.SL.1.1; SL.1.2; SL.1.3; SL.1.4; SL.1.5; SL.1.6

Instructional Resources:

- *Required*
  - Blank sticky notes, pencils
  - Paper and pencils for keeping score

Instructional Roles:

The classroom teacher and the school librarian may co-teach this lesson by coordinating independent reading, student group contributions, and assessment.

Procedure for Completion:

Step One: The school librarian will remind the students where in the library the fiction section is located, show them a picture book, and point out the author's last name and the spine label. They are asked if they notice something the author's last name and the spine label have in common and are guided to the shelving location of the book.

Step Two: Game Rules:

1. The students will be divided into table groups, given a pencil and blank sticky note, and assigned a number.

Adapted from an SLM learning plan by Karen Tukua. Cross Curricular: Games to Play with Paper Book Jackets. *School Library Media Activities Monthly*, Volume XXV, No. 5, January 2009, pp. 12–13.

2. Ask the students what their last name is, what letter it starts with, and have them write this letter on the blank sticky note.
3. The co-teachers will do the same thing, telling the students they will pretend to be a book, and place their sticky note in the appropriate shelving location.
4. When the school librarian says, "Ready, go," the Number Ones will begin the game by placing their sticky note in the correct shelving location.
5. The first student to correctly locate where they should be shelved receives 2 points for their group. Each student after that who correctly shelves their sticky note receives 1 point each.
6. The game continues until all students have "been shelved."
7. The table with the most points will be the first group to choose and check out independent reading books.

Completion of Lesson:

The game is complete when all students have found their book placement and the points are totaled.

Student Assessment/Reflection:

The rubrics for this activity may be part of a larger project assessment or utilized as a guide for student behavior, cooperation, and participation.

Professional Reflection—Librarian Notes:

This lesson is a fun review for younger students to become familiar with book location in the library. As students become more adept at locating books, other genres may be added to the game or it could be expanded to utilize the Paper Book Jackets developed in a later lesson.

Book Location Game Rubric

	Excellent	Satisfactory	Unsatisfactory
Correct Location	The student correctly identified the location of their initial.	The student needed assistance to identify the location of their initial.	The student did not participate in identifying the location of their initial.
Group Participation	The student was a positive contribution to the game.	The student needed encouragement to participate in the game.	The student did not participate in the game.
Staying on Task Daily	Student working as assigned and not disengaged or causing a disruption.	Student working well on assignment most days.	Student not on task daily or is a discipline problem.

Student Name:

Book Location Game Grade:

	Excellent	Satisfactory	Unsatisfactory
Correct Location			
Group Participation			
Staying on Task Daily			

SUGGESTED BIBLIOGRAPHY

Access to books in a variety of genres, such as:

EBooks
Fiction books
Expository books
Biographies
Reference books

LIBRARY/TECHNOLOGY   Grade Levels: K–3
Inquiry

Lesson Summary: The basics of this lesson can be used with students at different levels, helping them to identify what they already know and to build interest in and curiosity for the inquiry work in the future. It also guides them to develop questions about things they are curious about prior to the research process.

Standards Addressed:

AASL *Standards for the 21st Century Learner*

- Inquire, think critically, and gain knowledge (1.1.1–1.1.3; 1.2.1;1.2.6;1.4.2)
- Draw conclusions, make informed decisions, apply knowledge to new situations, and create new knowledge (2.1.1; 2.1.3; 2.1.5; 2.3.1; 2.4.1; 2.4.3)
- Share knowledge and participate ethically and productively as members of our democratic society (3.1.2; 3.2.1; 3.2.3; 3.3.2)
- Pursue personal and aesthetic growth (4.2.3; 4.3.1; 4.4.2)

Common Core State Standards

- CCSS.ELA-Literacy.L.K.1; L.K.5
- CCSS.ELA-Literacy.SL.K.1; SL.K.2; SL.K.3; SL.K.6
- CCSS.ELA-Literacy.L.1.1; L.1.4; L.1.6
- CCSS.ELA-Literacy.SL.1.1; SL.1.2; SL.1.3; SL.1.6
- CCSS.ELA-Literacy.L.2.1; L.2.3; L.2.4; L.2.6
- CCSS.ELA-Literacy.SL.2.1; SL.2.2; SL.2.3; SL.2.6
- CCSS.ELA-Literacy.L.3.1; L.3.3; L.3.4; L.3.6
- CCSS.ELA-Literacy.SL.3.1; SL.3.2; SL.3.3; SL.3.6

Instructional Resources:

- *Required*
  - Items from nature
  - Physical objects
  - Primary source documents, maps, or images from recommended Internet sources

All handouts are included in the Student Resource site found at http://www.abc-clio.com/Libraries Unlimited/product.aspx?pc=A4367P.

Instructional Roles:

The teacher and school librarian will meet to discuss an upcoming unit of study or research. They identify key ideas, themes, and questions that might arise in the unit. They will then identify a primary source (an object, document, map, or image) that will be used to introduce the See, Think, Wonder method. The focus of the activity is to elicit what students already know through a series of three scaffolded questions of increasing difficulty. When the activity is presented, one educator acts as the discussion facilitator and the other as the scribe.

Adapted from an SLM learning plan by Kristin Fontichiaro. Cross Curriculum: Awakening and Building Prior Knowledge with Primary Sources: See, Think, Wonder. *School Library Monthly*, Volume XXVII, Number 1, September–October 2010, pp. 14–15.

Procedure for Completion:

Step One: The students are learning in the classroom about early peoples. The children sit in a circle. One co-teacher creates a three-column chart based on the See, Think, Wonder method of inquiry:

- What do you see?
- What do you think?
- What do you wonder?

Step Two: One co-teacher takes an object, for example, a mastodon tooth, out of a canvas bag, saying, "I have something here, and I would like each of you to hold it and tell us one way that you would describe it. I'm going to start: 'I feel bumps.'" The tooth is passed around the circle with each child adding or repeating an attribute (e.g., bumpy, heavy, smooth, rough). The second teacher records the students' answers. The students are to share their thoughts with a partner about what they think the item is. They report their ideas, which are added to the chart.

Step Three—Completion: The co-teachers identify the object and ask the students: "What do you wonder? What questions do you have about this object?" The students again share ideas with their partner, then are brought back to the circle where their ideas are added to the chart. The co-teachers refer to the chart and add to it as the class inquiry builds and students discover information that answers their individual questions.

Completion of Project:

There is not a particular project attached to this lesson, but it is used as a base point for student inquiry and research.

Student Assessment/Reflection:

The purpose of this lesson is to build student enthusiasm and excitement about the project to come, and for the teachers to gain some understanding of students' current knowledge and curiosity in order to make the forthcoming inquiry work more resonant. Therefore, the teachers observe the conversation and use the questions and comments to guide their future lesson design and offer no formal assessment.

Professional Reflection—Librarian Notes:

This is an opportunity for the school librarian to be included in the curriculum process that may build on student inquiry. It is based on a process that can be transferred to a variety of topics that allows the school librarian to provide or share research tools that include images, tactile objects, and documents. The early elementary science lessons offer many opportunities to utilize this lesson, for example, feathers from local birds or leaves to identify trees.

Inquiry Sample Rubric			
	Excellent	Satisfactory	Unsatisfactory
Contribution to Class Discussion	The student volunteered and usefully contributed to the discussion.	The student contributed to the discussion but needed urging to respond.	The student did not contribute to the discussion.
Completed Practice Assignment	The assignment was organized and completed on time.	The assignment was not completed on time or missing some required elements.	The assignment was not complete or not handed in at all.
Staying on Task Daily	Student working as assigned and not disengaged or causing a disruption.	Student working well on assignment most days.	Student not on task daily or is a discipline problem.

Student Name:

Inquiry Sample Grade:

	Excellent	Satisfactory	Unsatisfactory
Contribution to Class Discussion			
Completed Practice Assignment			
Staying on Task Daily			

SUGGESTED BIBLIOGRAPHY

Various books and materials for the specific lesson being introduced.

Online Resources:

Calisphere: http://www.calisphere.universityofcalifornia.edu/
Library of Congress American Memory project: http://memory.loc.gov
Mastodon tooth: http://www.lakeneosho.org/More20.html
Mel Michigan eLibrary: http://mel.org/SPT–BrowseResourcesMichigana.php?ParentID=687
National Archives: http://www.archives.gov

LIBRARY

Book Jackets and Reviews

Grade Levels: K–6

Lesson Summary: This activity incorporates student independent reading, writing a book review, and creating a paper book jacket that can be used for future library games and lessons.

Standards Addressed:

AASL *Standards for the 21st Century Learner*

- Inquire, think critically, and gain knowledge (1.1.1–1.1.4; 1.2.2; 1.3.4; 1.4.2; 1.4.4)
- Draw conclusions, make informed decisions, apply knowledge to new situations, and create new knowledge (2.1.1; 2.1.2; 2.1.5; 2.1.6; 2.2.4; 2.3.1; 2.4.3; 2.4.4)
- Share knowledge and participate ethically and productively as members of our democratic society (3.1.3; 3.2.1; 3.2.2; 3.3.4; 3.4.2)
- Pursue personal and aesthetic growth (4.1.1–4.1.3; 4.1.5; 4.1.6; 4.1.8; 4.2.4; 4.3.1; 4.3.2; 4.4.1; 4.4.6)

Common Core State Standards

- CCSS.ELA-Literacy.RL.K.1; RL.K.2; RL.K.3; RL.K.4; RL.K.5; RL.K.6; RL.K.7; RL.K.9; RL.K.10
- CCSS.ELA-Literacy.RF.K.1; RF.K.2; RF.K.3; RF.K.4
- CCSS.ELA-Literacy.L.K.1; L.K.2; L.K.4; L.K.5; L.K.6
- CCSS.ELA-Literacy.SL.K.5
- CCSS.ELA-Literacy.W.K.1; W.K.5; W.K.6; W.K.7
- CCSS.ELA-Literacy.RL.1.1; RL.1.2; RL.1.3; RL.1.4; RL.1.5; RL.1.6; RL.1.7; RL.1.9; RL.1.10
- CCSS.ELA-Literacy.RF.1.1; RF.1.2; RF.1.3; RF.1.4
- CCSS.ELA-Literacy.L.1.1; L.1.2; L.1.4; L.1.5; L.1.6
- CCSS.ELA-Literacy.SL.1.5
- CCSS.ELA-Literacy.W.1.1; W.1.6
- CCSS.ELA-Literacy.RL.2.1; RL.2.2; RL.2.3; RL.2.5; RL.2.6; RL.2.7; RL.2.10
- CCSS.ELA-Literacy.RF.2.3; RF.2.4
- CCSS.ELA-Literacy.L.2.1; L.2.2; L.2.3; L.2.4; L.2.5; L.2.6
- CCSS.ELA-Literacy.W.2.1; W.2.6
- CCSS.ELA-Literacy.RL.3.1; RL.3.2; RL.3.3; RL.3.5; RL.3.6; RL.3.7; RL.3.10
- CCSS.ELA-Literacy.RF.3.3; RF.3.4
- CCSS.ELA-Literacy.L.3.1; L.3.2; L.3.3; L.3.4; L.3.5; L.3.6
- CCSS.ELA-Literacy.W.3.1; W.3.4; W.3.5; W.3.6; W.3.10
- CCSS.ELA-Literacy.RL.4.2; RL.4.3; RL.4.4; RL.4.5; RL.4.6; RL.4.10
- CCSS.ELA-Literacy.RF.4.3; RF.4.4
- CCSS.ELA-Literacy.L.4.1; L.4.2; L.4.3; L.4.4; L.4.5; L.4.6
- CCSS.ELA-Literacy.W.4.1; W.4.4; W.4.5; W.4.6; W.4.9; W.4.10
- CCSS.ELA-Literacy.RL.5.1; RL.5.2; RL.5.3; RL.5.4; RL.5.5; RL.5.6; RL.5.7; RL.5.9; RL.5.10
- CCSS.ELA-Literacy.RF.5.3; RF.5.4
- CCSS.ELA-Literacy.L.5.1; L.5.2; L.5.3; L.5.4; L.5.5; L.5.6
- CCSS.ELA-Literacy.W.5.1; W.5.4; W.5.5; W.5.6; W.5.9; W.5.10
- CCSS.ELA-Literacy.RL.6.1; RL.6.2; RL.6.3; RL.6.4; RL.6.5; RL.6.6; RL.6.10
- CCSS.ELA-Literacy.L.6.1; L.6.2; L.6.3; L.6.4; L.6.5; L.6.6
- CCSS.ELA-Literacy.W.6.4; W.6.5; W.6.6; W.6.9; W.6.10

Instructional Resources:

- *Required*
  - o Drawing paper, markers, crayons, colored pencils
  - o Book Review Outline handout
  - o Book Jacket Checklist handout
  - o Laminator
  - o Computer and word processing program access

All handouts are included in the Student Resource site found at http://www.abc-clio.com/Libraries Unlimited/product.aspx?pc=A4367P.

Instructional Roles:

The classroom teacher and the school librarian may co-teach this lesson, coordinating the independent reading, review writing, and creation of the book jackets. The lesson may be utilized with students in kindergarten through grade 6, with additional student assistance depending on the grade level.

Procedure for Completion:

Step One: The students will choose any book in the school library for independent reading. After they have completed the book they will write a book review, following the guidelines on the Book Review Outline handout. The co-teachers will check the Book Review handout prior to having the students type the reviews in a word processing program or write them on lined paper, depending on the grade level and word processing experience.

Step Two—Completion: The students will create a paper book jacket for their book. The co-teachers will encourage them to create something unique that captures the essence of the book in their opinion, will attract other students to read it, and is not like the original book cover.

Completion of Lesson:

The completed book jacket and book review will be submitted and the school librarian will laminate the book jacket.

Student Assessment/Reflection:

The completed book jacket and book review are the culminating activities of this lesson and are assessed using the rubric for the lesson. Observations and questions by the teacher and school librarian throughout the project will be included in the assessment process.

Professional Reflection—Librarian Notes:

The book reviews may be included in the school library website, as a part of a folder for students' use, or posted around the library or the classroom. The book jackets will be utilized in further library lessons.

Book Jackets and Reviews Rubric

	Excellent	Satisfactory	Unsatisfactory
Book Choice and Independent Reading	The student selected a grade-appropriate book independently.	The student selected a grade-appropriate book but needed assistance.	The student did not participate and did not select a book for independent reading.
Book Review	The student submitted a book review on time with all required elements.	The student submitted a book review that was not completed on time or was missing some required elements.	The assignment was not complete or not submitted.
Book Jacket	The book jacket was neat, creative, and included all required elements.	The book jacket was submitted late or did not include all required elements.	The book jacket was not submitted.
Staying on Task Daily	Student working as assigned and not disengaged or causing a disruption.	Student working well on assignment most days.	Student not on task daily or is a discipline problem.

Student Name:

Book Jackets and Reviews Grade:

	Excellent	Satisfactory	Unsatisfactory
Book Choice and Independent Reading			
Book Review			
Book Jacket			
Staying on Task Daily			

SUGGESTED BIBLIOGRAPHY

Brantley, C. L. *Writing Smart Junior: An Introduction to the Art of Writing.* Princeton, NJ: Princeton Review.

Kamberg, M. L. (2008). *The I Love to Write Book—Ideas & Tips for Young Writers.* Milwaukee, WI: Crickethol-
low Books.

Online Resources:

Biblionasium: https://www.biblionasium.com/
Scholastic: http://teacher.scholastic.com/activities/swyar/
SlimeKids: http://www.slimekids.com/book-reviews/

LIBRARY   Grade Levels: 2–6
Book Jackets Game

Lesson Summary: This activity serves to reinforce students' ability to locate information and books for both pleasure reading and research projects across the curriculum and locate the correct information for writing a citation.

Standards Addressed:

AASL *Standards for the 21st Century Learner*

- Inquire, think critically, and gain knowledge (1.1.1–1.1.4; 1.1.9; 1.2.2; 1.2.3; 1.3.4; 1.4.2; 1.4.4)
- Draw conclusions, make informed decisions, apply knowledge to new situations, and create new knowledge (2.1.1; 2.1.2; 2.1.5; 2.3.1; 2.4.3; 2.4.4)
- Share knowledge and participate ethically and productively as members of our democratic society (3.1.3; 3.2.1; 3.2.2; 3.2.3; 3.4.2)
- Pursue personal and aesthetic growth (4.1.1–4.1.6; 4.1.8; 4.2.4; 4.3.1; 4.3.2; 4.4.1; 4.4.6)

Common Core State Standards

- CCSS.ELA-Literacy.RL.2.1; RL.2.2; RL.2.3; RL.2.5; RL.2.6; RL.2.7; RL.2.10
- CCSS.ELA-Literacy.RF.2.3; RF.2.4
- CCSS.ELA-Literacy.SL.2.1; SL.2.2; SL.2.3; SL.2.6
- CCSS.ELA-Literacy.RL.3.1; RL.3.2; RL.3.3; RL.3.5; RL.3.6; RL.3.7; RL.3.10
- CCSS.ELA-Literacy.RF.3.3; RF.3.4
- CCSS.ELA-Literacy.SL.3.1; SL.3.2; SL.3.3; SL.3.4; SL.3.6
- CCSS.ELA-Literacy.RL.4.2; RL.4.3; RL.4.4; RL.4.5; RL.4.6; RL.4.10
- CCSS.ELA-Literacy.RF.4.3; RF.4.4
- CCSS.ELA-Literacy.SL.4.1; SL.4.2; SL.4.3; SL.4.6
- CCSS.ELA-Literacy.RL.5.1; RL.5.2; RL.5.3; RL.5.4; RL.5.5; RL.5.6; RL.5.7; RL.5.10
- CCSS.ELA-Literacy.RF.5.3; RF.5.4
- CCSS.ELA-Literacy.LSL.5.1; SL.5.2; SL.5.3; SL.5.6
- CCSS.ELA-Literacy.RL.6.1; RL.6.2; RL.6.3; RL.6.4; RL.6.5; RL.6.6; RL.6.10
- CCSS.ELA-Literacy.SL.6.1; SL.6.3; SL.6.6

Instructional Resources:

- *Required*
  - Paper Book Jackets
  - Paper and pencils for keeping score
  - Timer

Instructional Roles:

The classroom teacher and the school librarian may co-teach this lesson, coordinating the independent reading, student group contributions, and scoring. The lesson may be utilized with students in grades 2 through 6 with the co-teacher adapting the book genre to the appropriate grade level.

Adapted from an SLM learning plan by Karen Tukua. Cross Curricular: Games to Play with Paper Book Jackets. *School Library Media Activities Monthly*, Volume XXV, No. 5, January 2009, pp. 12–13.

Procedure for Completion:

Step One: The students will be divided into table groups and each student will be assigned a number. The co-teachers will decide which book genre to select from the paper book jackets (made by students in the Book Jacket and Review lesson). Table points will be given to the first person to locate where their paper book jacket would be shelved in the school library. The co-teachers will demonstrate the game to the students by using one of the Paper Book Jackets.

Step Two: Game Rules:

1. The school librarian shuffles the Paper Book Jackets and gives one to each table.
2. Students have 15 seconds for a "heads together" to discuss where the book is located.
3. Number Ones stand with their table's book jacket. The teacher says "Ready, go," and starts the timer.
4. The first table to correctly locate where their book jacket should be shelved receives 2 points. Each table after who correctly locates where their book would be shelved receives 1 point.
5. Continue the same process until all students have had an opportunity to "shelve" a Paper Book Jacket.
6. The table with the most points will be the first group to choose and check out independent reading books.

Completion of Lesson:

The lesson is a review and serves to reinforce student familiarity with the library and how to access the physical materials.

Student Assessment/Reflection:

The rubrics for this activity may be part of a larger project assessment or utilized as a guide for student behavior, cooperation, and participation.

Professional Reflection—Librarian Notes:

This lesson may be expanded as students become more adept at locating books with other genres being added to the selections. Using real books, students can locate information needed to write citations. For example, the first student to find the copyright date in their book earns table points.

Book Jackets Game Rubric			
	Excellent	Satisfactory	Unsatisfactory
Student Participation	The student was a positive contribution to the game.	The student needed encouragement to participate in the game.	The student did not participate in the game.
Accuracy of Shelving	The student contributed toward a positive group outcome.	The student needed assistance in finding the correct location.	The student did not participate in the activity.
Staying on Task Daily	Student working as assigned and not disengaged or causing a disruption.	Student working well on assignment most days.	Student not on task daily or is a discipline problem.

Student Name:

Book Jackets Game Grade:

	Excellent	Satisfactory	Unsatisfactory
Student Participation			
Accuracy of Shelving			
Staying on Task Daily			

SUGGESTED BIBLIOGRAPHY

Access to books in a variety of genres, such as:

EBooks
Fiction books
Expository books
Biographies
Reference books

LIBRARY
Library Orientation

Grade Levels: 3–6

Lesson Summary: This activity provides students with the opportunity to practice oral reading in a fun, nonthreatening way while focusing on the rules and procedures for the school library.

Standards Addressed:

AASL *Standards for the 21st Century Learner*

- Inquire, think critically, and gain knowledge (1.1.2; 1.1.4; 1.1.6; 1.1.9)
- Draw conclusions, make informed decisions, apply knowledge to new situations, and create new knowledge (2.1.5; 2.1.6; 2.3.1)
- Share knowledge and participate ethically and productively as members of our democratic society (3.1.2; 3.1.3; 3.1.5; 3.2.3)
- Pursue personal and aesthetic growth (4.1.1; 4.2.4)

Common Core State Standards

- CCSS.ELA-Literacy.RF.3.3; RF.3.4
- CCSS.ELA-Literacy.SL.3.1; SL.3.3; SL.3.6
- CCSS.ELA-Literacy.RF.4.3; RF.4.4
- CCSS.ELA-Literacy.SL.4.1; SL.4.3; SL.4.6
- CCSS.ELA-Literacy.RF.5.3; RF.5.4
- CCSS.ELA-Literacy.SL.5.1; SL.5.3; SL.5.6
- CCSS.ELA-Literacy.SL.6.1; SL.6.2; SL.6.6

Instructional Resources:

- *Required*
  - Who Has … Library Orientation cards, cut up, glued on file cards, and laminated
  - Library Orientation Matching handout
  - Selection of library-related, age-appropriate read-aloud stories, suggestions provided in the Bibliography section

All handouts are included in the Student Resource site found at http://www.abc-clio.com/Libraries Unlimited/product.aspx?pc=A4367P.

Instructional Roles:

The school librarian creates the Who Has … Library Orientation cards and leads the game, and the classroom teacher may provide assistance during the execution of the game and in guiding students in reading the cards for fluency.

Procedure for Completion:

Lesson: The school librarian will read an age-appropriate story about a library; some suggestions are offered in the Bibliography section. The librarian will introduce the Library Orientation game, shuffle the

Adapted from an SLM learning plan by Catherine Trinkle. Who Has … Library Orientation? *School Library Monthly,* Volume XXVI, Number 1, September 2009, p. 11.

Who Has ... Library Orientation cards, and distribute one to each student. The content of the cards can be changed to align with the rules and procedures of individual school libraries.

The students will be allowed a few minutes to read their cards to themselves, with the co-teachers assisting as needed. To meet the differentiated needs of students, the less difficult cards should be given to students who need more support when reading aloud.

After students have familiarized themselves with their cards, the school librarian will ask who has the first card. That student raises his or her hand and will be asked to begin by reading the card. The student who has the answer to the first question responds and asks the next question until all students have read and responded. The final answer is "This is the Last Card!"

Completion: The next time the students are in the library they will complete the Library Matching handout to assess their retention of the rules and procedures of the library.

Completion of Lesson:

The Library Orientation Matching handout may be a culminating evaluation of the lesson.

Student Assessment/Reflection:

The purpose of this lesson is to introduce or review rules and procedures in the library. The instructors will observe the game and ask questions as it proceeds. The Library Orientation Matching handout may also be used as an assessment.

Professional Reflection—Librarian Notes:

The content of the Orientation cards may be directed at a particular grade level as well as adapted to individual school libraries. It may be used at the beginning of the school year or as a mid-year review.

Library Orientation Rubric

	Excellent	Satisfactory	Unsatisfactory
Who Has ... Card Game	The student participated in the game enthusiastically and read fluently.	The student contributed to the game but needed urging to respond.	The student did not participate in the game.
Library Orientation Matching	The assignment was organized and completed correctly.	The assignment was not completed on time or was incorrect.	The assignment was not complete or not handed in at all.
Staying on Task Daily	Student working as assigned and not disengaged or causing a disruption.	Student working well on assignment most days.	Student not on task daily or is a discipline problem.

Student Name:

Library Orientation Grade:

	Excellent	Satisfactory	Unsatisfactory
Who Has ... Card Game			
Library Orientation Matching			
Staying on Task Daily			

SUGGESTED BIBLIOGRAPHY

Clifford, E. (2004). *Help! I'm a Prisoner in the Library*. New York, NY: HMH Books for Young Readers.

Enderle, D. (2010). *The Library Gingerbread Man*. Madison, WI: Upstart Books.

Finn, C. (2007). *Manners in the Library*. Mankato, MN: Picture Window Books.

Lies, B. (2008). *Bats at the Library*. New York, NY: HMH Books for Young Readers.

Lindbergh, R. (2011). *Homer, the Library Cat*. Somerville, MA: Candlewick Press.

Meddour, W. (2014). *How the Library (Not the Prince) Saved Rapunzel*. London: Frances Lincoln Children's Books.

Rosenstock, B. (2013). *Thomas Jefferson Builds a Library*. Honesdale, PA: Calkins Creek Books.

Stewart, S. (2008). *The Library Paperback*. New York, NY: Square Fish.

Wexler, D. (2014). *The Forbidden Library*. New York, NY: Kathy Dawson Books.

Williams, S., & Kellogg, S. (2001). *Library Lil*. New York, NY: Puffin.

Online Resources:

School Library 2.0: http://readinginstruction.pbworks.com/w/page/13185454/Who%20Has

LIBRARY/TECHNOLOGY   **Grade Levels:** 4–6
Inquiry

Lesson Summary: The basics of this lesson can be used with students at different levels, helping them to identify what they already know and to build interest in and curiosity for the inquiry work in the future. It also guides them to develop questions about things they are curious about prior to the research process.

Standards Addressed:

AASL *Standards for the 21st Century Learner*

- Inquire, think critically, and gain knowledge (1.1.1–1.1.3; 1.2.1;1.2.6;1.4.2)
- Draw conclusions, make informed decisions, apply knowledge to new situations, and create new knowledge (2.1.1; 2.1.3; 2.1.5; 2.3.1; 2.4.1; 2.4.3)
- Share knowledge and participate ethically and productively as members of our democratic society (3.1.2; 3.2.1; 3.2.3; 3.3.2)
- Pursue personal and aesthetic growth (4.2.3; 4.3.1; 4.4.2)

Common Core State Standards

- CCSS.ELA-Literacy.L.4.1; L.4.2; L.4.4; L.4.6
- CCSS.ELA-Literacy.SL.4.1; SL.4.2; SL.4.3
- CCSS.ELA-Literacy.L.5.1; L.5.3; L.5.4; L.5.6
- CCSS.ELA-Literacy.SL.5.1; SL.5.2; SL.5.3
- CCSS.ELA-Literacy.L.6.1; L.6.3; L.6.4; L.6.6
- CCSS.ELA-Literacy.SL.6.1; SL.6.2

Instructional Resources:

- *Required*
  - Color photos of "Lincoln's Pockets"
  - Primary source documents, maps, or images from recommended Internet sources
  - Three-column chart, whiteboard, or chalkboard

All handouts are included in the Student Resource site found at http://www.abc-clio.com/Libraries Unlimited/product.aspx?pc=A4367P.

Instructional Roles:

The teacher and school librarian will meet to discuss an upcoming unit of study or research. They identify key ideas, themes, and questions that might arise in the unit. They will then identify a primary source (an object, document, map, or image) that will be used to introduce the See, Think, Wonder method. The focus of the activity is to elicit what students already know through a series of three scaffolded questions of increasing difficulty. When the activity is presented, one educator acts as the discussion facilitator and the other as the scribe.

Adapted from an SLM learning plan by Kristin Fontichiaro. Cross Curriculum: Awakening and Building Prior Knowledge with Primary Sources: See, Think, Wonder. *School Library Monthly*, Volume XXVII, Number 1, September–October 2010, pp. 14–15.

Procedure for Completion:

Step One: Students are about to begin a study of the Civil War. In advance of the lesson the co-teachers print out color photos of each of the nine items that were in Abraham Lincoln's pockets at the time of his assassination (found on "Lincoln's Pockets" images in the Bibliography section). A PowerPoint presentation with each of the nine items is created as well as a three-column chart based on the See, Think, Wonder method of inquiry:

- What do you see?
- What do you think?
- What do you wonder?

Step Two: The first picture is passed around the class and projected on a screen. The instructors facilitate the question "What do you see?" Each student will add or repeat an attribute while one of the co-teachers lists the students' answers on the three-column chart. The students share their thoughts with a partner about what they think the item is. They report their ideas, which are also added to the chart. This process is repeated for each of the objects.

Step Three—Completion: The students are informed that all of the objects are related and they must figure out how. If no one guesses the correct answer, the instructors reveal that all of the items were in Lincoln's pockets when he was assassinated. The final question would be: what can they learn about Lincoln as a person from these items? Did those details make them more eager to learn about the historical events that led up to his assassination?

Completion of Project:

There is not a particular project attached to this lesson, but it is used as a base point for student inquiry and research.

Student Assessment/Reflection:

The purpose of this lesson is to build student enthusiasm and excitement about the project to come, and for the teachers to gain understanding of students' current knowledge and curiosity in order to make the forthcoming inquiry work more resonant. Therefore, the teachers observe the conversation, use the questions and comments to guide their future lesson design, and offer no formal assessment.

Professional Reflection—Librarian Notes:

This is an opportunity for the school librarian to be included in the curriculum process that may build on student inquiry. It is based on a process that can be transferred to a variety of topics that allows the school librarian to provide or share research tools that include images, tactile objects, and documents.

Inquiry Sample Rubric			
	Excellent	Satisfactory	Unsatisfactory
Contribution to Class Discussion	The student volunteered and usefully contributed to the discussion.	The student contributed to the discussion but needed urging to respond.	The student did not contribute to the discussion.
Completed Practice Assignment	The assignment was organized and completed on time.	The assignment was not completed on time or missing some required elements.	The assignment was not complete or not handed in at all.
Staying on Task Daily	Student working as assigned and not disengaged or causing a disruption.	Student working well on assignment most days.	Student not on task daily or is a discipline problem.

Student Name:

Inquiry Sample Grade:

	Excellent	Satisfactory	Unsatisfactory
Contribution to Class Discussion			
Completed Practice Assignment			
Staying on Task Daily			

SUGGESTED BIBLIOGRAPHY

Cary, B. (2011). *Meet Abraham Lincoln.* New York, NY: Random House Books for Young Readers.

Doeden, M. (2009). *The Civil War: An Interactive History Adventure.* Mankato, MN: Capstone Press.

Edison, E. (2013). *Abraham Lincoln.* Mankato, MN: Capstone Classroom.

Fay, G. (2011). *Why We Fought: The Civil War.* Mankato, MN: Capstone Classroom.

Freedman, R. (1989). *Lincoln: A Photobiography.* New York, NY: HMH Books for Young Readers.

Kolpin, A., & Kolpin, M. (2015). *The Story of the Civil War.* Mankato, MN: Capstone Classroom.

McPherson, J. M. (2002). *Fields of Fury: The American Civil War.* New York, NY: Atheneum Books for Young Readers

Pascal, J. (2008). *Who Was Abraham Lincoln?* New York, NY: Grosset & Dunlap.

Ratliff, T., & Salarya, D. (2013). *You Wouldn't Want to Be a Civil War Soldier!* London: Children's Press.

Stone, T. L. (2005). *DK Biography: Abraham Lincoln.* New York, NY: DK Children.

Online Resources:

Calisphere: http://www.calisphere.universityofcalifornia.edu/

Library of Congress American Memory project: http://memory.loc.gov

"Lincoln's Pockets" images: http://memory.loc.gov/ammem/collections/stern-lincoln/objects.html

Mel Michigan eLibrary: http://mel.org/SPT–BrowseResourcesMichigana.php?ParentID=687

National Archives: http://www.archives.gov

LIBRARY   **Grade Levels:** 5–6

Graphic Novel–Book–Movie

Lesson Summary: This lesson provides students the opportunity to enjoy the same story in various formats and analyze the differences and similarities in the story based on the format they are using.

AASL *Standards for the 21st Century Learner:*

- Inquire, think critically, and gain knowledge (1.1.2; 1.1.6; 1.1.9; 1.2.3; 1.3.4; 1.4.4)
- Draw conclusions, make informed decisions, apply knowledge to new situations, and create new knowledge (2.1.1; 2.1.2; 2.1.5)
- Share knowledge and participate ethically and productively as members of our democratic society (3.1.1; 3.1.2; 3.1.3; 3.2.1; 3.2.2; 3.2.3; 3.3.2; 3.4.3)
- Pursue personal and aesthetic growth (4.1.1; 4.1.3; 4.1.4; 4.1.6; 4.2.4; 4.3.2; 4.4.1–4.4.3)

Common Core State Standards

- CCSS.ELA-Literacy.RL.5.1; RL.5.2; RL.5.3; RL.5.4; RL.5.5; RL.5.6; RL.5.7; RL.5.10
- CCSS.ELA-Literacy.SL.5.1; SL.5.2; SL.5.6
- CCSS.ELA-Literacy.RL.6.1; RL.6.2; RL.6.3; RL.6.4; RL.6.5; RL.6.6; RL.6.7; RL.6.10
- CCSS.ELA-Literacy.SL.6.1; SL.6.2; SL.6.6

Instructional Resources:

- *Required*
  - Access to a computer, document camera, and presentation hardware
  - *Howl's Moving Castle* by Diana Wynne Jones
  - *Howl's Moving Castle* video, 2004, directed by Hayao Miyazaki
  - Multiple copies of *Howl's Moving Castle Film Comic, Vol. 1* by Hayao Miyazaki
  - Book to Video Analysis handout

All handouts are included in the Student Resource site found at http://www.abc-clio.com/Libraries Unlimited/product.aspx?pc=A4367P.

- *Recommended*
  - *Howl's Moving Castle Film Comic, Vol. 2* by Hayao Miyazaki
  - *Howl's Moving Castle Film Comic, Vol. 3* by Hayao Miyazaki
  - *Howl's Moving Castle Film Comic, Vol. 4* by Hayao Miyazaki
  - Miyazaki, H. (2005). *The Art of Howl's Moving Castle*. San Francisco, CA: VIZ Media

Instructional Roles:

The school librarian and teacher co-facilitate student learning by guiding the students through analysis of the same story presented in various formats.

Procedure for Completion:

Step One: The students will view the movie *Howl's Moving Castle*. It may take several library classes to complete the movie, and they will begin independent reading of *Howl's Moving Castle* by Diana Wynne Jones as an outside the class assignment throughout the lesson.

Step Two: The school librarian will read the graphic novel *Howl's Moving Castle Film Comic, Vol. 1* by Hayao Miyazaki to the students while projecting the pages on the screen.

Step Three: The students will be separated into pairs to complete the Book to Video Analysis handout. In this step the pairs will work together to compare the graphic novel to the video.

Step Four—Completion: Each pair will share their Book to Video Analysis handout with the rest of the class. The final assignment for the lesson will be to individually complete a Book to Video Analysis on the independently read *Howl's Moving Castle* to the video.

Completion of Project:

The expectation of this project is for the students to complete independent reading of the novel *Howl's Moving Castle*, one individual Book to Video Analysis handout, and one paired Book to Video Analysis handout.

Student Assessment/Reflection:

The two Book to Video Analysis handouts are the objects of the main student assessment and are based on the rubric for the project. Conversations with the teacher and school librarian throughout the process will also be included in the assessment process.

Professional Reflection—Librarian Notes:

An expansion to this lesson would be to have the students take a familiar story, folk tale, myth, or fairy tale and develop it into a movie, play, or graphic novel.

Graphic Novel–Book–Movie Rubric

	Excellent	Satisfactory	Unsatisfactory
Paired Worksheet	The student contributed to the assignment accurately and with effort.	The student contributed minimally to the assignment or inaccurately.	The student did not contribute to the assignment.
Individual Worksheet	The assignment was organized, accurate, and completed on time.	The assignment was not completed on time or missing some required elements.	The assignment was not handed in.
Independent Reading	The student clearly demonstrated that they completed the independent reading.	The student did not complete the independent reading.	The student did not do any of the independent reading.
Staying on Task Daily	Student working as assigned and not disengaged or causing a disruption.	Student working well on assignment most days.	Student not on task daily or is a discipline problem.

Student Name:
Graphic Novel–Book–Movie Grade:

	Excellent	Satisfactory	Unsatisfactory
Paired Worksheet			
Individual Worksheet			
Independent Reading			
Staying on Task Daily			

SUGGESTED BIBLIOGRAPHY

Howl's Moving Castle. Dir. Hayao Miyazaki. Perfs. Jean Simmons, Christian Bale. Walt Disney Home Entertainment, 2004.

Jones, D. W. (2008). *Howl's Moving Castle*, Reprint edition. New York, NY: Greenwillow Books.

Jones, D. W. (2014). *World of Howl Collection: Howl's Moving Castle, House of Many Ways, Castle in the Air*. New York, NY: Greenwillow Books.

Miyazaki, H. (2005). *The Art of Howl's Moving Castle*. San Francisco, CA: VIZ Media.

Miyazaki, H. (2005). *Howl's Moving Castle Film Comic, Vol. 1*. San Francisco, CA: VIZ Media.

Miyazaki, H. (2005). *Howl's Moving Castle Film Comic, Vol. 2*. San Francisco, CA: VIZ Media.

Miyazaki, H. (2005). *Howl's Moving Castle Film Comic, Vol. 3*. San Francisco, CA: VIZ Media.

Miyazaki, H. (2005). *Howl's Moving Castle Film Comic, Vol. 4*. San Francisco, CA: VIZ Media.

Napier, S. J. (2005). *Anime from Akira to Howl's Moving Castle: Experiencing Contemporary Japanese Animation*. New York, NY: Palgrave Macmillan.

Online Resource:

Diana Wynne Jones website: http://www.leemac.freeserve.co.uk/

TECHNOLOGY

Website Evaluation

Lesson Summary: This lesson allows students the chance to evaluate websites and come to a conclusion regarding their authenticity based on their own sleuthing skills.

AASL *Standards for the 21st Century Learner:*

- Inquire, think critically, and gain knowledge (1.1.1–1.1.8; 1.2.1–1.2.7; 1.3.2; 1.3.3; 1.3.5; 1.4.1–1.4.4)
- Draw conclusions, make informed decisions, apply knowledge to new situations, and create new knowledge (2.1.1–2.1.5; 2.2.1; 2.2.3; 2.3.1; 2.4.1; 2.4.3)
- Share knowledge and participate ethically and productively as members of our democratic society (3.1.4; 3.1.6; 3.3.1; 3.4.1; 3.4.2)
- Pursue personal and aesthetic growth (4.1.6; 4.2.1)

Common Core State Standards

- CCSS.ELA-Literacy.RI.5.2; RI.5.3; RI.5.4; RI.5.5; RI.5.6; RI.5.7; RI.5.9; RI.5.10
- CCSS.ELA-Literacy.RI.6.1; RI.6.2; RI.6.3; RI.6.7; RI.6.8; RI.6.9; RI.6.10

Instructional Resources:

- *Required*
  - Online and presentation access
  - Evaluating a Website handout
  - Evaluating Resources handout
  - Online computer access for each student
  - Access to http://www.shsu.edu/~lis_mah/documents/TCEA/hoaxtable.html

All handouts are included in the Student Resource site found at http://www.abc-clio.com/Libraries Unlimited/product.aspx?pc=A4367P.

Instructional Roles:

The school librarian and teacher co-teach the lesson. The school librarian introduces the lesson and, along with the teacher, answers any questions students may have throughout their learning experience. This lesson will be a lead-in to student research projects.

Procedure for Completion:

Day One: Students are introduced to the acronym DUPED (Date Published or last updated; URL of Website; Pop-up ads or ads on the webpage; Email Address to contact someone; Designer or publisher of website) to evaluate a website and are provided the DUPED handout for reference. The co-teachers utilize the http://www.shsu.edu/~lis_mah/documents/TCEA/hoaxtable.html website, choose one of the sites, and guide the students in evaluating the authenticity of the website.

Day Two—Completion: Students have been assigned a research project and begin to search online resources. They are to find five online resources and complete the Evaluating Resources handout.

Adapted from an SLM learning plan by Tina S. Laramie. Cross Curricular: DUPED? Website Evaluation. *School Library Monthly*, Volume 28, Number 3, December 2011, pp. 53–54.

Completion of Project:

Completion of Evaluating Websites handout.

Student Assessment/Reflection:

The DUPED group work handout and student contribution to the class discussion will be part of the student assessment. Completion of the Evaluating Websites handout evaluation and conversations with the teacher and school librarian throughout the lesson will also be included in the assessment process.

Professional Reflection—Librarian Notes:

The DUPED acronym assists students in deciphering information to decide if the website is reliable and provides a quick and easy reference point. This lesson may also be used as a review and reminder lesson for checking authentic online sources.

Website Evaluation Rubric

	Excellent	Satisfactory	Unsatisfactory
DUPED Group Worksheet	The student volunteered, contributed to the discussion, and completed the worksheet.	The student contributed to the discussion but needed urging to respond or may not have completed the worksheet accurately.	The student did not contribute to the discussion and did not complete the worksheet.
Evaluating Resources Handout	The assignment was organized, accurate, and completed on time.	The assignment was not completed on time or missing some required elements.	The assignment was not complete or not handed in at all.
Staying on Task Daily	Student working as assigned and not disengaged or causing a disruption.	Student working well on assignment most days.	Student not on task daily or is a discipline problem.

Student Name:

Website Evaluation Grade:

	Excellent	Satisfactory	Unsatisfactory
DUPED Group Worksheet			
Evaluating Resources Handout			
Staying on Task Daily			

SUGGESTED BIBLIOGRAPHY

Adcock, D. (2008). *Evaluating Information.* New York, NY: Heinemann.

Asslen, K. C. (2013). *Smart Research Strategies: Finding the Right Sources.* Mankato, MN: Capstone Classroom.

Livingstone, S. (2009). *Children and the Internet.* New York, NY: Merriam Webster/Polity.

Scheibe, C., & Rogow, F. (2011). *The Teacher's Guide to Media Literacy: Critical Thinking in a Multimedia World.* New York, NY: Corwin.

Online Resources:

Builder, "How dangerous is DHMO?": http://www.informationliteracy.org/builder/view/2469

Hoax sites gathered by Dr. Mary Ann Bell: http://www.shsu.edu/~lis_mah/documents/TCEA/hoaxtable.html

Original lesson plan: http://www.informationliteracy.org/plans/view/489/back/0

S.O.S. for Information Literacy: http://www.informationliteracy.org

TECHNOLOGY

Movie Creation

Grade Levels: 5–6

Lesson Summary: In this lesson students use technology to exhibit their understanding of the inference process and cinema techniques through the creation of an iMovie.

AASL *Standards for the 21st Century Learner:*

- Inquire, think critically, and gain knowledge (1.1.1–1.1.9; 1.2.1–1.2.7; 1.3.1–1.3.5; 1.4.1–1.4.4)
- Draw conclusions, make informed decisions, apply knowledge to new situations, and create new knowledge (2.1.1–2.1.6; 2.2.4; 2.3.1)
- Share knowledge and participate ethically and productively as members of our democratic society (3.1.1–3.1.4; 3.1.6; 3.2.1–3.2.3; 3.3.1; 3.3.4)
- Pursue personal and aesthetic growth (4.1.8; 4.2.3; 4.3.2; 4.3.4)

Common Core State Standards

- CCSS.ELA-Literacy.L.5.1; L.5.3; L.5.4; L.5.8
- CCSS.ELA-Literacy.SL.5.1; SL.5.2; SL.5.5; SL.5.6
- CCSS.ELA-Literacy.L.6.1; L.6.3; L.6.4; L.6.6
- CCSS.ELA-Literacy.SL.6.1; SL.6.2; SL.6.5; SL.6.6

Instructional Resources:

- *Required*
  - Access to iMovie and computers
  - Video cameras
  - Storyboard handout
  - Camera Shots handout
  - A copy of *The Landlady* by Roald Dahl

All handouts are included in the Student Resource site found at http://www.abc-clio.com/Libraries Unlimited/product.aspx?pc=A4367P.

Instructional Roles:

The school librarian and teacher co-teach the lesson. The teacher will teach the inference process, introduce and facilitate the use of an inference flowchart, and introduce the project-based unit to the students. The school librarian will introduce iMovie and camera, including angles and shots, and facilitate recognition of copyright and citations.

Procedure for Completion:

Day One: Students will have a previous lesson and understanding of format and usage of a screenplay. The classroom teacher introduces the inference process with a question like, "How do you know your chair will hold your weight?" and records the student responses on the board or chart paper. The students will read *The Landlady* by Roald Dahl and chart the faulty inference of the main character, Billy, in pairs. Answers are shared with the class and misconceptions clarified.

Adapted from an SLM learning plan by Caroline Arp. English: Things Are Not Always as They Seem. *School Library Monthly*, Volume 28, Number 3, December 2011, pp. 55–57.

Day Two: The school librarian teaches students how to download a video, import it to iMovie, add transitions and text, and export it using tutorials or an instructional video.

Days Three–Four: Students create their screenplays, working in pairs, and the teacher reviews the format and screenplay. Students will revise the screenplays as needed.

Day Five: The school librarian reviews the camera shot and angle and storyboard processes and reminds students about copyright. Students complete the Storyboard handout and the Sample Camera Shots handout. The co-teachers check storyboards and answer questions.

Day Six—Completion: Students complete their iMovies by filming, editing, and adding music and voice-over with assistance from the classroom teacher and school librarian.

Completion of Project:

Completion of the iMovie.

Student Assessment/Reflection:

The classroom teacher and the school librarian assess the projects using the rubric. Conversations with and observations by the teacher and school librarian throughout the lesson will also be included in the assessment process.

Professional Reflection—Librarian Notes:

This is an extensive project that will require co-planning with the classroom teacher. The project can be as extensive or as simple as necessary for the classroom demographic. Allowing students the opportunity to explore movie-making provides an opportunity for project-based learning and student-led inquiry.

Screenplay Evaluation Rubric

	Excellent	Satisfactory	Unsatisfactory
Screenplay Content	Screenplay is well constructed and developed. Good dialog and storyline.	Screenplay is well constructed with minor lapses in dialog and storyline that may detract from audience comprehension.	The student did not complete the assignment.
Screenplay Organization	Screenplay is consistently well organized and is clear and coherent.	Screenplay is basically organized, somewhat clear and coherent, but may lack logical order.	Screenplay was not completed or generally disorganized and not presented in a logical manner.
Staying on Task	Student working as assigned and not disengaged or causing a disruption.	Student working well on assignment most days.	Student not on task daily or is a discipline problem.

Student Name:

Screenplay Grade:

	Excellent	Satisfactory	Unsatisfactory
Screenplay Content			
Screenplay Organization			
Staying on Task Daily			

iMovie Evaluation Rubric

	Excellent	Satisfactory	Unsatisfactory
iMovie Storyboard	Storyboard is complete with all components and reflects depth in comprehension of subject.	Storyboard is complete and reflects some understanding of the assignment.	The student did not complete a storyboard.
iMovie Creativity and Transitions	A variety of transitions, text, and music make the movie run smoothly and create a finished product.	An acceptable amount of transitions, text, and music allow the movie to flow but minor gaps are apparent.	No movie was created or one with no transitions, text, or music.
iMovie Use of Camera Angles	Camera angles used are varied and appropriate for scenes and add meaning to the overall purpose of the movie.	Camera angles are used appropriately for scenes but are not varied enough to add meaning.	No movie was created or one with only one camera angle, and it detracts from the meaning of the movie.
Staying on Task	Student working as assigned and not disengaged or causing a disruption.	Student working well on assignment most days.	Student not on task daily or is a discipline problem.

Student Name:

iMovie Grade:

	Excellent	Satisfactory	Unsatisfactory
iMovie Storyboard			
iMovie Creativity and Transitions			
iMovie Use of Camera Angles			
Staying on Task Daily			

SUGGESTED BIBLIOGRAPHY

Frost, S. (2011). *Kids Guide to Movie Making: How Kids Can Produce and Direct Their Own Movies That Audiences Will Love*. CreateSpace Independent Publishing Platform.

Ohler, J. B. (2013). *Digital Storytelling in the Classroom: New Media Pathways to Literacy, Learning, and Creativity*. Thousand Oaks, CA: Corwin Press.

Palser, B., & Wittekind, E. (2012). *Exploring Media Literacy*. Mankato, MN: Compass Point Books.

Online Resources:

iMovie Tutorials: http://www.apple.com/support/mac-apps/imovie/

The Landlady by Roald Dahl: http://www.nexuslearning.net/books/holt-eol2/collection%203/landlady.htm

Inference Clips:

http://www.teachertube.com/video/inference-17098

http://www.teachertube.com/video/observation-vs-inference-189914

Citation and Copyright:

http://lib.trinity.edu/lib2/cite_nontrad_mla.php

https://owl.english.purdue.edu/owl/section/2/

http://www.copyrightkids.org/

http://www.cyberbee.com/cb_copyright.swf

Cinematography and Music Websites:

http://www.freeplaymusic.com/

http://www.freesound.org/

http://www.mediacollege.com/video/camera/angles/

http://www.mediacollege.com/video/shots/

Chapter 6

Art and Music

ART   **Grade Levels:** K–2

Snowflakes

Lesson Summary: This lesson will include a study of the book *Snowflake Bentley* by Jacqueline Briggs Martin. Students will design and create snowflakes for the classroom and school library.

Standards Addressed:

AASL *Standards for the 21st Century Learner*

- Inquire, think critically, and gain knowledge (1.1.1; 1.1.2; 1.1.3; 1.1.6; 1.4.4)
- Draw conclusions, make informed decisions, apply knowledge to new situations, and create new knowledge (2.1.5; 2.2.4; 2.3.1)
- Share knowledge and participate ethically and productively as members of our democratic society (3.1.2; 3.3.4)
- Pursue personal and aesthetic growth (4.1.1; 4.1.3; 4.1.8)

Common Core State Standards

- CCSS.ELA-Literacy.RL.K.1; RL.K.3; RL.K.4; RL.K.5; RL.K.6; RL.K.7; RL.K.10
- CCSS.ELA-Literacy.RI.K.1; RI.K.2; RI.K.4; RI.K.5; RI.K.6; RI.K.7; RI.K.10
- CCSS.ELA-Literacy.SL.K.1; SL.K.2; SL.K.3; SL.K.5; SL.K.6
- CCSS.ELA-Literacy.RL.1.1; RL.1.3; RL.1.4; RL.1.5; RL.1.6; RL.1.7; RL.1.10
- CCSS.ELA-Literacy.RI.1.1; RI.1.2; RI.1.3; RI.1.4; RI.1.5; RI.1.6; RI.1.7; RI.1.10
- CCSS.ELA-Literacy.SL.1.1; SL.1.2; SL.1.3; SL.1.5; SL.1.6
- CCSS.Math.Content.1.G.A.3
- CCSS.ELA-Literacy.RL.2.1; RL.2.3; RL.2.5; RL.2.7; RL.2.10
- CCSS.ELA-Literacy.RI.2.1; RI.2.2; RI.2.4; RI.2.5; RI.2.6; RI.2.7; RI.2.8; RI.2.10
- CCSS.ELA-Literacy.SL.2.1; SL.2.2; SL.2.3; SL.2.6
- CCSS.Math.Content.2.G.A.3

Instructional Resources:

- *Required*
  - *Snowflake Bentley* by Jacqueline Briggs Martin
  - Access to a computer and presentation hardware or Smartboard
  - White paper, scissors
  - String or fishing line

All handouts are included in the Student Resource site found at http://www.abc-clio.com/Libraries Unlimited/product.aspx?pc=A4367P.

Instructional Roles:

This is a lesson that the school librarian may facilitate or it can be co-taught with the classroom teacher or art instructor.

Procedure for Completion:

Step One: The school librarian will read *Snowflake Bentley* by Jacqueline Briggs Martin to the class and utilize a document camera to enlarge the pages so the students can see the additional nonfiction details as well as the woodcut prints of the illustrations. The school librarian will facilitate a discussion of Wilson Bentley's life and fascination with snowflakes and share some of the information presented on the author website, the Snowflake Bentley website, and the Snowflake Bentley Museum website.

Step Two: The school librarian will project the directions on How to Make a Paper Snowflake and demonstrate the procedure while guiding the students in folding white paper, cutting appropriately, and creating a snowflake.

Step Three—Completion: The students will continue making snowflakes while listening to another story such as *The Mitten, The Big Snow,* or *The Snowy Day.*

Completion of Project:

The students will make several snowflakes, which will be hung around the school library or classroom.

Student Assessment/Reflection:

The story time, paper snowflakes, and student contribution to the class discussion are based on the rubric. Teacher observations throughout the process are included in the assessment.

Professional Reflection—Librarian Notes:

There are many opportunities to incorporate lessons with this book in other subject areas including science and weather; math, symmetry, and tessellations; science and snow crystal patterns; art and photography; computer-designed snowflakes; English and poetry; and spreadsheets to compare snowfall.

Snowflake Bentley Rubric

	Excellent	Satisfactory	Unsatisfactory
Listened to the Story and Contributed to the Discussion	The student listened well and contributed to the discussion in a positive way.	The student needed reminding to listen and encouragement to participate.	The student did not pay attention or contribute to the discussion.
Followed Directions to Make the Snowflake	The student followed cutting and folding directions without assistance.	The student needed assistance while cutting and folding the paper.	The student did not complete the assignment.
Completed Snowflake	The student completed a pretty and creative snowflake.	The student needed assistance while completing the snowflake.	The student did not complete a snowflake.
Staying on Task Daily	Student working as assigned and not disengaged or causing a disruption.	Student working well on assignment most days.	Student not on task daily or is a discipline problem.

Student Name:

Snowflake Bentley Grade:

	Excellent	Satisfactory	Unsatisfactory
Listened to the Story and Contributed to the Discussion			
Followed Directions to Make the Snowflake			
Completed Snowflake			
Staying on Task Daily			

SUGGESTED BIBLIOGRAPHY

Bentley, W. A. (2000). *Snowflakes in Photographs*. New York, NY: Dover.

Brett, J. (1999). *The Mitten*. New York, NY: G. Putnam & Sons.

Briggs, R. (1979). *The Snowman*. New York, NY: Random House.

Cassino, M. (2009). *The Story of Snow: The Science of Winter's Wonder*. San Francisco, CA: Chronicle Books.

Hader, B., & Hader, E. (1993). *The Big Snow*. New York, NY: Aladdin.

Keats, E. J. (1961). *The Snowy Day*. New York, NY: Viking Press.

Martin, J. B., & Azarian, M. (1998). *Snowflake Bentley*. Boston, MA: Houghton Mifflin.

Shulevitz, U. (1998). *Snow*. New York, NY: Farrar, Straus & Giroux.

Online Resources:

Jacqueline Briggs Martin website: http://www.jacquelinebriggsmartin.com/contact/index.html

Mary Azarian website: http://www.maryazarian.com/index.html

Snowflake Bentley website: http://www.snowflakebentley.com/

Snowflake Bentley Museum: http://snowflakebentley.com/museum2.htm

MUSIC

"This Land Is Your Land"

Grade Levels: 1–3

Lesson Summary: This lesson will be taught in conjunction with a holiday such as Veteran's Day, Memorial Day, Patriots Day, or Labor Day. Students will be taught the song "This Land Is Your Land" and will explore the meaning behind the lyrics, the background of the composer, and the historical background of the era.

Standards Addressed:

AASL *Standards for the 21st Century Learner*

- Inquire, think critically, and gain knowledge (1.1.1; 1.1.2; 1.1.3; 1.1.4; 1.1.5; 1.4.4)
- Share knowledge and participate ethically and productively as members of our democratic society. (3.1.1; 3.1.2; 3.1.5; 3.2.3; 3.3.1; 3.3.2; 3.3.4)
- Pursue personal and aesthetic growth. (4.1.1; 4.1.8; 4.2.1; 4.2.2; 4.2.3; 4.4.1; 4.4.2; 4.4.3; 4.4.4)

Common Core State Standards

- CCSS.ELA-Literacy.RL.1.1; RL.1.2; RL.1.3; RL.1.4; RL.1.5; RL.1.6; RL.1.10
- CCSS.ELA-Literacy.RI.1.1; RI.1.2; RI.1.3; RI.1.4; RI.1.6; RI.1.7; RI.1.8; RI.1.10
- CCSS.ELA-Literacy.RL.2.1; RL.2.4; RL.2.7; RL.2.10
- CCSS.ELA-Literacy.RI.2.1; RI.2.3; RI.2.4; RI.2.6; RI.2.7; RI.2.10
- CCSS.ELA-Literacy.RL.3.3; RL.3.4; RL.3.5; RL.3.6; RL.3.7; RL.3.10
- CCSS.ELA-Literacy.RI.3.1; RI.3.2; RI.3.3; RI.3.4; RI.3.7; RI.3.8; RI.3.10

Instructional Resources:

- *Required*
  - *This Land Is Your Land* illustrated by Kathy Jakobsen
  - Music and accompaniment for the song are included in the back of the picture book
  - Access to a document reader or overhead projector to view the illustrations on a screen

Instructional Roles:

As co-teachers in this lesson, the music teacher will take the lead in teaching the students the words and tune to the song "This Land Is Your Land." The school librarian will read the book *This Land Is Your Land* illustrated by Kathy Jakobsen and introduce the students to the background of the story and the period in history when it was written.

Procedure for Completion:

Day One: The school librarian will read *This Land Is Your Land* to the students while projecting the book illustrations on a screen. The co-teachers will provide further background information that will include facts about the composer, why he wrote the song, and some historical data.

Day Two—Completion: The music teacher will prepare the students to sing the song "This Land Is Your Land" at an assembly for Memorial Day, Veterans Day, Flag Day, D-Day, or other patriotic holiday.

Completion of Project:

Students' presentation of the song to an audience.

Student Assessment/Reflection:

The song in concert is the object of the main student assessment and is based on the rubric for the project. Questions asked during the discussion presentation and conversations with the teacher and school librarian throughout the process will also be included in the assessment process.

Professional Reflection—Librarian Notes:

The book *This Land Is Your Land* includes a tribute to Woody Guthrie by Pete Seeger. This may be a good place to begin gathering information to share with the students about the United States at the time the song was written. Other suggestions would be to include a discussion on the variety of landscapes across the United States that are reflected in the illustrations of the book. Students may be invited to share observations about places they have visited or special aspects of where they live.

"This Land Is Your Land" Rubric

	Excellent	Satisfactory	Unsatisfactory
Step One: Listen to the Story and Participate in the Discussion	The student is attentive and participates constructively in the discussion.	The student is listening to the story but not participating in the discussion.	The student is not paying attention or not participating in the discussion with relevant comments.
Step Two: Learn the Song	The student learns the words and tune to the song.	The student only knows part of the song.	The student does not know the song.
Step Three: Participate in the Concert	The student is present, well behaved, and singing in the concert.	The student is present but may not be attentive or participate in the singing.	The student does not attend or participate in the concert.
Staying on Task Daily	The student is working as assigned and not disengaged or causing a disruption.	The student is working well and paying attention most of the time.	The student is not on task daily or is a discipline problem.

Student Name:

"This Land Is Your Land Grade":

	Excellent	Satisfactory	Unsatisfactory
Step One: Listen to the Story and Participate in the Discussion			
Step Two: Learn the Song			
Step Three: Participate in the Concert			
Staying on Task Daily			

From *The Common Core in Action: Ready-to-Use Lesson Plans for K–6 Librarians* by Deborah J. Jesseman. Santa Barbara, CA: Libraries Unlimited. Copyright © 2015.

SUGGESTED BIBLIOGRAPHY

Cella, C. (2013). *Memorial Day*. Mankato, MN: Capstone Classroom.

Frost, H. (2000). *Memorial Day*. Mankato, MN: Capstone Classroom.

Guthrie, W., & Jakobsen, K., ill. (1998). *This Land Is Your Land*. Canada: Little, Brown.

Murphy, P. J. (2002). *Our National Holidays*. Mankato, MN: Capstone Classroom.

Rissman, R. (2011). *Veterans Day*. Mankato, MN: Capstone Classroom.

Rissman, R. (2011). *Memorial Day*. Mankato, MN: Capstone Classroom.

ART   **Grade Levels:** 4–6

Block Prints

Lesson Summary: In this lesson the students will design snow scenes for a block print art project while relating the project to the illustrator of the book *Snowflake Bentley* by Jacqueline Briggs Martin.

Standards Addressed:

AASL *Standards for the 21st Century Learner*

- Inquire, think critically, and gain knowledge (1.1.1; 1.1.2; 1.1.3; 1.1.6; 1.4.4)
- Draw conclusions, make informed decisions, apply knowledge to new situations, and create new knowledge (2.1.5; 2.2.4; 2.3.1)
- Share knowledge and participate ethically and productively as members of our democratic society (3.1.2; 3.3.4)
- Pursue personal and aesthetic growth (4.1.1; 4.1.3; 4.1.8)

Common Core State Standards

- CCSS.ELA-Literacy.RL.4.1; RL.4.2; RL.4.3; RL.4.4; RL.4.7; RL.4.10
- CCSS.ELA-Literacy.RI.4.1; RI.4.2; RI.4.3; RI.4.4; RI.4.5; RI.4.7; RI.4.8; RI.4.10
- CCSS.ELA-Literacy.SL.4.1; SL.4.2
- CCSS.ELA-Literacy.RL.5.1; RL.5.2; RL.5.3; RL.5.4; RL.5.5; RL.5.6; RL.5.7; RL.5.10
- CCSS.ELA-Literacy.RI.5.1; RI.5.2; RI.5.3; RI.5.4; RI.5.5; RI.5.8; RI.5.10
- CCSS.ELA-Literacy.SL.5.1; SL.5.2
- CCSS.ELA-Literacy.RL.6.1; RL.6.2; RL.6.4; RL.6.6; RL.6.10
- CCSS.ELA-Literacy.RI.6.1; IR.6.2; RI.6.3; RI.6.4; RI.6.5; RI.6.6; RI.6.7; RI.6.10
- CCSS.ELA-Literacy.SL.6.1; SL.6.2

Instructional Resources:

- *Required*
  - *Snowflake Bentley* by Jacqueline Briggs Martin
  - Access to a computer and presentation hardware
  - Balsa wood or florist foam
  - Fat primary pencil or large stylus
  - Cork or thread spool
  - Paint, paintbrush, light paint roller
  - Construction paper, practice paper, newsprint paper
  - Block Print Project handout

All handouts are included in the Student Resource site found at http://www.abc-clio.com/Libraries Unlimited/product.aspx?pc=A4367P.

Instructional Roles:

The art teacher and the school librarian will co-teach this lesson. The art teacher will guide the students in the development of the block print, and the school librarian will share the story and background of the main character and his study of snowflakes.

Procedure for Completion:

Day One: The school librarian will read *Snowflake Bentley* by Jacqueline Briggs Martin to the class and utilize a document camera to enlarge the pages so the students can see the additional nonfiction details as well as the woodcut prints of the illustrations. The co-teachers will facilitate a discussion of Wilson Bentley's life and fascination with snowflakes. They will also share some of the information presented on the author website, the Snowflake Bentley website, and the Snowflake Bentley Museum website.

Day Two: The co-teachers will provide basic background on the illustrator, Mary Azarian, and the art of woodcut printing. The students will begin to sketch a basic drawing to create their own block print design to be completed using the directions in the Block Print Project handout.

Day Three: The co-teachers will approve each student sketch and provide them with balsa wood or florist foam and a tool to press out their design.

Day Four—Completion: Students will spread the paint on their block and press it onto newsprint or other practice paper. When the design and paint thickness is to their satisfaction, they will print on the final colored construction paper.

Completion of Project:

The block print art drawing is the final project and will be hung in the library, classroom, or school hallways.

Student Assessment/Reflection:

The completed printing is the object of the main student assessment and is based on the rubric. Conversations and observations with the teacher and school librarian throughout the process will also be included in the assessment process.

Professional Reflection—Librarian Notes:

There are many opportunities to incorporate this book in other subject areas including science and weather; math, symmetry, and tessellations; science and snow crystal patterns; art and photography; computer-designed snowflakes; English and poetry; and spreadsheets to compare snowfall.

Snowflake Bentley Rubric

	Excellent	Satisfactory	Unsatisfactory
Preprint Sketch	Work was creative and completed on time.	Work completed but the student needed assistance in creating the design.	Work not completed.
Block Design Imprint	Work was creative and completed on time.	Work completed but the student needed a lot of assistance.	Work not completed.
Completed Print	Work was creative and completed on time.	Work completed but required additional assistance.	Work not completed.
Staying on Task Daily	Student working as assigned and not dis-engaged or causing a disruption.	Student working well on assignment most days.	Student not on task daily or is a discipline problem.

Student Name:

Snowflake Bentley Grade:

	Excellent	Satisfactory	Unsatisfactory
Preprint Sketch			
Block Design Imprint			
Completed Print			
Staying on Task Daily			

SUGGESTED BIBLIOGRAPHY

Bentley, W. A. (2000). *Snowflakes in Photographs.* New York, NY: Dover.

Briggs, R. (1979). *The Snowman.* New York, NY: Random House.

Cassino, M. (2009). *The Story of Snow: The Science of Winter's Wonder.* San Francisco, CA: Chronicle Books.

Libbrecht, K. (2010). *The Secret Life of a Snowflake: An Up-Close Look at the Art and Science of Snowflakes.* London/New York, NY: Voyageur Press.

Libbrecht, K. (2006). *Ken Libbrecht's Field Guide to Snowflakes.* London/New York, NY: Voyageur Press.

Martin, J. B., & Azarian, M. (1998). *Snowflake Bentley.* Boston, MA: Houghton Mifflin.

Online Resources:

Jacqueline Briggs Martin website: http://www.jacquelinebriggsmartin.com/contact/index.html

Mary Azarian website: http://www.maryazarian.com/index.html

Snowflake Bentley website: http://www.snowflakebentley.com/

Snowflake Bentley Museum: http://snowflakebentley.com/museum2.htm

MUSIC   Grade Levels: 4–6
Military Anthems

Lesson Summary: The students will learn the words and music to several of the military anthems attached to the armed forces of the United States and sing at an assembly. The students will conduct background research on one of the branches of the armed forces that includes a minimum of five facts.

Standards Addressed:

AASL *Standards for the 21st Century Learner*

- Inquire, think critically, and gain knowledge (1.1.1–1.1.4; 1.1.8; 1.1.9; 1.2.2; 1.2.3; 1.3.5; 1.4.2; 1.4.4)
- Draw conclusions, make informed decisions, apply knowledge to new situations, and create new knowledge (2.1.2; 2.1.3; 2.2.1; 2.2.4; 2.3.1)
- Share knowledge and participate ethically and productively as members of our democratic society (3.1.1; 3.1.3; 3.1.6; 3.3.4)
- Pursue personal and aesthetic growth (4.1.6; 4.2.1)

Common Core State Standards

- CCSS.ELA-Literacy.RI.4.1; RI.4.2; RI.4.3; RI.4.4; RI.4.5; RI.4.9
- CCSS.ELA-Literacy.W.4.2; W.4.4; W.4.5; W.4.7; W.4.9; W.4.10
- CCSS.ELA-Literacy.RI.5.1; RI.5.3; RI.5.4; RI.5.5; RI.5.6; RI.5.7; RI.5.9
- CCSS.ELA-Literacy.W.5.2; W.5.4; W.5.5; W.5.7; W.5.9; W.5.10
- CCSS.ELA-Literacy.RI.6.1; RI.6.3; RI.6.7; RI.6.8; RI.6.9
- CCSS.ELA-Literacy.RH.6-8.4; RH.6-8.5; RH.6-8.8
- CCSS.ELA-Literacy.W.6.2; W.6.4; W.6.5; W.6.6; W.6.7; W.6.9; W.6.10

Instructional Resources:

- *Required*
  - Words and music to:
    – "The Caisson Song," official song of the U.S. Army
    – "Anchors Aweigh," official song of the U.S. Navy
    – "The Marines' Hymn," official hymn of the Marine Corps
    – "The Army Air Corps Song," official song of the Army Air Corps, now the U.S. Air Force
    – *"Semper Paratus,"* official song of the U.S. Coast Guard
  - Research tools including books, encyclopedias, and online resources
  - Five Facts handout

All handouts are included in the Student Resource site found at http://www.abc-clio.com/Libraries Unlimited/product.aspx?pc=A4367P.

Instructional Roles:

This lesson will be co-taught by the music teacher and the school librarian. The music teacher will take the lead in teaching the students the words and tunes of the military songs, and the school librarian will share resources and guide the students in their research on the various branches of the U.S. armed forces.

Procedure for Completion:

Day One: The school librarian will provide brief background information on each of the branches of the U.S. armed forces and guide the students in the research process. The students will choose a topic from a slip of paper drawn out of a hat. They will begin to research one branch of the military and conclude with a written report that expands on five facts they find interesting in their investigation.

Day Two: The music teacher will prepare the students to sing a selection of songs at an assembly for Memorial Day, Veterans Day, Flag Day, D-Day, or other patriotic holiday.

Day Three—Completion: The students will continue to research their topic and complete the Five Facts handout. When this handout has the approval by the co-teachers, the students will write a single-page paper on their topic.

Completion of Project:

Students will submit a written report based on the five facts they have researched and sing at an assembly.

Student Assessment/Reflection:

The song in concert and the paper are the objects of the main student assessment and are based on the rubric for the project. Questions asked during the research process and conversations with the teacher and school librarian throughout the process will also be included in the assessment.

Professional Reflection—Librarian Notes:

The school librarian may assist the teacher with expanded lessons that include the U.S. national anthem and Armed Forces anthems such as:

"The Caisson Song"—official song of the U.S. Army
"Anchors Aweigh"—official song of the U.S. Navy
"The Marines' Hymn"—official hymn of the Marine Corps
"The Army Air Corps Song"—official song of the Army Air Corps, now the U.S. Air Force
"*Semper Paratus*"—official song of the U.S. Coast Guard

Military Anthems Rubric

	Excellent	Satisfactory	Unsatisfactory
Step One: Complete the Research Paper	Student completed the assignment with all requirements.	The paper is handed in on time but is missing part of the requirements.	Student has not handed in an assignment or the assignment is incomplete.
Step Two: Learn the Song	Student learns the words and tune to the song.	Student only knows part of the song.	Student does not know the song.
Step Three: Participate in the Concert	Student is present, well behaved, and singing in the concert.	Student is present but may not be attentive or participate in the singing.	Student does not attend or participate in the concert.
Staying on Task Daily	Student is working as assigned and not disengaged or causing a disruption.	Student working well and paying attention most of the time.	Student not on task daily or is a discipline problem.

Student Name:
Military Anthems Grade:

	Excellent	Satisfactory	Unsatisfactory
Step One: Complete the Research Paper			
Step Two: Learn the Song			
Step Three: Participate in the Concert			
Staying on Task Daily			

SUGGESTED BIBLIOGRAPHY

Berne, E. C. (2013). *Today's U.S. Marines*. Washington, DC: CPB.

Braulick, C. A. (2005). *The Blue Angels*. Mankato, MN: Blazers Capstone.

Braulick, C. A. (2005). *The U.S. Air Force Thunderbirds*. Mankato, MN: Blazers Capstone.

Braulick, C. A. (2005). *The U.S. Army Golden Knights*. Mankato, MN: Blazers Capstone.

Braulick, C. A. (2007). *The U.S. Army National Guard*. Mankato, MN: Blazers Capstone.

Burgan, M. (2013). *Today's U.S. Air Force*. Washington, DC: CPB.

Cella, C. (2013). *Memorial Day*. Mankato, MN: Capstone Classroom.

Ferrish, M. (2014). *Star-Spangled Banner*. Baltimore, MD: Johns Hopkins University Press.

Frost, H. (2000). *Memorial Day*. Mankato, MN: Capstone Classroom.

Kenney, K. L. (2013). *Today's U.S. National Guard*. Washington, DC: CPB.

Llanas, S. G. (2011). *Women of the U.S. Navy: Making Waves*. Reston, VA: Snap (now Association Media & Publishing).

Murphy, P. J. (2002). *Our National Holidays*. Mankato, MN: Capstone Classroom.

Nardo, D. (2013). *Today's U.S. Army*. Washington, DC: CPB.

Nobbman, D. V. (2002). *Patriotic Music Companion Fact Book: The Chronological History of Our Favorite Traditional American Patriotic Songs*. Anaheim, CA: Centerstream.

Raum, E. (2009). *The Star Spangled Banner in Translation: What It Really Means*. Mankato, MN: Capstone Classroom.

Online Resource:

http://www.hampton.lib.nh.us/hampton/history/military/legionpost35/armedforcessongs.htm

ART   **Grade Levels:** 4–6

Chasing Vermeer

Lesson Summary: In this lesson the book *Chasing Vermeer* will be read to the students, and they will examine copies of the paintings by Vermeer to determine their own conclusion about the puzzle in the book and write letters stating these conclusions.

Standards Addressed:

AASL *Standards for the 21st Century Learner*

- Inquire, think critically, and gain knowledge (1.1.1–1.1.9; 1.2.1–1.2.7; 1.3.4; 1.3.5; 1.4.1–1.4.4)
- Draw conclusions, make informed decisions, apply knowledge to new situations, and create new knowledge (2.1.1–2.1.6; 2.2.1–2.2.4; 2.3.1–2.3.3; 2.4.1–2.4.4)
- Share knowledge and participate ethically and productively as members of our democratic society (3.3.1–3.3.6)
- Pursue personal and aesthetic growth (4.1.1–4.1.5; 4.2.1–4.2.6; 4.3.2; 4.3.4)

Common Core State Standards

- CCSS.ELA-Literacy.RL.4.1; RL.4.2; RL.4.3; RL.4.4; RL.4.6; RL.4.7; RL.4.10
- CCSS.ELA-Literacy.L.4.1; L4.2; L.4.3; L4.4
- CCSS.ELA-Literacy.W.4.1; W.4.2; W.4.3; W.4.4; W.4.4; W.4.5; W.4.6; W.4.8; W.4.9; W.4.10
- CCSS.ELA-Literacy.RL.5.1; RL.5.2; RL.5.3; RL.5.4; RL.5.5; RL.5.6; RL.5.7; RL.5.10
- CCSS.ELA-Literacy.L.5.1; L.5.2; L.5.3; L.5.4; L.5.5; L.5.6
- CCSS.ELA-Literacy.W.5.1; W.5.2; W.5.3; W.5.4; W.5.5; W.5.6; W.5.8; W.5.9; W.5.10
- CCSS.ELA-Literacy.RL.6.1; RL.6.2; RL.6.3; RL.6.10
- CCSS.ELA-Literacy.L.6.1; L.6.2; L.6.3; L.6.4; L.6.5; L.6.6
- CCSS.ELA-Literacy.W.6.1; W.6.2; W.6.3; W.6.4; W.6.5; W.6.6; W.6.8; W.6.9; W.6.10

Instructional Resources:

- *Required*
  - *Chasing Vermeer* by Blue Balliett
  - Computer access
  - Student printouts of pentominoes found on the websites http://www.blueballiettbooks.com/teachers.html and http://www.scholastic.com/blueballiett/holdfast.htm
  - Student printouts of Tommy's letters in code to Calder, found at the beginning of the book
  - Large poster with the above code to post for all students to view

Instructional Roles:

The art teacher and the school librarian will co-teach this unit. The art teacher will provide background for the artist and paintings. The school librarian will read the book in consecutive sessions and guide the students as they research paintings of Vermeer and use the interactive websites for the book and author.

Procedure for Completion:

Day One: The school librarian will read Chapters 1–6 in *Chasing Vermeer* to the students. The poster of Calder and Tommy's code is displayed or projected, and students must translate the code of Tommy's letter and explore the Reader's Challenge provided by the author and illustrator, both of which are in the book. The students will be introduced to the online resources for the book and participate in the interactive lessons.

Day Two: The school librarian will read Chapters 7–12 in *Chasing Vermeer* to the students. The students will be divided into small groups with access to photos of Vermeer's paintings, books, or websites to further examine the paintings and determine their own solutions to the puzzle.

Day Three: The school librarian will read Chapters 13–18 in *Chasing Vermeer* to the students. The school librarian and teacher co-teach a brief lesson on the structure of letter writing.

Day Four—Completion: The school librarian will read Chapters 19–24 in *Chasing Vermeer* to the students. They will utilize the information they explored in the small groups and write a letter stating their position on the authenticity of the Vermeer paintings and why.

Completion of Project:

The student-written letters will be the final product of this lesson.

Student Assessment/Reflection:

The completed letter is the object of the main student assessment and is based on the rubric. Conversations among student groups and with the teacher and school librarian throughout the process will also be included in the assessment process.

Professional Reflection—Librarian Notes:

There are many additional options for lessons with this book that the school librarian may utilize or encourage the students to pursue. Some of these ideas are codes, pentominoes, roman numerals, and mysteries. The school librarian may collaborate with teachers to explore the incorporation of a variety of subjects into this novel study.

Chasing Vermeer Rubric

	Excellent	Satisfactory	Unsatisfactory
Step One: Letter Is Properly Written	Work completed as assigned on time.	Work completed but not on time or essential elements are missing.	Work not completed or having several revisions before moving to the next step.
Step Two: Statement of Problem and Student Answer	Work completed on time with the problem and answer included in the response.	Work not completed on time or missing elements.	Work not completed.
Step Three: Answer Justification	Work completed on time and the justification is reasonable.	Work completed but not on time or an illogical conclusion has been made.	Work not completed or not explained.
Staying on Task Daily	Student working as assigned and not disengaged or causing a disruption.	Student working well on assignment most days.	Student not on task daily or is a discipline problem.

Student Name:
Chasing Vermeer Grade:

	Excellent	Satisfactory	Unsatisfactory
Step One: Letter Is Properly Written			
Step Two: Statement of Problem and Student Answer			
Step Three: Answer Justification			
Staying on Task Daily			

From *The Common Core in Action: Ready-to-Use Lesson Plans for K–6 Librarians* by Deborah J. Jesseman. Santa Barbara, CA: Libraries Unlimited. Copyright © 2015.

SUGGESTED BIBLIOGRAPHY

Balliett, B. (2004). *Chasing Vermeer*. New York, NY: Scholastic.

Cesar, S. (2014). *Twenty-Four Johannes Vermeer's Paintings for Kids* [Kindle Edition]. Amazon Digital Services.

deWinter, J. (2010). *Amazing Tricks of Real Spies*. Mankato, MN: Capstone Classroom.

National Gallery of Art. (2013). *An Eye for Art: Focusing on Great Artists and Their Work*. Chicago, IL: Chicago Review Press.

Nilsen, A. (2000). *Art Fraud Detective: Spot the Difference, Solve the Crime!* New York, NY: Kingfisher.

Racza, B. (2010). *The Vermeer Interviews: Conversations with Seven Works of Art*. Portland, OR: First Avenue Editions.

Venezia, M. (2002). *Johannes Vermeer (Getting to Know the World's Greatest Artists)*. New York, NY: Children's Press.

Wheelock, A., & Broos, B. (1995). *Johannes Vermeer*. Washington, DC: National Gallery of Art.

Wood, A. (2013). *Johannes Vermeer (Artists Through the Ages)*. New York, NY: Windmill Books.

Online Resources:

http://www.blueballiettbooks.com/teachers.html

http://www.scholastic.com/blueballiett/holdfast.htm

Chapter 7

Health and Character Education

CHARACTER EDUCATION   Grade Levels: K–1
            Friendship

Lesson Summary: The lesson allows students to interpret a story about friendship while making it relevant to their own lives. They will learn about friendship while developing skills for listening, reading comprehension, personal transfer, and artistic expression and connection.

Standards Addressed:

AASL *Standards for the 21st Century Learner*

- Inquire, think critically, and gain knowledge (1.1.2; 1.1.9; 1.2.2; 1.4.2; 1.4.4)
- Draw conclusions, make informed decisions, apply knowledge to new situations, and create new knowledge (2.1.5; 2.1.6; 2.2.4; 2.3.1)
- Share knowledge and participate ethically and productively as members of our democratic society (3.1.3; 3.1.5; 3.2.1; 3.3.4)
- Pursue personal and aesthetic growth (4.1.1; 4.1.8; 4.3.1)

Common Core State Standards

- CCSS.ELA-Literacy.RL.K.1; RL.K.3; RL.K.4; RL.K.7; RL.K.9; RL.K.10
- CCSS.ELA-Literacy.RF.K.1; RF.K.2; RF.K.3
- CCSS.ELA-Literacy.SL.K.1; SL.K.2; SL.K.3; SL.K.4; SL.K.5; SL.K.6
- CCSS.ELA-Literacy.RL.1.1; RL.1.3; RL.1.4; RL.1.6; RL.1.7; RL.1.9; RL.1.10
- CCSS.ELA-Literacy.RF.1.1; RF.1.2; RF.1.3
- CCSS.ELA-Literacy.SL.1.1; SL.1.2; SL.1.3; SL.1.4; SL.1.6

Instructional Resources:

- *Required*
  - *The Wishing Ball* by Elisa Kleven
  - Large squares of gray construction paper or newsprint
  - Multicolor chalk and pastels
  - Baby wipes

Adapted from an SLM learning plan by Samantha Roslund. Reading/Language Arts: What Do You Look for in a Friend? *School Library Monthly*, Volume 29, Number 4, January 2013, pp. 54–55.

    o Access to computer and projector or Smartboard
    o Whiteboard or easel chart

    All handouts are included in the Student Resource site found at http://www.abc-clio.com/Libraries Unlimited/product.aspx?pc=A4367P.

Instructional Roles:

    The school librarian and the classroom teacher collaborate in this lesson with both educators leading the students in discussion, drawing, and writing activities.

Procedure for Completion:

Step One: The school librarian introduces *The Wishing Ball* by explaining about the three characters in the story: Nellie the Lonely Cat (show them an illustration featuring Nellie), Ernst the Tender Crocodile (show Ernst illustration), and the Tricky Crow (show crow illustration) and reads the story to the class. Upon conclusion of the story, the teachers will explain to students that everyone needs help from a friend from time to time. When Nellie the Cat and Ernst the Alligator found each other they were so happy because they both got what they wished for—a new friend.

Step Two: The co-teachers will ask the students to share qualities they might look for in a friend, and these characteristics are written and displayed on the board or easel. Then the children will draw their own sidewalk chalk friend and answer the following questions asked by the co-teachers:

- What are the characteristics of a friend?
- What are they drawing?
- Have they named their sidewalk chalk friend?

Completion: When everyone has finished their chalk friends, have the students lay the drawings next to each other to create a pretend sidewalk. Invite them to walk along the sidewalk and look at everyone's drawings.

Completion of Project:

    The final product will be the drawings and their responses to question of important characteristics in a friend and the chalk friend's name.

Student Assessment/Reflection:

    The completed drawing will be the object of the main student assessment and is based on the rubric for the project. Conversations with the teacher and school librarian throughout the process are important in the assessment process.

Professional Reflection—Librarian Notes:

This lesson can be adapted for an outside activity if the weather cooperates and may be an expansion of the lesson. The school librarian can develop a resource center for character education books, displaying friendship books during this lesson.

Friendship Rubric

	Excellent	Satisfactory	Unsatisfactory
Step One: Listening to the Story	Student was actively engaged in the story lesson.	Student listened but had to be reminded to pay attention.	Student did not listen well and did not understand the point of the story.
Step Two: Creating and Naming the Chalk Friend	Student completed the drawing with all components included.	Student did not complete the drawing on time or was missing some component of the assignment.	Student did not complete the drawing.
Step Three: Characteristics of Friendship	Work completed on time and correct.	Work completed but with assistance.	Work not completed or incorrect.
Staying on Task	Student working as assigned and not disengaged or causing a disruption.	Student working well on assignment most of the time.	Student not on task or was a disciplinary problem.

Student Name:

Friendship Grade:

	Excellent	Satisfactory	Unsatisfactory
Step One: Listening to the Story			
Step Two: Creating and Naming the Chalk Friend			
Step Three: Characteristics of Friendship			
Staying on Task Daily			

SUGGESTED BIBLIOGRAPHY

Hobbs, J. A., & Rush, J. C. (1997). *Teaching Children Art.* Long Grove, IL: Waveland Press.

Kleven, E. (2006). *The Wishing Ball.* New York, NY: Macmillan.

Sipe, L. R. (2007). *Storytime: Young Children's Literary Understanding in the Classroom.* New York, NY: Teacher's College Press.

HEALTH   Grade Levels: 3–6

Research into Diseases

Lesson Summary: This lesson provides students with the knowledge to explain the difference between communicable and noncommunicable diseases, defines hereditary diseases, discusses ways in which technology can be used to help students find information about personal health, and analyzes the way in which peers influence healthy and unhealthy choices.

Standards Addressed:

AASL *Standards for the 21st Century Learner*

- Inquire, think critically, and gain knowledge (1.1.1–1.1.8; 1.2.2; 1.2.4; 1.2.6; 1.2.7; 1.3.3; 1.3.4; 1.3.5; 1.4.2; 1.4.4)
- Draw conclusions, make informed decisions, apply knowledge to new situations, and create new knowledge (2.1.1; 2.1.2; 2.1.3; 2.1.4; 2.1.6; 2.2.3; 2.2.4; 2.3.1; 2.4.3)
- Share knowledge and participate ethically and productively as members of our democratic society (3.1.1; 3.1.3; 3.1.5; 3.1.6; 3.3.4)
- Pursue personal and aesthetic growth (4.1.4; 4.1.6; 4.2.1; 4.4.2; 4.4.4)

Common Core State Standards

- CCSS.ELA-Literacy.RI.3.1; RI.3.3; RI.3.4; RI.3.5; RI.3.7; RI.3.9; RI.3.10
- CCSS.ELA-Literacy.W.3.2; W.3.4; W.3.5; W.3.6; W.3.7; W.3.10
- CCSS.ELA-Literacy.RI.4.2; RI.4.3; RI.4.4; RI.4.5; RI.4.7; RI.4.9; RI.4.10
- CCSS.ELA-Literacy.W.4.2; W.4.4; W.4.5; W.4.6; W.4.7; W.4.9; W.4.10
- CCSS.ELA-Literacy.RI.5.1; RI.5.3; RI.5.4; RI.5.5; RI.5.7; RI.5.8; RI.5.9; RI.5.10
- CCSS.ELA-Literacy.W.5.2; W.5.4; W.5.5; W.5.6; W.5.7; W.5.9; W.5.10
- CCSS.ELA-Literacy.RI.6.1; RI.6.2; RI.6.3; RI.6.4; RI.6.6; RI.6.7; RI.6.8; RI.6.9; RI.6.10
- CCSS.ELA-Literacy.W.6.2; W.6.4; W.6.5; W.6.6; W.6.7; W.6.9; W.6.10

Instructional Resources:

- *Required*
  - Access to computers and online resources
  - Graphic Organizer handout
  - T-Chart example
  - *The Lemonade Club* by Patricia Polacco
  - Writing materials or computer access and word processing software

All handouts are included in the Student Resource site found at http://www.abc-clio.com/Libraries Unlimited/product.aspx?pc=A4367P.

- *Recommended:*
  - *Make Lemonade* by Virginia Euwer Wolff

Instructional Roles:

The school librarian and the classroom teacher will co-teach this lesson with both educators guiding the students in discussion and the research and writing process.

Adapted from an SLM learning plan by Catherine Trinkle. Text-to-Self Connection: *The Lemonade Club* and Research into Diseases. Count? *School Library Media Activities Monthly*, Volume XXV, No. 3, November 2008, pp. 12–14.

Procedure for Completion:

Step One: To help the students make the connection between what they are researching and their own self, ask them to think about health problems they have experienced or that a family member or friend has experienced. Then have them write about the experience but assure them that what they write will be personal unless they choose to share with the class. While students are writing the co-teachers will be walking around and checking to make sure they are on task and answer any questions they might have.

Step Two: The school librarian will read *The Lemonade Club* to the students. The co-teachers will encourage class discussion with topics such as:

- Compare Miss Wichelman's classroom to their classroom.
- Ask the students what they dream about when they grow up. They should think about the question first and then talk with another student about their future dreams.
- What does the phrase, "when life hands you lemons, make lemonade" mean?
- Have they heard this phrase before?
- What do they think it means?
- Will they share some examples?
- Why did Marilyn's classmates shave their heads?
- Define the word "empathy" and ask the students to think about whether they would have been one of the classmates who shaved his or her head in order to show their empathy.

Step Three—Completion: The co-teachers will define communicable and noncommunicable diseases, displaying a T-Chart on large paper, and have students provide examples of each. Each student will choose one disease to research, complete the Graphic Organizer handout utilizing online and library resources, and write a paper based on the information noted on the Graphic Organizer.

Completion of Project:

The research paper and Graphic Organizer handout are the culminating activities for this lesson. The length and extent of research is dependent on the grade level or classroom requirements.

Student Assessment/Reflection:

The main student assessment is based on the rubric for the research paper, Graphic Organizer handout, and student contribution to the class discussions. Observations and conversations by the teacher and school librarian throughout the process will be included in the assessments.

Professional Reflection—Librarian Notes:

The content and rubric in this lesson are intended to be adapted to the focus grade level, utilizing appropriate content. For the upper elementary students discuss Marilyn's comment at the beginning of the story, "I would do just about anything to be thin!" Although Marilyn did not purposefully diet, she expressed a feeling many preadolescents and adolescents share. This could lead to a class discussion about anorexia.

Research into Diseases Rubric

	Excellent	Satisfactory	Unsatisfactory
Discussion Participation	The student fully participated in discussions with positive contributions.	The student had to be encouraged to participate in discussions or did not contribute positively.	The student did not participate in any of the class discussions.
Graphic Organizer Handout	The handout was organized, accurate, and completed on time.	The handout was not completed on time or missing some required elements.	The handout was not completed or not handed in at all.
Written Research Paper	The paper was accurate and completed on time.	The paper was not completed on time and may not include all requirements.	The paper was not completed or is missing major elements.
Staying on Task Daily	Student working as assigned and not disengaged or causing a disruption.	Student working well on assignment most days.	Student not on task daily or is a disciplinary problem.

Student Name:

Research into Diseases Grade:

	Excellent	Satisfactory	Unsatisfactory
Discussion Participation			
Graphic Organizer Handout			
Written Research Paper			
Staying on Task Daily			

From *The Common Core in Action: Ready-to-Use Lesson Plans for K–6 Librarians* by Deborah J. Jesseman. Santa Barbara, CA: Libraries Unlimited. Copyright © 2015.

SUGGESTED BIBLIOGRAPHY

Kehret, P. (2006). *Small Steps: The Year I Got Polio.* Park Ridge, IL: Albert Whitman.

Krull, K. (2000). *Wilma Unlimited: How Wilma Rudolph Became the World's Fastest Woman.* New York, NY: HMH Books for Young Readers.

Polaccco, P. (2007). *The Lemonade Club.* New York, NY: Philomel.

Wolff, V. W. (1993). *Make Lemonade.* New York, NY: Henry Holt.

Online Resources:

KidsHealth: http://www.kidshealth.org

New York State Department of Health, Communicable Disease Fact Sheets: http://www.health.state .ny.us/diseases/communicable

New York State Department of Health, Diseases and Conditions: Information about Diseases, Viruses, Conditions, and Prevention: http://www.health.state.ny.us/diseases/

CHARACTER EDUCATION
My Hero

Grade Levels: 4–5

Lesson Summary: In this lesson students will choose a "hero" to research and report on. The result will be the development of a graphic novel.

Standards Addressed:

AASL *Standards for the 21st Century Learner*

- Inquire, think critically, and gain knowledge (1.1.1–1.1.5; 1.1.7; 1.1.8; 1.2.2–1.2.4; 1.2.6; 1.3.3; 1.3.5; 1.4.4)
- Draw conclusions, make informed decisions, apply knowledge to new situations, and create new knowledge (2.1.1–2.1.4; 2.1.6; 2.2.1; 2.2.4; 2.3.1; 2.4.1)
- Share knowledge and participate ethically and productively as members of our democratic society (3.1.1; 3.1.3; 3.1.4; 3.1.6; 3.3.4; 3.4.2)
- Pursue personal and aesthetic growth (4.1.6; 4.3.2; 4.3.4; 4.4.2)

Common Core State Standards

- CCSS.ELA-Literacy.RI.4.1; RI.4.2; RI.4.3; RI.4.4; RI.4.5; RI.4.6; RI.4.9; RI.4.10
- CCSS.ELA-Literacy.L.4.1; L.4.2; L.4.3; L.4.4; L.4.6
- CCSS.ELA-Literacy.W.4.2; W.4.4; W.4.5; W.4.6; W.4.7; W.4.9; W.4.10
- CCSS.ELA-Literacy.RI.5.2; RI.5.3; RI.5.4; RI.5.5; RI.5.6; RI.5.7; RI.5.9; RI.5.10
- CCSS.ELA-Literacy.L.5.1; L.5.2; L.5.3; L.5.4; L.5.6
- CCSS.ELA-Literacy.W.5.2; W.5.4; W.5.5; W.5.7; W.5.9; W.5.10

Instructional Resources:

- *Required*
  - Computer access
  - Access to a computer program that allows uploading of pictures and inserting "bubbles" for conversation, minimally Microsoft Office but preferably Comic Life or Kidspiration
  - Access to online resources including copyright-free image uploads
  - Hero Notes handout
  - Storyboard Template handout

All handouts are included in the Student Resource site found at http://www.abc-clio.com/Libraries Unlimited/product.aspx?pc=A4367P.

- *Recommended*
  - Comic Life software
  - Kidspiration software
  - Access to a binding machine or funds to have the students' work bound

Instructional Roles:

The classroom teacher and school librarian will co-teach this lesson. The classroom teacher may define the assignment, and the school librarian will facilitate research and resources.

Procedure for Completion:

Day One: The school librarian will read *Especially Heroes* to the students and facilitate a discussion to explain the social situations in 1964 that align with the book. The students will begin work on their Hero Notes handout by choosing who they want to write about and begin their research.

Days Two–Three: Guided by the teacher and school librarian, students will research their "hero," utilizing reference sources including library books and online materials.

Days Four–Five: The instructors will demonstrate the development of a storyboard as a means of planning the report. Students will develop their individual storyboards utilizing the Storyboard Template handout.

Day Six—Completion: Students will complete their projects using the software available to them. If they are not experienced in the software program to develop their graphic novel pages, time must be spent teaching these skills. If students are experienced with the software program, they will complete the project individually.

Completion of Project:

The graphic novel pages will be handed in, and the school librarian will bind them or have them bound.

Student Assessment/Reflection:

The student assessment is based on the rubric for the project and conversations with the teacher and school librarian throughout the process.

Professional Reflection—Librarian Notes:

The school librarian may want to share some of the resources that include successful people who have overcome adverse conditions such as *Extraordinary People with Disabilities* by Kent and Quinlan. This is a good lesson to remind students of copyright issues, utilize free images, and [provide practice in] citing sources.

My favorite definition of a hero is from T. A. Barron and can be found at http://tabarron.com /young-heroes/:

"Heroism is about character. inner qualities such as courage, perseverance, faith, compassion, humility, and humor. What it's absolutely not about is fame and glory: That's how we get terribly confused in our society, obscuring the great difference between a hero and a celebrity."

My Hero Rubric			
	Excellent	Satisfactory	Unsatisfactory
Step One: Notes Worksheet	The Notes Worksheet was completed as assigned.	The Notes Worksheet was completed but not on time or missing elements.	The Notes Worksheet was not complete or not handed in at all.
Step Two: Storyboard Template	The template was organized and completed on time.	The template was not completed on time or missing some required elements.	The template was not complete or not handed in at all.
Step Three: Completed Graphic Novel	Work completed on time, accurate, and creative.	Work not completed on time and may not include all requirements.	Work not completed or is missing major elements.
Staying on Task Daily	Student working as assigned and not disengaged or causing a disruption.	Student working well on assignment most days.	Student not on task daily or is a disciplinary problem.

Student Name:

My Hero Grade:

	Excellent	Satisfactory	Unsatisfactory
Step One: Notes Worksheet			
Step Two: Storyboard Template			
Step Three: Completed Graphic Novel			
Staying on Task Daily			

SUGGESTED BIBLIOGRAPHY

Bingham, J. (2012). *Animal Heroes.* Mankato, MN: Capstone Classroom.

Childhood of Famous Americans Series. New York, NY: Aladdin Press.

Elder, J. (2005). *Different Like Me: My Book of Autism Heroes.* London: Jessica Kingsley.

Kent, D., & Quinlan, K. A. (1997). *Extraordinary People with Disabilities.* New York, NY: Children's Press.

Kroll, V. (2003). *Especially Heroes.* Grand Rapids, MI: Eerdmans Books for Young Readers.

Meltzer, B. (2012). *Heroes for My Daughter.* New York, NY: HarperCollins.

Meltzer, B. (2010). *Heroes for My Son.* New York, NY: HarperCollins.

Snodgrass, M. E. (2008). *Beating the Odds: A Teen Guide to 75 Superstars Who Overcame Adversity.* Santa Barbara, CA: ABC-CLIO/Greenwood.

Online Resource:

T. A. Barron website: http://tabarron.com/young-heroes/

CHARACTER EDUCATION
Does Character Really Count?

Grade Levels: 5–6

Lesson Summary: This lesson identifies the "Six Pillars of Character" and has the students connect these characteristics to biographies of real people.

Standards Addressed:

AASL *Standards for the 21st Century Learner*

- Inquire, think critically, and gain knowledge (1.1.1–1.1.4; 1.1.8; 1.1.9; 1.4.2; 1.4.4)
- Draw conclusions, make informed decisions, apply knowledge to new situations, and create new knowledge (2.1.1; 2.1.2; 2.1.3; 2.1.5; 2.1.6; 2.2.3; 2.2.4; 2.3.1)
- Share knowledge and participate ethically and productively as members of our democratic society (3.1.1; 3.1.3; 3.1.5; 3.2.1; 3.3.4)
- Pursue personal and aesthetic growth (4.1.1; 4.1.2; 4.1.4; 4.1.8; 4.3.2; 4.4.1; 4.4.2)

Common Core State Standards

- CCSS.ELA-Literacy.RI.5.1; RI.5.2; RI.5.3; RI.5.4; RI.5.8; RI.5.10
- CCSS.ELA-Literacy.W.5.1; W.5.4; W.5.5; W.5.6; W.5.9; W.5.10
- CCSS.ELA-Literacy.RI.6.1; RI.6.2; RI.6.3; RI.6.4; RI.6.5; RI.6.6; RI.6.10
- CCSS.ELA-Literacy.W.6.2; W.6.4; W.6.5; W.6.6; W.6.9; W.6.10

Instructional Resources:

- *Required*
  - Access to a variety of biographies and autobiographies
  - Access to online resources; suggestions located in the Bibliography section
  - Who's That handout
  - KWLH handout
  - *Wilma Unlimited: How Wilma Rudolph Became the World's Fastest Woman* by Kathleen Krull
  - Document reader and projector or Smartboard

All handouts are included in the Student Resource site found at http://www.abc-clio.com/Libraries Unlimited/product.aspx?pc=A4367P.

Instructional Roles:

The school librarian and the classroom teacher will co-teach this lesson with both educators guiding the students in discussion and introduction of the KWLH charts, the character traits they want to emphasize, and the research and writing process.

Procedure for Completion:

Step One: Using the Character Counts website and free downloads, the co-teachers introduce "The Six Pillars of Character" (Trustworthiness, Respect, Responsibility, Fairness, Caring, Citizenship) to the students. The characteristics are discussed and students share examples of how the pillars apply to everyday life. The Know-Want-Learn-How handout is projected on a screen and the first two columns are completed as a group.

The school librarian reviews the concept of biography and autobiography, reminds the students of where they are located in the library, and reads aloud *Wilma Unlimited: How Wilma Rudolph Became the World's Fastest Woman* by Kathleen Krull. The third column of the K-W-L-H chart is completed: "What we learned about the six pillars of character and our biographical figure."

Step Two: The co-teachers will lead the students in completing the Who's That handout for Wilma Rudolph. The students will choose a biography or autobiography that appeals to them and begin reading.

Step Three—Completion: Students will complete the K-W-L-H handout, the Who's That handout, and write an essay describing the six pillars of character as they apply to their biographical figure.

Completion of Project:

The K-W-L-H handout, the Who's That handout, and an essay are the culminating activities of the lesson.

Student Assessment/Reflection:

The main student assessment is based on the rubric for the K-W-L-H handout, the Who's That handout, and the written essay. Observations and conversations by the teacher and school librarian throughout the process will be included in the assessments.

Professional Reflection—Librarian Notes:

This lesson is adapted from one that utilized "The Six Pillars of Character" but may simply transfer into another character education program. Some examples of the various programs are located in the Bibliography section, Online Resources.

Character Counts Rubric

	Excellent	Satisfactory	Unsatisfactory
K-W-L-H Handout	The handout was completed as assigned.	The handout was completed but not on time or missing elements.	The handout was not completed or not handed in at all.
Who's That Handout	The handout was organized, accurate, and completed on time.	The handout was not completed on time or missing some required elements.	The handout was not completed or not handed in at all.
Written Essay	The essay was completed on time, accurate, and creative.	The essay was not completed on time and may not include all requirements.	The essay was not completed or is missing major elements.
Staying on Task Daily	Student working as assigned and not disengaged or causing a disruption.	Student working well on assignment most days.	Student not on task daily or is a disciplinary problem.

Student Name:

Character Counts Grade:

	Excellent	Satisfactory	Unsatisfactory
K-W-L-H Handout			
Who's That Handout			
Written Essay			
Staying on Task Daily			

From *The Common Core in Action: Ready-to-Use Lesson Plans for K–6 Librarians* by Deborah J. Jesseman. Santa Barbara, CA: Libraries Unlimited. Copyright © 2015.

SUGGESTED BIBLIOGRAPHY

Adler, D. A. (1990). *A Picture Book of George Washington* (Picture Book Biography). New York, NY: Holiday House.

Adler, D. A. (1997). *A Picture Book of Jackie Robinson* (Picture Book Biography). New York, NY: Holiday House.

Adler, D. A. (1990). *A Picture Book of Abraham Lincoln* (Picture Book Biography). New York, NY: Holiday House.

Childhood of Famous Americans Series. New York, NY: Aladdin Press.

Elder, J. (2005). *Different Like Me: My Book of Autism Heroes.* London: Jessica Kingsley.

Kent, D., & Quinlan, K. A. (1997). *Extraordinary People with Disabilities.* New York, NY: Children's Press.

Kroll, V. (2003). *Especially Heroes.* Grand Rapids, MI: Eerdmans Books for Young Readers.

Krull, K. (2000). *Wilma Unlimited: How Wilma Rudolph Became the World's Fastest Woman.* New York, NY: HMH Books for Young Readers.

Meltzer, B. (2012). *Heroes for My Daughter.* New York, NY: HarperCollins.

Meltzer, B. (2010). *Heroes for My Son.* New York, NY: HarperCollins.

Snodgrass, M. E. (2008). *Beating the Odds: A Teen Guide to 75 Superstars Who Overcame Adversity.* Santa Barbara, CA: ABC-CLIO/Greenwood.

Online Resources:

Center for Character and Responsibility: http://www.bu.edu/education/caec/

Character Counts: http://charactercounts.org/sixpillars.html

CharacterEd.net: http://www.charactered.net/

Character.org: http://www.character.org/

Don't Laugh at Me program: http://www.operationrespect.org/index2.php

Free Character Education resources: http://advancepublishing.com/freeCharacterEducation.html

Good Character.com: http://www.goodcharacter.com/

Internet4Classrooms: http://www.internet4classrooms.com/character_ed.htm

The Center for the 4th and 5th Rs (Respect and Responsibility): http://www.cortland.edu/character/

CHARACTER EDUCATION   Grade Levels: 5–6
Body Image

Lesson Summary: This lesson focuses on a healthy body image for upper elementary students. Connecting real life and graphic novel images, students will be guided to focus on what they can do to have a healthy outlook.

Standards Addressed:

AASL *Standards for the 21st Century Learner*

- Inquire, think critically, and gain knowledge (1.1.1; 1.1.2; 1.1.3; 1.1.6; 1.1.8; 1.1.9; 1.2.4; 1.2.5; 1.3.5; 1.4.4)
- Draw conclusions, make informed decisions, apply knowledge to new situations, and create new knowledge (2.1.1; 2.1.2; 2.1.4; 2.1.5; 2.1.6; 2.2.1; 2.2.4; 2.3.1)
- Share knowledge and participate ethically and productively as members of our democratic society (3.1.1; 3.1.4; 3.1.5; 3.1.6; 3.2.2; 3.2.3; 3.3.2; 3.3.3; 3.3.4; 3.3.5)
- Pursue personal and aesthetic growth (4.1.5; 4.1.8; 4.2.2; 4.3.1)

Common Core State Standards

- CCSS.ELA-Literacy.L.5.1; L.5.2; L.5.3; L.5.4; L.5.6
- CCSS.ELA-Literacy.SL.5.1; SL.5.2; SL.5.6
- CCSS.ELA-Literacy.W.5.3; W.5.10
- CCSS.ELA-Literacy.L.6.1; L.6.2; L.6.3; L.6.4; L.6.6
- CCSS.ELA-Literacy.SL.6.1; SL.6.2; SL.6.3; SL.6.6
- CCSS.ELA-Literacy.W.6.3; W.6.10

Instructional Resources:

- *Required*
  - Various magazines for students to cut out
  - Scissors, newsprint paper, markers, glue
  - Access to online resources that include free avatars
  - Access to an assortment of graphic novels, manga, anime, and computer game avatars
  - Mirror, Mirror handout
  - Positive Reminder handout
  - Document reader and projector or Smartboard

All handouts are included in the Student Resource site found at http://www.abc-clio.com/Libraries Unlimited/product.aspx?pc=A4367P.

Instructional Roles:

The school librarian and the health teacher will co-teach this lesson with both educators guiding the students empathically and productively through the process.

Procedure for Completion:

Day One: The co-teachers will show the students pictures of characters from graphic novels, manga, anime, or computer games and facilitate a discussion about the shapes and forms of the typical graphic character. The teachers will demonstrate the creation of an avatar from one of the free websites listed in the Bibliography section, and students will create their own avatar. When the students have completed their creation, the teachers will check it and print it. The students will cut it out, glue it to the Mirror, Mirror handout, and write a paragraph indicating why they created their avatar with those specific characteristics.

Step Two: Form same-sex groups with 4–5 students in each group and provide each group with two pieces of newsprint and markers. Each group will make a list of parts of the body they are not satisfied with. The females will title their list "Girls Often Do Not Like …" and the males will title their list "Boys Often Do Not Like … ." The groups will use the magazines to cut out pictures of people they think are attractive and make a collage with the second piece of paper. When the groups have completed the assignment the co-teachers will hang the lists and collages side-by-side on the walls around the library, and the students will walk around to view them.

The students will come back to their seats and the co-teachers will facilitate a discussion about what the lists and collages may indicate. For example, if several male lists include height, the discussion might include comments like:

- Some groups listed height as one thing boys may not like about their own body.
- Some of the collages include lots of tall men.
- What does that say about men who are short or of medium height?
- Can they still be attractive?
- Do you think that only tall men are attractive?

Day Three: The co-teachers will utilize some of the discussion points included in the lesson and provide thought-provoking questions for the students to ask themselves and to discuss. After the discussion, the students will complete the Positive Reminder handout.

Completion of Project:

The culminating exercise is the class discussion and Positive Reminder handout.

Student Assessment/Reflection:

The main student assessment is based on the rubric for the group activity, the Mirror, Mirror handout, and the Positive Reminder handout. Observations and conversations by the teacher and school librarian throughout the process will be included in the assessments.

Professional Reflection—Librarian Notes:

Since discussing body image may be embarrassing or uncomfortable for some students, sensitivity is needed when addressing this topic. The school librarian should have extra resources, such as those listed in the Bibliography, at age-appropriate levels to assist students with further questions. This lesson may also be tied to a nutrition unit with the focus on a healthy body image rather than fat, thin, or in between.

Body Image Rubric

	Excellent	Satisfactory	Unsatisfactory
Group Assignment	The handout was completed as assigned.	The handout was completed but not on time or missing elements.	The handout was not complete or not handed in at all.
Mirror, Mirror Handout	The handout was organized, accurate, and completed on time.	The handout was not completed on time or missing some required elements.	The handout was not complete or not handed in at all.
Positive Reminder Handout	The essay was completed on time, accurate, and creative.	The essay was not completed on time and may not include all requirements.	The essay was not completed or is missing major elements.
Staying on Task Daily	Student working as assigned and not disengaged or causing a disruption.	Student working well on assignment most days.	Student not on task daily or is a disciplinary problem.

Student Name:
Body Image Grade:

	Excellent	Satisfactory	Unsatisfactory
Group Assignment			
Mirror, Mirror Handout			
Positive Reminder Handout			
Staying on Task Daily			

SUGGESTED BIBLIOGRAPHY

Assortment of various graphic novels

Blume, J. (1986). *Blubber.* New York, NY: Yearling.

Davis, B. (1999). *What's Real, What's Ideal: Overcoming a Negative Body Image.* Center City, MN: Hazelden Press.

Douglas, A., & Douglas, J. (2006). *Body Talk: The Straight Facts on Fitness, Nutrition, and Feeling Great About Yourself!* Toronto, ON: Owlkids Books.

Grimes, N. (2012). *Halfway to Perfect: A Dyamonde Daniel Book.* New York, NY: Putnam.

Kirberger, K. (2003). *No Body's Perfect.* New York, NY: Scholastic.

Larimore, W., & Wohleer, A. S. (2013). *The Ultimate Girls' Body Book: Not-So-Silly Questions About Your Body.* Grand Rapids, MI: Zonderkidz.

Madaras, L., & Gilligan, P. (2008). *On Your Mark, Get Set, Grow!: A "What's Happening to My Body?" Book for Younger Boys.* New York, NY: William Morrow.

Moe, B. (1999). *Understanding the Causes of a Negative Body Image.* Center City, MN: Hazelden Press.

O'Leary, S. (2013). *Girl to Girl: Honest Talk About Growing Up and Your Changing Body.* San Francisco, CA: Chronicle Books.

Paley, R., Norwich, G., & Mar, J. (2010). *The Body Book for Boys.* New York, NY: Scholastic.

Palser, B. (2012). *Selling Ourselves: Marketing Body Images.* Mankato, MN: Compass Point Books.

Rosinsky, N. M. (2009). *Write Your Own Graphic Novel.* Mankato, MN: Compass Point Books.

Rutledge, J. Z. (2007). *Picture Perfect: What You Need to Feel Better About Your Body.* Deerfield Beach, FL: HCI.

Online Resources:

Avatar Creator Sites

http://avachara.com/avatar/
http://bitstrips.com/create/character/
http://mybluerobot.com/create-your-own-avatar/
http://www.faceyourmanga.com/editmangatar.php

Mirror, Mirror Handout

Use one of the following websites to obtain a free "Mirror, Mirror" image for this activity:

http://ninidamour.blogspot.com/2012/07/mirror-mirror-frame-free-vintage-clip.html

http://pixabay.com/en/frame-mirror-picture-baroque-empty-308791/

http://www.clipartpanda.com/categories/oval-frame-clipart

References

Andrews, S., & Gann, L. (2011). Into the Curriculum Learning Plans: Science: Everyday Weather. *School Library Monthly*, Volume 28, Number 2, November 2011, pp. 52–53.

Andrews, S., & Gann, L. (2011). Into the Curriculum Learning Plans: Science: Weather or Not? *School Library Monthly*, Volume 28, Number 2, November 2011, pp. 53–55.

Arp, C. (2011). Into the Curriculum Learning Plans: English: Things Are Not Always as They Seem. *School Library Monthly*, Volume 28, Number 3, December 2011, pp. 55–57.

Bautz, K. (2012). Into the Curriculum Learning Plans: Math/Science: Pattern Storytime. *School Library Monthly*, Volume 28, Number 8, May–June 2012, p. 50.

Bell, A. (2007). Into the Curriculum Learning Plans: Math/Reading/Language Arts: Writing and Reading and Graphs, Oh My! *School Library Media Activities Monthly*, Volume XXIV, Number 7, March 2008, pp. 11–12.

Bell, A. (2007). Into the Curriculum Learning Plans: Language Arts/Science/Math: Animal and Number Poetry. *School Library Media Activities Monthly*, Volume XXIII, Number 8, April 2007, pp. 11–12.

Brodie, C. (2009). Connect the Book: *Make Way for Ducklings* by Robert McCloskey. *School Library Media Activities Monthly*, Volume XXV, Number 8, April 2009, pp. 33–35.

Brownlee, A. (2012). Into the Curriculum Learning Plans: English/Language Arts: Persuasive Reading with Newspaper Editorials. *School Library Monthly*, Volume 28, Number 6, March 2012, pp. 55–57.

Case, V. (2012). Into the Curriculum Learning Plans: Social Studies: Global Tooth Fairies. *School Library Monthly*, Volume XXVIII, Number 5, February 2012, http://www.schoollibrarymonthly.com/curriculum/Case2012-v28n5p54.html.

Cassel, P. (2012). Into the Curriculum Learning Plans: Science/Language Arts: "Getting Buggy" with David Biedrzycki. *School Library Monthly*, Volume 28, Number 8, May–June 2012, pp. 53–55.

Chilcoat, L. (2012). Into the Curriculum Learning Plans: Social Studies: WWI Primary and Secondary Sources and a Novel. *School Library Monthly*, Volume 28, Number 7, April 2012, pp. 55–57.

Ciciora, R. (2010). Into the Curriculum Learning Plans: Social Studies: Information Detectives. *School Library Monthly*, Volume XXVII, Number 2, November 2010, pp. 18–20.

Common Core State Standards Initiative, http://www.corestandards.org/

Congelio, M. (2012). Into the Curriculum Learning Plans: Science/Technology: Problem Solving. *School Library Monthly*, Volume 29, Number 1, September–October 2012, pp. 53–54.

Creekmore, M. (2012). Into the Curriculum Learning Plans: English/Social Studies: A Sweet Recipe for Change. *School Library Monthly*, Volume 28, Number 6, March 2012, pp. 52–55.

Deskins, L. (2010). Into the Curriculum Learning Plans: Science: What Is That Hiding in My Backyard? (And, Can I Keep It?). *School Library Monthly*, Volume XXVII, Number 2, November 2010, pp. 15–16.

Evans, J. (2007). Into the Curriculum Learning Plans: Reading/Language Arts: It's the Great Pumpkin Fiction, Nonfiction Lesson. *School Library Media Activities Monthly*, Volume XXIV, Number 2, October 2007, pp. 17–18.

Fawcett, D. L. (2012). Into the Curriculum Learning Plans: English/Language Arts: Adjectives about Us! *School Library Monthly*, Volume 28, Number 4, January 2012, pp. 52–53.

Fontichiaro, K. (2010). Cross Curriculum: Awakening and Building Prior Knowledge with Primary Sources: See, Think, Wonder. *School Library Monthly*, Volume XXVII, Number 1, September–October 2010, pp. 14–15.

Griffin, E. (2011). Into the Curriculum Learning Plans: English/Language Arts: Advice for Anansi. *School Library Monthly*, Volume XXVII, Number 5, February 2011, pp. 12–14.

Jesseman, D. (2014). Into the Curriculum: *Dinotopia* and a New Society. *School Library Monthly*, Volume 30, Number 6, March 2014, p. 53.

Jesseman, D. (2012). Into the Curriculum: Math/Geometry Quilting and the Underground Railroad. *School Library Monthly*, Volume 28, Number 8, May–June.

Kebetz, L. (2009). Retro-Lesson Plan: Looking at Our Heroes: Does Character Really Count? (SLMAM, January 2000). *School Library Media Activities Monthly*, Volume XXV, Number 7, June 2009, p. 11.

Labaire, E. (2009). Into the Curriculum Learning Plans: Science: Our Class Pet: A Dinosaur? *School Library Media Activities Monthly*, Volume XXV, Number 10, June 2009, pp. 12–13.

Laramie, T. S. (2011). Into the Curriculum Learning Plans: Cross Curricular: DUPED? Website Evaluation. *School Library Monthly*, Volume 28, Number 3, December 2011, pp. 53–54.

O'Keefe, A. (2011). Into the Curriculum Learning Plans: Science: Our Class Pet: A Dinosaur? *School Library Monthly*, Volume 28, Number 1, September–October 2011, p. 55.

O'Keefe, A. (2010). Into the Curriculum Learning Plans: Science: Postcards from the Solar System. *School Library Monthly*, Volume 28, Number 4, January 2012, pp. 50–51.

Purcell, M. (2013). Into the Curriculum Learning Plans: English Language Arts: Lights, Cameras, Action, and Books!: A Book Trailer. *School Library Monthly*, Volume 29, Number 4, January 2013, pp. 56–58.

Rascoe, J. M. (2008). Into the Curriculum Learning Plans: Social Studies: Women Who Paved the Way. *School Library Monthly*, Volume XXIV, Number 6, February 2008, pp. 18–23.

Reigelsperger, L. (2010). Into the Curriculum Learning Plans: Social Studies/Language Arts: Learning about Abraham Lincoln Using Fiction and Nonfiction Materials. *School Library Monthly*, Volume XXVII, Number 1, September–October 2010, pp. 16–17.

Roslund, S. (2013). Into the Curriculum Learning Plans: Reading/Language Arts: What Do You Look for in a Friend? *School Library Monthly*, Volume 29, Number 4, January 2013, pp. 54–55.

Scribner, K. (2010). Into the Curriculum Learning Plans: Science: Let's Take a Weather Trip. *School Library Monthly*, Volume XXVII, Number 1, September–October 2010, pp. 18–19.

"Standards for the 21st Century Learner." Chicago, IL: American Association of School Librarians. http://www.ala.org/aasl/standards-guidelines/learning-standards.

Taylor-Fox, H., & Rose, D. (2011). Into the Curriculum Learning Plans: Social Studies: Almanacs Reveal State Secrets. *School Library Monthly*, Volume 28, Number 3, December 2011, pp. 52–53.

Tolson, M. (2010). Into the Curriculum Learning Plans: Reading/Language Arts: All Aboard! Your Own Polar Express. *School Library Monthly*, Volume XXVII, Number 3, December 2010, pp. 18–20.

Trinkle, K. (2008). Into the Curriculum: Text-to-Self Connection: *The Lemonade Club* and Research into Diseases. Count? *School Library Media Activities Monthly*, Volume XXV, Number 3, November 2008, pp. 12–14.

Trinkle, C. (2009). Cross Curriculum: Who Has ... Library Orientation? *School Library Monthly*, Volume XXVI, Number 1, September 2009, p. 11.

Tukua, K. (2009). Into the Curriculum Learning Plans: Cross Curricular: Games to Play with Paper Book Jackets. *School Library Media Activities Monthly*, Volume XXV, Number 5, January 2009, pp. 12–13.

Index

About the Author

DEBORAH J. JESSEMAN, MLS, PhD, is a tenured professor of education and school library and information studies at Minnesota State University, Mankato, MN. She has been a school librarian, a business education and math teacher, and a university professor and program coordinator. Her published works include the *School Library Media Certification by State* handbook for *School Library Monthly* and the *International Collaborative Curriculum Development Project*. Jesseman holds a master's degree in Library Science from Indiana University and a doctorate in Educational Studies: Higher Education Administration from the University of Nebraska–Lincoln.